CHASING THE DREAM
- A NEW LIFE
ABROAD

An anthology of travel stories

CURATED BY ALYSON SHELDRAKE

Tadornini Publishing

Copyright © 2021 Alyson Sheldrake

Cover Artwork by Darkmoon-Art. Copyright © 2021.

Website: www.darkmoon-art.com

Cover Design Alyson Sheldrake Copyright © 2021

All photographs and images provided by the authors concerned. Copyright © 2021

Published by Tadornini Publishing, 2021

Formatted by AntPress.org

First Edition

Paperback ISBN: 9798515973209

Hardback ISBN: 9798515973971

Large Print Paperback ISBN: 9798515975692

The author asserts the moral right under the Copyright, Designs and Patents Act 1988 to be identified as the author of this work.

All rights reserved.

No part of this publication may be reproduced in any form or by any electronic or mechanical means, including information storage and retrieval systems, without the prior written consent of the author, except for the use of brief quotations in a book review.

This is a work of creative nonfiction. All the contributors to this book have tried to recreate events, places, and conversations from their memories as truthfully as their recollection permits. All persons in this book are actual people. There are no composite or fictional characters. Some names have been changed to protect the innocent (or the guilty!).

Contents

Introduction *Alyson Sheldrake*	5
1. Get Your Coats, We're Going to Buy Chickens! *Victoria Twead*	7
2. Doing Things the Dutch Way *Val Poore*	23
3. Waking up in Japan *Todd Wassel*	39
4. An Unplanned Adventure in the Hills of Umbria *Clare Pedrick*	51
5. Global Nomads *Linda Decker*	67
6. Finding the Dream *Nick Albert*	83
7. From Bench Life to French Life *Beth Haslam*	101
8. Mountain Dreams *Roy Clark*	119
9. A Toilet Behind the Sofa (and other stories) *Lisa Rose Wright*	135
10. "You lived where?" *Lucinda E Clarke*	153
11. From the Garden of England to the Foothills of the French Pyrenees *Nikki McArthur*	169
12. A Fridge too Far *Rob Johnson*	183
13. A Long Way to the Castanets *Jean Roberts*	199
14. Born to be an Expat *Ann Patras*	215
15. Winter Fruit *Vernon Lacey*	231
16. Travel is in my DNA *Rachel Caldecott*	243
17. In Sight of Aconcagua *Ronald Mackay*	259

18. Tuscan Dreams	277
Tonia Parronchi	
19. Melbourne – the Wonder Down Under	291
Simon Michael Prior	
20. Living the Algarve Dream	313
Alyson Sheldrake	
About the Authors	327
Itchy Feet – Tales of travel and adventure	339
We Love Memoirs	341
Acknowledgements and Dedication	343
Free Photo Album	345
Keeping in Touch	347
About the Curator	349
Your Review	351

Introduction
ALYSON SHELDRAKE

Moving abroad can feel like a daunting prospect. For many people, though, it can seem like a dream life; the chance to pack up and start again somewhere new—and preferably somewhere warm and sunny.

"You're so lucky! I wish I could live abroad."

"I bet you spend all day lying in a hammock on the beach, sipping cocktails in the sun."

"Have you got a swimming pool?"

These are all comments many of us that live abroad have heard many times.

Sadly, the reality is usually quite different. Moving to a new country often involves battling with bureaucracy, renovating a ruin, struggling to decipher a new language, learning about a different culture and customs, and missing family and friends.

But there is joy and laughter too, and a deep sense of satisfaction. A new, often simpler way of life; self-sufficiency, and a different, often less stressful existence are available if you are willing to take the plunge.

I tried my best to articulate my own journey and feelings in two travel memoirs, written and published in 2020. *Living the Dream – in* the Algarve, Portugal and the sequel, *Living the Quieter Algarve Dream* were initially created from the content of the blog my husband and I set up about our move to live in the Algarve, Portugal. They were joined by another volume, *A New Life in the Algarve Portugal – An anthology of life stories*, in 2021, the third book in my *Algarve Dream Series*.

I also joined a fantastic group on Facebook called *We Love Memoirs* and discovered a whole new world of memoir writing. I made friends with so many other writers who were also documenting and recording their new lives abroad. And so this book, and the *Travel Stories Series*, was born.

In this anthology I have invited nineteen other authors to join me and share their unique stories with you. They cover the globe, with stories of planned moves with families to new overseas postings, to rash spur-of-the-moment property purchases abroad. Young lives, second chancers, midlife movers and retirement dreamers are all included in the pages of this book.

There are New York Times bestselling authors here, alongside brand-new writers with their first book recently published. All have been chosen specifically because of their ability to tell a good story, and to entertain you. At the end of each chapter you can find out more about the books each author has written, allowing you to discover a whole new selection of travel memoirs to enjoy.

Making the move to live abroad, often leaving homes, jobs, families, and friends behind, is not an easy decision to make. But it is a choice that can lead to wonderful new opportunities to live a different, often less stressful, more peaceful way of life. Maybe you will read these stories and be inspired too.

Please note that most of the chapters are written in British English. Some of the contributors, however, use US English. I have tried to stay faithful to their background, whilst editing gently, and I hope their voices come through the pages for you.

Happy reading!

Alyson Sheldrake
June 2021

1

Get Your Coats, We're Going to Buy Chickens!
VICTORIA TWEAD

"We are so lucky that Father Lenny is going to let us all take a good look around the church," I said to Green Class. Cross-legged on the carpet, twenty-two little faces looked up at me.

"We are all going to walk in a nice line, holding hands, all the way to St Mary's church," I announced.

A hand shot up.

"Yes, Jovi?"

"I gotta wing-mirror!"

Suddenly there was excitement in the air.

"That's nice, Jovi," I started, "but …"

"From a car."

The class gasped. "I found it by the road. I got it in my bag! Shall I get it?"

All the four and five-year-olds swung round to stare at Jovi.

"No way!"

"Don't believe you!"

"Lessee it!"

"Go on, get it!"

"Thank you, Jovi, that's *really* exciting," I interrupted. "You can get it at Show and Tell before home time and we'll all have a good look at it. Now, sit down nicely and I'll tell you all about our church visit."

Green Class looked disappointed. They sighed and fidgeted. I realised I'd been upstaged by a wing-mirror. Life is not easy for a substitute teacher.

"Are we ready to go, Mrs Thompson?" I asked my friend and teaching assistant, Juliet. "Any absentees?"

"Just one. Laura's big sister gave me this note."

I tore the envelope open and unfolded the sheet of paper within.

Please excuse Laura for being absent from school. She was sick again so I took her to the doctor and had her shot.

"Laura won't be joining us today," I told the class.

"Miss, why not?" asked Harry.

"She's having an injection."

Harry made a face and jabbed Jovi's forearm with a pointy finger.

I passed the note back to Mrs Thompson to read and deal with. I didn't dare make eye contact. Sometimes we laughed so much one of us had to leave the classroom or the assembly hall.

"I don't want to hold hands with Jovi," said Marie. "He smells of guinea pigs."

Walking twenty-two small children safely from school to church along a busy road was never going to be easy. Mrs Thompson brought up the rear, making sure that no child was distracted and strayed away. A volunteer mother kept an eye on the middle of the line.

I recalled Sports Day not long ago when I had been called in to supervise Green Class. We began with the running race along clearly defined, white-painted lanes. I lined them up and shouted, "Ready, Steady, GO!"

Twenty-two children galloped away.

All in different directions, north, south, east and west.

It took a good ten minutes to round them up again.

The memory made me glad to have help as we crossed a busy road and entered the cool church. Father Lenny was waiting, his hands clasped.

"Welcome!" he beamed.

"Say hello to Father Lenny," I said.

"Hello-Father-Lenny," chanted Green Class.

"Welcome, Green Class, it's very nice to have you here." Father Lenny's eyes twinkled. "You can go wherever you like in the church. This is God's house and He loves little children. If you have any questions, just ask me and ..."

But it was too late. Twenty-two children stampeded into the church and Father Lenny could only stand back.

"Green Class!" I shrilled.

No response.

With a sense of impending doom, we followed the class inside.

There were small children everywhere. Two had found the stone font and little hands were splashing in the water.

"Father Lenny! What's this water for?"

"Ah, I'm glad you asked, dears. It's holy water. We sprinkle it on babies' heads …"

Marie pulled a face. "My mummy has a proper baby bath for my baby sister. Do you want to borrow it?"

Father Lenny and I opened our mouths to speak but Marie and her little friend had lost interest and were scampering away. Father Lenny laughed.

Mrs Thompson and I did our best to control and educate but it was a losing battle. No corner of the church was left unexplored. Children ran down the central aisle, played hide-and-seek behind the altar and climbed the steps to the pulpit.

I suppose I shouldn't have worried because Father Lenny was having a lovely time. The benevolent smile never left his face and his eyes twinkled more than ever. At last I looked at my watch.

"We'd better round them up," I said to Mrs Thompson. "I see it's raining again. It's going to be a wet walk back."

"Yup. Have you seen what Father Lenny is doing?"

"No?"

"He's playing peek-a-boo with Susie around the confessional curtains. He was playing zoos with Jovi and Matthew under the altar cloth earlier. They were roaring tigers in a cage and Father Lenny was the zookeeper."

Definitely time to go.

As a casual teacher, I never knew how my day would pan out. I could be supervising four-year-olds, or a class of sixteen-year-old boys doing metalwork. It was never boring but it was exhausting.

I began to dream about leaving it all behind. Maybe moving abroad, starting a new life in the sun, living simply and enjoying a slower, less stressful pace of life. Joe was nearing retirement and that would be a perfect time, wouldn't it? The problem was, it was my dream, not his.

If I had remained silent and carried on secretly dreaming about moving to Spain, we'd probably still be in West Sussex today. But one wet August Bank Holiday, I voiced my dream.

"For goodness' sake, why on *earth* would we want to move to Spain?" Joe asked in horror.

And that's when I wrote The List.

I love lists. They used to call me Schindler at work because of my list-making. I hoped this one would convince my husband that we should leave Britain and move abroad. *Reasons to move to Spain*, I titled it, and underlined it twice.

'Sunny weather' came first, of course. The climate. If you are English, you'll know how wonderful English summer days are when the sun warms your pale skin and the sky is blue with little white puffs of clouds scudding past. But days like these are as rare as hen's teeth. I dreamed of living somewhere where the sun shone every day. A place where a pre-arranged barbecue wouldn't be rained off. I dreamed of paddling in turquoise Mediterranean waters instead of the freezing, grey English Channel.

So that particular Bank Holiday day in August, as Joe napped on the couch, I stared out of the window at the leaden sky and fantasised about living in Spain. I watched the greasy raindrops chase each other down the window pane and I yearned to chase my dream.

My list was a work of art and my points, combined with my inability to talk about anything else for weeks, finally wore Joe down. He agreed we should move to Spain.

"Just for five years, mind. Let's see how it goes."

I smile now when I think of my naivety. Just find a nice house, I thought, then move in and enjoy the beautiful weather. Easy.

No more central heating, no ice on the car's windscreen and no black ice on the roads. No thick winter coats and no hats and scarves needed because in Spain, it never gets cold, does it?

Well, yes, actually it does.

In some ways, I was right. For instance, we didn't have central heating when we moved to Spain and neither did any of our neighbours.

Actually, that's not quite true, either. A few years after we moved to El Hoyo, a millionaire moved into the village and installed central heating in one room. A single radiator was heated by a paraffin-fuelled boiler and the villagers marvelled at it.

"English! Have you seen Alejandro's new heating system?" asked

Paco, our next-door neighbour. "Come, I will take you to his house. You must see this invention!"

He showed us the millionaire's monstrous radiator bolted to the wall. "Feel it! It is hot! I'm sure you have never seen anything like that!"

Joe and I admired it politely and didn't mention that nearly every house in Britain has radiators and central heating.

We moved to Spain in mid-summer and the cottage we bought had a log-burning stove. We couldn't imagine we'd ever need to light it. But, to our surprise, when our first winter arrived, we began lighting that fire every evening, a little earlier each day. The previous owners had left some firewood which soon became as precious to us as gold-dust.

And we thought we had left cold weather behind.

That first year, one cold morning, when the sky was a clear, steely blue and frost crunched underfoot, Paco pounded on our front door with his fist.

"English! Get your coats," he ordered. "We are going to buy chickens!"

We didn't know the first thing about hens. We'd only been in Spain for a few months and had hardly begun work on our house. We didn't even have a kitchen yet.

"Do we want chickens?" Joe whispered to me.

"Maybe one day, but we're not ready yet, are we?"

But Paco was already sitting in his old Landrover on the street outside our front door, revving the engine, work-worn fingers drumming impatiently on the steering wheel. Reluctantly, we climbed in and the Landrover lurched off and climbed out of the valley. Into the mountains he drove, past more tumbledown whitewashed villages just like ours, until we reached a sprawling building with cars and tractors parked in front.

"This is it!" said Paco. "They sell good chickens here."

We allowed Paco to march us inside but we weren't permitted to stop and look around. Oh no. Like obedient children, we followed as he passed out of a back door and headed towards a separate barn.

The deafening noise hit us first, then the smell. We entered and gasped at the rows of cages piled up on top of each other, each housing up to five cramped, unhappy birds.

"We'll take that one, that one and those," said Paco to the assistant, who grabbed the unfortunate birds by the legs, pulling them out of the cages and holding them hanging upside-down.

Five minutes later we owned eight young chickens: six brown, and two white. The assistant packed them into a cardboard box and taped it down. Then he stabbed the cardboard repeatedly with his penknife.

"Air-holes," he explained, grinning.

I just hoped he hadn't stabbed one of our poor hens.

"You will buy some chicken food, a feeder and a water container now," announced Paco and led the way back into the shop. "You will put them into your chicken coop and soon you will have eggs."

Chicken coop? Joe and I exchanged glances. Unfortunately, we'd recently dismantled part of the old outhouse in our orchard and used the timber for firewood. We had no idea that Paco had assumed that this shack would be our new chicken coop.

Back home, he strode purposefully across the orchard.

"Pah!" he said in surprise when he saw the remains of the outhouse. "Never mind, we can fix it."

He insisted that our new chickens would be absolutely fine in the rickety lean-to that remained. He pulled some chicken-wire across the front, and hey presto! We had a chicken coop.

I'll never forget that first day, as our eight girls were gently tipped out of their cardboard box and landed, blinking on the ground.

They'd never been outside before. They'd never seen the sky or felt anything beneath their feet but wire mesh. Now they huddled together, fearful of this strange, quiet, new world. How baffling not to be deafened by the noise of hundreds of their sisters in cages just like theirs. Now there was no asbestos roof above them or harsh electric light. They stood like statues, their feet sinking into clover and grass, in soft daylight, a mountain breeze ruffling their feathers.

We were transfixed, watching.

"Pah!" said Paco, rolling his eyes.

He clearly thought we were quite insane, staring at the chickens. He strode away and left us to it.

Slowly, slowly, the girls gained confidence and began to peck at the odd blade of grass. They stretched their wings and even took a few uncertain steps.

We stayed with them all that first day, watching as they learned that grass was good to eat and that they could walk and scratch the ground. They discovered their feeder was topped up with never-ending delicious grain. They sipped the water, tipping their heads back to allow it to run down their throats.

Slowly, a strange thing happened.

Joe and I unexpectedly fell utterly in love with them.

Throughout that first day, their characters emerged. Who would have thought that chickens have very different, individual personalities? We didn't! It was fascinating to watch the bossy one become Top Hen. There was a shy one, a noisy one, a flighty one and another who squawked in alarm at every new thing she discovered. Two brown ones were always together and were so similar we called them the No-Name Twins, and we gave names to the others, chuckling at their antics.

"Brr, it's getting really cold," said Joe at last, rubbing his hands together.

"The fire's made. It just needs lighting. Let's just watch to make sure they settle down for the night."

When the winter sun stained the sky pink and sank behind the mountain, our new girls began to crane their heads this way and that. Then one of the white ones spotted the branch that Paco had wedged to form a roost. Up she flapped and called her sisters to join her. One by one, they made their way up until each chicken was settled on the branch, claws clamped.

"Amazing, they still have the instinct to roost off the ground, even though they've never had the chance to do it before!" Joe remarked.

"They couldn't even stretch their wings before. I'm so glad we've been able to give eight of them a much better life," I said.

We didn't know then that we would become addicted to keeping chickens. We didn't know then that we'd visit the horrible chicken shop many more times, buying more chickens to roam on our pastures. Becoming chicken farmers and selling eggs had not been on my list at all. And I certainly didn't know that one day, Joe would bring home Cocky, the feisty little cock who wanted to tear us all to shreds.

But I digress. I was explaining how guaranteed sunshine was one of the main reasons we moved to sunny Andalucía. As that night rolled in, our eight girls fluffed out their feathers, gave contented little sighs and put their heads under their wings. We secured the wire mesh to protect them from foxes as they slept, and, satisfied that our girls were tucked up and happy, we walked back to the house to light the fire.

How could we know that we had picked the one night when something incredible was about to happen? We slept, oblivious, totally unaware of what was happening outside.

Our bedroom was a cave. It was warm but windowless so we can be forgiven for not knowing anything was amiss until we arose and tried to boil the electric kettle for a cup of coffee the next morning.

"The kettle's not working," I said, puzzled.

"Nor is the light," said Joe, trying the switch. "We don't have any electricity, I wonder why?"

He opened the shutters of the living room window and our jaws dropped. The world was silent. A blindingly white blanket of snow smothered the mountains. Snow in southern Spain? Surely that wasn't possible?

"The chickens!" I gasped.

"I'll go out and check," said Joe, but he couldn't open the front door because snow was piled up against it, chest high.

After much pushing, we managed to open the back door and after he had pulled on his old army boots and donned several sweaters, Joe slowly made his way to the orchard. It was a difficult trek because the snowdrifts hid obstacles, but he finally reached the place where he was pretty sure the chicken coop had been. To his horror, the chicken shelter was one gigantic snowdrift.

You'll be glad to hear that our girls survived the heaviest snowfall in living memory. Our village was totally cut off and we couldn't leave the valley for days. We had no electricity, water or telephone, but we survived too.

So I'd advise anybody chasing their dream, who thinks moving abroad guarantees sunnier climes, to pause and check. Is the weather as good as you think, all the year-round? Don't read the tourist descriptions and take it at face value, like we did.

✿ℬ✿ℜ✿

Property in England is notoriously expensive, so it probably wasn't surprising that 'cheap houses' figured on my list of reasons to move to Spain. We ultimately fell in love with a cottage much cheaper than anything we could afford in England. It was also much less expensive than modern Spanish houses. But there was a reason for that.

Our cottage was quirky with strange rooms leading off other rooms, cave rooms hacked out of the mountainside and no proper kitchen. We cheerfully reckoned we could easily sort that but hadn't understood how old Spanish houses are constructed. No bricks were used in the building of our house. Instead, large flints and stones were held together by mud, forming strong walls that are never flat or square. Often a rock would fall out of the wall and soil poured out onto our floors. Patching walls became a regular job.

Our roofs were constructed from corrugated asbestos. Hard to believe, nowadays, but true.

Paco's brother-in-law, Fausto, worked in construction. He kindly offered to look at our cottage and give us the benefit of his advice. He arrived with his beautiful five-year-old daughter, which was useful because little Marisa was learning English at pre-school. Our Spanish was still poor and Fausto's English was non-existent.

"We'd like to make this window into a door, and build a terrace on that roof," Joe explained waving his arms. "What do you think? Is that possible?"

Fausto scratched his chin thoughtfully. Then he shook his head with regret and delivered his verdict in quick words to his daughter.

"My father, he say not possible," piped up Marisa, hopping from one foot to the other. "My father, he say all the house not strong. My father, he say better make house like this." She clapped her hands together. "Then make new."

"Knock the house down and start again?" I echoed.

Little Marisa had found a hole in the wall and was poking at it, picking out little bits of masonry that tumbled to the floor. "Yes, my father he say this house she is rubbish."

We were horrified, but with hindsight, Fausto was right. We'd probably have saved ourselves a fortune by knocking down our beloved cottage and starting again, but I'm so glad we didn't. We adored that house and loved every quirky corner. Even when the roof leaked, or we couldn't find the underground cesspit.

Anyway, if we'd followed Fausto's advice and arranged to demolish the house in order to rebuild, the houses on either side would probably have collapsed. Perhaps it was a good thing we didn't go down that route.

Living in the country was high on the list I made that August day in England. My wish was granted, and our cottage was set halfway up the mountainside, overlooking olive and almond groves and the village cemetery. When we eventually built our roof terrace, we had a 360° view. We could see the ocean in the distance and watch the sun set over the mountains. Across the valley, the winding road down to the village was clearly visible. Looking down, we could watch the village's daily activity below, much of which ended up in the pages of the books I would subsequently write.

The doctor visited once a week, but the villagers were robust and rarely needed medical attention.

"Where is the doctor's surgery?" we asked in the early days.

"Pah!" said Paco. "There is no surgery. The doctor usually uses Marcia Estoban's living room."

The nearest shops were down the mountain half an hour away, but we didn't mind. White vans selling bread and fresh produce drove down into our valley several times a week, beeping their horns so villagers knew when they arrived. The village cats recognised the beep of the fish van and assembled in the village square, eager for scraps that often flew through the air in their direction.

The village ticked along in tune with the seasons, year by year. We came to recognise the sound of olives being knocked from the trees and almonds being de-husked. We were given masses of oranges, peaches and watermelons in season and we helped our neighbours press grapes for wine in late September.

Our days were filled with sunshine, fiestas, village gossip, fresh mountain air and hard work. My wish for country life was granted.

I recall that near the top of my list were the words 'friendly people', because I knew from past holidays in Spain that the Spanish are a warm, sociable race. In England, I barely knew my neighbours.

From the first day we moved into the village, friendly people surrounded us. Perhaps I would have preferred it if the mayor hadn't pursued me quite so relentlessly for private 'English lessons' in the Town Hall. Or if our neighbours, the Ufartes, hadn't been so determined to leave their children in our care.

But the villagers' kindness and generosity overwhelmed us and we often found gifts of fresh produce left on our doorstep or hanging from our door handle. Our next-door neighbours, Paco and Carmen, were an absolute delight. Nothing was too much trouble for them. They invited us to all their family gatherings and we wanted for nothing.

I'd also written something like 'delicious Spanish food' on my list. That particular dream certainly came true.

Most of the time.

"English!" bellowed Paco one day. "Carmen has cooked *manos de cerdo* for the family and all our cousins are waiting. You will come and eat!"

No invitation. It was an order.

We thanked him and prepared to follow him next door.

"What's that?" asked Joe when Paco had gone.

"Um, I think that translates to 'hands of pig'."

"What?"

"Pigs' trotters."

"You are kidding."

I shook my head, thinking longingly of the nice, crisp stir-fry I'd planned for supper.

"Ah, there you are!" said Paco when we arrived. "Here, help yourself to stuffed tomatoes. Our son grew them."

The tomatoes were delicious but I couldn't tear my eyes away from the cauldron in the middle of the table. White pigs' trotters bobbed in a murky brown ocean.

"I always have the tail," roared Paco, and fished it out from amongst the trotters with his fingers. "Unless you would like it?"

"No, no," we said hurriedly, "you have it!"

Paco grasped one end and stripped the meat from the bone by pulling it through his teeth. We watched, mesmerised.

"Pah! That was good! Carmen, serve the *manos* to the English!"

Spanish people don't object to food gone cold, so by the time we were served, a trotter complete with knuckle sat on each of our plates in a pool of congealed fat and pale chickpeas.

"Thank you so much," I trilled, patting my stomach, "but I'm full already. I don't think I could manage that."

Carmen looked disappointed but took my trotter away. The spotlight was on Joe and the atmosphere was electric with anticipation. Carmen stood poised, smoothing her apron, waiting expectantly. Paco refilled our wine glasses. Silence fell.

Joe was brave. He seized the trotter as he had seen Paco do, and pulled off a piece of cold fat with his teeth. He chewed courageously and smiled at Carmen who beamed with pleasure and turned back to the kitchen. Paco clapped Joe on the back and refilled everyone's glasses again. The cousins cheered in approval and everyone started talking at once. Joe masticated valiantly, using the wine to wash down the rubbery lumps of gristle. At last his plate was clear and Joe leaned back in relief.

Carmen appeared again with saucepan and ladle. "*¿Te gustó?* Did you like it?" she asked.

I couldn't resist. "He loved it!" I piped up. "He said he'd like some more."

There was murder in Joe's eyes as yet again the ladle descended to his plate.

On that wet August day long ago when I wrote my list, I had no idea what the future would bring. If we'd known that one day we would not only live in a tiny mountain village, but own probably the most dangerous cockerel in Spain, we would have snorted with laughter and disbelief. If we'd known we'd help rescue a vulture and that, one day, I would urge my husband to relieve himself, *in public*, on our friend's leg, would we have made that move?

Probably not.

But I'm very glad we chased the dream.

Perhaps I would have preferred it if we hadn't knocked over the village fountain on our moving-in day. Or if a mother cat hadn't given birth to kittens on our doorstep. Or we hadn't caused village ladies to fight outside our gate.

But life was certainly never dull. I'm even glad that the villainous Cocky came into our lives. He had the heart of a lion, the stamina of Casanova but the temper of a Tasmanian Devil. Come too close, and he would fly into a rage, hurling his vast vocabulary of chicken swear words at all and sundry. Nobody was safe from Cocky's wrath. It didn't matter that we were the hands that fed him; we were ambushed daily. Passing villagers were attacked and Cocky drew blood on numerous occasions. Something had to be done.

Sadly, there isn't space here to describe Cocky's shocking crimes or what eventually happened to him. Or why our neighbours, the Ufartes, became the talk of the village. Or why we had to move a car full of tomato plants in the dead of night. Or who stole all our chickens, and why. Or why Joe tended our grapevine in the nude and bought forty peaches by mistake. And how my teaching assistant, Juliet Thompson, and Sue, another teacher from my former life, became the Gin Twins and visited the village every year, often behaving as badly as the children in Green Class.

I only meant to produce one book about the village, but life was much too eventful, hilarious and colourful not to write about, and so the series continues to grow, much to Joe's horror.

And please don't think that pigs' trotters are the best example of delicious Spanish cooking. The village ladies kindly shared other, much more palatable recipes and so I'll end with a popular crowd-pleaser from the series. And I urge you, if you have a dream, chase it, even if your husband, or wife, thinks it's the worst idea he or she has ever heard.

Grumpy's Garlic Mushrooms

Ingredients (serves 4)

- 50ml (2 fl oz) extra virgin olive oil
- 250g (8oz) fresh mushrooms (sliced)
- 4-6 cloves of garlic (chopped or sliced)
- 3 tablespoons dry Spanish sherry
- 2 tablespoons lemon juice
- Large pinch of dried chili flakes
- Large pinch of paprika
- Salt, freshly ground pepper
- Chopped parsley to garnish

Method

1. Heat the oil in a frying pan and fry the mushrooms over a high heat for 2 or 3 minutes. Stir constantly.
2. Lower the heat and add the garlic, lemon juice, sherry, salt and pepper.
3. For a milder flavour you can leave it at that if you like. But if you like a few 'fireworks', now is the time to add the dried chili and paprika as well.
4. Cook for another 5 minutes or so until the garlic and mushrooms have softened, then remove from the heat.
5. Sprinkle with chopped parsley and divide up into pre-heated little dishes.
6. Serve with plenty of fresh, crusty bread to mop up the seriously garlicky juices.

The Old Fools Series
by Victoria Twead

This delightful series by New York Times bestselling author, Victoria Twead, begins with *Chickens, Mules and Two Old Fools* and describes retiring to a tiny Spanish mountain village and becoming reluctant chicken farmers. Eight books and ten years later, the series continues to grow.

• The Telegraph – "a colourful glimpse of Andalucían life with a psychopathic chicken or two … charming … funny."

• HarperCollins – "laugh-out-loud funny … especially the Spanish women heckling over eggs from the English … the interspersion of recipes is charming."

• The Catalunya Chronicle – "Weeks later, you will be standing at your kitchen window doing the dishes and recall some fleeting scene with chickens or mules or two old fools and laugh out loud all over again."

**For more information, visit her website:
www.victoriatwead.com**

2

Doing Things the Dutch Way
VAL POORE

Before I settled permanently in the Netherlands in 2001, I lived in Gauteng on South Africa's Highveld, the name given to the high-altitude plateau on which the country's commercial and political capitals are built.

My home was in Krugersdorp, a satellite town to the west of Johannesburg with an impressive elevation of more than 1700 metres. In spite of the risks and dangers for which Johannesburg is notorious, South Africa suited me well in every way: the colourful, hospitable people; the wonderful, sunshiny weather; the rich, exotic wildlife; and the natural environment that was so close by. In a word (or three), I loved it.

How was it then that I came to find myself living in the Dutch city of Rotterdam, around 90% of which is between five and six metres below sea level? It also happens to be chilly, wet and windy, a total contrast to everything I knew and valued in my former life, and yet somehow I learned to feel at home here.

It seems crazy now, but the reason I managed to adapt as well as I did had much to do with a collection of rusting rivets and iron, all held somewhat precariously together in a historic Dutch barge. But before I get to that, perhaps I should provide a bit more background. In 1997 my then husband was a scriptwriter and producer in the corporate video industry and was finding it difficult to win projects in his field in the new South Africa. So when he was offered a twelve-month contract with a film company in Amsterdam, he jumped at the opportunity. I stayed behind with our two daughters, four cats, and two dogs, the idea being that he would earn the money needed to set up his own business at home. It seemed like a good plan that would salvage both his career and his finances.

However, towards the end of his contract he changed his mind. I remember the day I received the news because it was the proverbial bucket of cold water over my hopes and happiness.

It was in the early days of social media and we were using a programme called ICQ, a text-only chat platform. We couldn't upload photos and we didn't have emoticons either, so it was all a bit basic to say the least.

"How would you feel about coming to the Netherlands?" my other half wrote.

"Ooh, for a visit? Yes, please!" I replied.

"No, not a visit. Permanently."

"I'm sorry. I don't understand."

"I don't want to come back to South Africa."

"Oh."

For that 'Oh', read a great big howl, which of course I couldn't express on ICQ, especially as I was at work at the time.

As you might have gathered, I was shocked to the core, and it took me some time to process the idea. I knew very little about the Netherlands and felt I couldn't make a decision immediately, so I did what all cowards do when put under pressure. I stalled.

"I have to talk to the girls," I wrote back. "And even if we can come, you know I have to give notice at work. At least three months." It wasn't true, but as I said, I was stalling.

When I broached the subject with my daughters, they were at first resistant, much to my relief. That made it easy; I could just refuse. But then they changed their minds and started to like the idea. What made it worse was that I began to see certain benefits in moving as well. I can't remember what they were now but probably things like being a complete family again, not having to be responsible for everything, not having to pay all the bills myself; that kind of thing.

In the end, and after much agonising over the pros and cons, I agreed. But it was with more than a little sadness we packed our bags, organised transport for the cats and dogs and flew to the Netherlands to join my husband in Rotterdam, where he'd moved in the interim.

I will admit I was disappointed it wasn't Amsterdam, but he'd been encouraged to transfer to Rotterdam by the Arts Council to help develop the cultural profile of the city. In other words, they gave him a grant, which was a pretty powerful incentive for a struggling filmmaker with an independent streak. As a result, we arrived in the Netherlands' largest port and commercial centre to start the new year in 1999.

At first I wasn't so enamoured of the city; it was everything I've mentioned—you know, cold, wet and windy. It was also too modern for my tastes; not my kind of place at all. In fact, I was pretty depressed to begin with and went through plenty of remorse over what we'd left behind. 'If only' became my daily but unspoken mantra. Everything in Holland seemed so grey and drab after the vivid skies and golden grasses on the Highveld, especially in the middle of winter. It was hardly 'chasing the dream'.

But after we'd been in Rotterdam for a few weeks, I discovered a whole new and different kind of world, and life began to look up.

My change of heart came about because my husband had an office on the waterside in one of Rotterdam's working harbours. I was fascinated by the commercial barges that came in, mostly just to stay overnight. They often moored up against the quay outside the door and I would walk along beside them, surreptitiously peeking through the net curtains of the windows in their rear cabins. I was intrigued and felt like Alice in my own wonderland. It was such a novelty to realise entire families actually lived in the spacious accommodation behind the wheelhouse, just like a floating apartment.

Anyway, I was so taken by the idea of people both living and working on their barges that when my other half suggested we should buy one ourselves, I didn't hesitate—this being in spite of the fact I hated sea travel, loathed being wet and abhorred the cold. In my excitement I suppose I conveniently forgot about those minor details; however, there was a snag.

"How on earth can we afford it?" I asked. "Those barges are huge, and anyway, we could never take up their lifestyle. We don't have a clue about transporting goods."

"Don't be daft," my husband scoffed. "We wouldn't get one like the big commercials. There are plenty of older, smaller barges around, and lots of them are lived on. They even call them houseboats."

"Really?"

"Yes. There were loads in Amsterdam. We've just got to find out where they are here and start looking."

In our subsequent search, we discovered the Oude Haven, a harbour dedicated to the restoration of historic barges right in the heart of Rotterdam. And this was what sealed the deal for me; I was bowled over to put it mildly. It was even more appealing than the commercial harbours because the late 19th and early 20th century barges in the Oude Haven were so beautiful. The history of the waterways I learned from talking to some of the residents there was also incredibly interesting. I fell hopelessly for the romance of living on an old boat and all that went with it. As for the community living there, I found their alternative approach to life appealed to me no end.

Anyway, to cut a long story short, the reunion with my husband was ultimately not a success, but my adaptation to this new way of life was.

Leaving out the complicated murk of what became marital misery, it was in 2001 that I found myself living on my own in the Oude Haven on a rented 1920s Dutch barge. By this time, my husband had moved away, one daughter had returned to South Africa and the other had found her own niche in Dutch life. Considering my dislike for all the damp and chilly stuff, my decision to stay in the harbour says a lot for the sheer magical appeal of the barging community.

I was charmed by the quirky characters who became my neighbours. I was also captivated by the grace and form of the barges: the tall-masted *tjalks* and *klippers*, the sleek *luxe motors* and the muscular tugboats. The enthusiasm for preserving these gorgeous vessels as symbols of Dutch heritage was inspiring. Above all, I loved the whole lifestyle; so much so I bought my own historic barge to restore at the end of the year, which in essence concludes the tale of how and why I moved from South Africa and settled in Rotterdam.

But of course there's more to life in the Netherlands than the Oude Haven and my barge, and if I'd been otherwise unhappy, I doubt if I'd have stayed. Luckily, I had a good job as a freelance

English teacher, a new relationship, and a daughter nearby, so these factors played a persuasive role in my decision.

That said, it was still a challenge to make a new life in a new country as a forty-five-year-old divorcee. And quite apart from rebuilding a boat and grappling with a new language, I had to go through a steep cultural learning curve, a factor I hadn't initially taken into account.

Many English speakers arrive in the Netherlands believing the culture of the Dutch is at least similar to Britain's, if not the same. I'm not sure why they believe this. Perhaps it's the historical links; you know, William of Orange and all that. Maybe it's because the Dutch speak English so well and seem so easy going. I think, however, anyone who comes here with that notion is in for a surprise. The culture of the Netherlands is a world (or at least a Channel) away from England's and it can take some time to adjust to it.

To understand the differences, it's a good idea to know something about the country's past in order to make sense of its present. Firstly, this is a land formed by its own people and their common history has moulded their character. There's a well-known saying that 'God made the world but the Dutch made Holland,' for which they can be justly proud.

Collectively over the centuries, they built dykes against the sea, created vast stretches of arable land where formerly there was only water, and developed the polders (as this new ground is called) into an agricultural power house. To achieve this, they had to work together on an equal basis; indeed, egalitarianism is at the core of Dutch culture. As a consequence, the fundamental principle of their approach to life is that no one is superior to anyone else, which has the effect of making them fervently individualistic as well. Yes, I know it sounds strange, but it's one of many paradoxes in this country.

The other deeply ingrained cultural influence in the Netherlands is Calvinism, that rather severe, puritanical Protestant religion of the 16th century. Calvin struck fertile ground in these Lowlands. His message appealed to the people's hard-working egalitarianism and distaste for hierarchy.

The result of combining their belief in equality with a faith that rejected the pomp, ceremony and structure of the Catholic church provided all the ingredients for making the Dutch who they are today. Calvinism had an ethos that must have suited the Dutch mentality even for those who were still Catholics, which is another of those paradoxes.

✧✧✧✧✧

So now I've got that bit of history out of the way, it will probably help to explain a few of the cultural contrasts between the Netherlands and the Anglo-Saxon world. It's a bit of a cliché by now but the first of these has to be the renowned Dutch directness. Most people seem to know about it, but being aware of the Dutch tendency to give you their opinion without cushions is not quite the same as experiencing it.

This particular quirk can take a bit of getting used to, especially for those of us from the UK, where beating around the bush is a national pastime and we have our own built-in code book to decipher what people actually mean when they're talking to us. We can therefore be a bit shocked by the unmitigated truth when it is delivered as an unexpected side swipe.

Of course it's probably rooted in the deep-seated sense of equality Dutch people have. Historically, courtesy (the English softening technique) was derived from courtly behaviour which I suppose was not considered necessary when everyone was equal.

My first encounter with this directness was when I was chatting to Marja, a friend of mine, and bemoaning the amount of time I had to spend marking assignments for my work as a language teacher.

"It's such a demanding job," I sighed.

"Well, you chose to do it, so you can't complain, can you?" she said with almost painful candour.

I winced, but she was right. I was only looking for some empathy, but fake emotion is not a Dutch thing, so if they don't feel it you don't get it; they are far too practical and honest. I should have looked elsewhere.

However, I'm now so used to living here I'm almost suspicious when I go back to the UK or South Africa and encounter what sounds remarkably like double-speak to me. It really does. I haven't completely given up my English prevarication, but I've just got used to not expecting it from others.

My Dutch friends are lovely, kind people, and I have a lot of fun with them. Nonetheless, they are mystified and sometimes irritated by my tentative requests and diplomatic verbal meanderings, most of which leave more room for negotiation than I ever intend.

For instance, there was the time I was teaching at a bank in Amsterdam and wanted to ask if I could copy some handouts.

"Would it be possible if I could just make use of a photocopier for a few minutes?" I asked in what I thought was a normal, polite manner.

"Do you want to copy those documents you're holding?"

"Well, yes, I was wondering if that would be okay?"

"What are you trying to say, Val? Do you want to make some copies or not?"

"Erm, well, yes please."

"Then why don't you just say what you mean without all this decoration?"

"But I can't," I wailed. "It just won't come out."

"Agh! You English and your politeness. No wonder we never understand you!"

We all laughed, and I got my copies, but I also received a worthwhile lesson in Dutch culture. They genuinely didn't understand my approach to what I felt was an awkward situation and misinterpreted my hedged remarks.

It took me some time to learn to deflect the blows of their more candid comments. Mind you, I'm less sensitive than I was at first and I don't flinch anymore when a chance remark delivered with the bluntness of a sledgehammer knocks me off balance. I am used to it; I don't take umbrage or creep off and lick my wounds, because I know this is simply Dutch honesty and there's no intention to hurt or harm.

I think I've even picked up some of their directness myself. It saves both time and 'clue chasing' because everything is so much clearer. The day I realised no one meant to be rude to me and there was no malice intended, I started appreciating the intrinsic integrity of the approach.

What this attitude also means is that business dealings are generally honest. That's not to say there are no dirty dealings or dishonest practices, but they aren't as common as they were in either of my former homes and they're exposed pretty promptly. On the whole, you can trust sales and service people, who are normally efficient, straightforward, and friendly.

This inherent Dutchness also applies to being paid for your work. As a freelance teacher and trainer, I've never had to go to a lawyer to get paid. There's a saying that *'afspraak is afspraak'* which loosely means 'an agreement is an agreement' and you're honour bound to keep it. I've noticed that people who cheat on that rule soon get a bad name, which is broadcast far and wide. The Netherlands is a small country and news travels fast—especially over the internet.

So although the reputation of being direct is true, there is another stereotypical reputation that isn't. It's the one we've all heard of: the Dutch are stingy and mean, which I can categorically refute. In my experience they are frugal and careful but that isn't the same thing at all. Their culture is one of thrift (remember those Calvinists?) and I often think the old expression, 'waste not, want not' is at the basis of their attitude to money, but they are immensely generous people too.

In 2019 the Netherlands was among the top ten charity donors in the world, and on a personal level, I was overwhelmed by the kindness of the harbour residents who gave me so much when I was starting out with nothing.

But there's one cultural anomaly I encountered quite early during my working life here that's proved to be a double-edged sword. It's what some writers call 'flat country' politics, which applies as much in companies as it does in government. In theory, because equality (flatness) is the standard by which everything has to be measured, consensus in all decision making is the key. Now I'm sure no one would argue against the value of such a principle, would they?

In practice, however, it has its downsides. For example, meetings can last forever and are a painful and tortuous process because everyone, and I mean everyone, has an equal say. Yes, it's a wonderful ideal, but if you're sitting in a meeting which has already overrun because of the need for said consensus, and then just at the point of reaching an agreement the office junior suddenly voices an objection … well, let's say it can lead to varying levels of insanity. This is because you know, you just know, the whole issue will have to be discussed all over again until the office junior is happy.

I've been a freelancer the entire time I've lived here and this strict adherence to consensus politics is the main reason I've remained self-employed. I nearly succumbed to having a contract once, but after I'd been to one of these meetings, I saw the light and made my escape.

Don't get me wrong; I love the notion that every single person's opinion is important, I really do, but sometimes the nasty dictator in me wants to shout them all down and force them into a decision they might not all agree with … just once … just to save time.

Cultural challenges aside, I should emphasise there are many more upsides to life in the Netherlands than downsides. The first and probably most obvious of these for me was the feeling of safety.

After spending ten years in the crime capital of South Africa, I was used to living in a state of high alert. We would double lock and double check everything: doors, windows and gates in our houses. Then anything that could be stolen had to be hidden away, mobile phones and car radios in particular. We didn't dare take our eyes off a thing. I remember the day I put my prescription sunglasses down in the bank; they were gone the second I turned away to look at something else. That was the way of life I was accustomed to, so coming to the Netherlands was quite a shock in that sense as well, albeit a good one.

All of a sudden I felt safe—not that I trusted it at first; it took me ages to stop barricading myself into my boat and keeping the windows closed in the car, but eventually I relaxed and realised robberies and break-ins weren't an inevitable part of life.

Okay, bicycles are the exception when it comes to theft. I had eight stolen from me over the first nine years I lived here. Yes, let that sink in a moment. The theft was so bad at one time there was even a bill in Parliament to address the problem (absolutely true). But when you know the Prime Minister cycles to work every day, it's an indication of how important bikes are to most Dutch people. It's not nearly as bad now, though, and I haven't lost a bike since around 2009. Or perhaps I'm just a bit wiser—I now have four sturdy locks, even on my old bone-shaker.

On that subject I have to say I am fascinated by the Dutch biking culture. Being a late starter on two wheels, I am riveted by the skill of these versatile Dutch cyclists who seem to be able to perform impossible deeds on a bike. They give each other lifts, carry ridiculous amounts of baggage, and can often be seen leading a second bike as well.

My favourite pastime is to watch young mothers cycling with one child in a kiddy seat at the front, another at the back, and often a dog on a lead as well. They then weave their way through the traffic as if it's the most natural thing in the world. Their dexterity is such I often think that when they're born, they whizz out of the chute on tiny bikes and never look back. I like the idea, anyway.

Even better, everyone rides them: the police, politicians, businessmen, couriers, grandmothers, parents, children and students. When I take my car in for a service, the garage offers me a loan bike. Companies give their employees bikes as perks and you can claim the cost of a new bike against tax; it is so much part of the Dutch way of life.

Granted cycling is very safe here because of the huge network of cycle lanes that traverse the country. And of course it's flat, which helps tremendously; the only hills within miles of Rotterdam are the bridges over the rivers, and they're not all that taxing either.

The Dutch love of skating is another thing that has delighted me since I came here. As soon as there's enough natural ice to bear their weight, the Dutch rush to don their skates and head out to play. It just makes me smile. From tiny tots to octogenarians, they're all out there.

There's much less fuss about whether or not the ice is thick enough than there is elsewhere because much of the time even a big puddle will do, and no one's going to drown in that. Then if the winter isn't cold enough for natural ice, they make their own by freezing over random pieces of ground just so people can skate their little hearts out. I wish I had the courage to do it too.

However, a big surprise for me is how I've grown to love the flat Dutch landscape which has been so instrumental in forming the country's culture. Yes, I miss the mountains of South Africa, but these calm, pastoral flatlands have their own soothing beauty. What's more, the sky is as much part of the scenery as the land and is often stunning. It isn't any wonder that so many artists of the past came to the Netherlands to paint the 'Dutch light'.

I also love the trees along the dykes and the tall, waving reeds that line the drainage ditches and canals. I love the water everywhere; I *really* love that. The boats, barges, quaint bridges and huge commercial waterways alike are my soul food. The fact that river traffic takes priority over roads seems totally right to me, and I never mind waiting even up to twenty minutes for a bridge to open for the barges to pass through. If I'm late for work, well so be it. Everyone gets caught sometimes; it's a regular occurrence in all Dutch towns.

The Dutch attitude to pets is also something I appreciate immensely. They accept that dogs are part of the family and you can take your pet pooch anywhere on public transport. Most hotels welcome dogs too and there are plenty of restaurants where the family four-pawed friend is allowed, water bowl and biscuits provided.

We won't mention the poo on the pavements though. Alright, we will. Unfortunately, despite the threat of fines and the plethora of places where dogs are invited to do their business, many people are still surprisingly careless or even uncaring about letting their pets foul the pavements without picking up after them. It's definitely something to watch out for.

❁❦✧◈✧

What else, then? Well, the Netherlands has many beautiful old towns. Some of my favourites are Dordrecht, Zierikzee and Middelburg to the south of Rotterdam, and Deventer, Utrecht and Zwolle to the north east. They are gorgeous places ribboned with canals, harbours, and old boats. With their historic centres still intact, the picture of traditional Dutch life they present is enchanting. Most have cobbled streets and quaint, narrow gabled houses with tall windows. Often they have flowers in boxes outside, hollyhocks growing up through the paving cracks, and bicycles leaning haphazardly against walls and doorways. There is a kind of ramshackle but elegant charm about all these towns and I love them.

There is also much more trust than I have ever experienced anywhere else. Just recently, my partner and I were walking through Leiden (which is quite a large city) and someone had put a small table outside their front door with pots of jam in a box. There was a small notice politely asking takers to put the money in the tin provided. Now in rural areas I imagine this is quite common in most European countries, but in a large, cosmopolitan town? I would guess that's pretty rare.

Lastly, I love Rotterdam. It's my city and although I get tired of the noise in the Oude Haven at times, it really is a special and unique place to live. The centre is alive, vibrant and constantly changing. It's a standard joke that anyone coming to Rotterdam might ask, "What's that building over there?" and the Rotterdammer will say, "I don't know; it wasn't there last week!"

I enjoy walking through the market early in the morning, across the square behind the church and along the back alleys into the Meent, one of the busy shopping streets. When the city is waking up and the cafés and bars are opening, there is a special atmosphere of fresh expectancy. Oh and yes, I love the river (predictable, I know). It is the lifeblood of the country. If the Netherlands were a body, Rotterdam would be its heart and the river its main artery. Wonderful.

There are of course things I don't like: the weather for one (I know—I've already mentioned that), but then I don't think I'd like that anywhere much in Europe. For me, South Africa had the perfect climate and was a tough act to follow. I don't like the bureaucracy much either; it's a pain, it's frustrating and mind-numbing. The Blasted Dienst (*Belastingdienst* aka the tax office) is the worst because they have access to so much of our private information, a fact which came as a shock to me after the relative anonymity we enjoyed in South Africa. But in truth it probably isn't any worse than the UK and is almost certainly not as bad as France and Spain from what I've heard.

Another thing I don't much care for is the do-it-yourself approach to healthcare. There's no National Health Service and everyone is obliged to have medical insurance, but I'm afraid it doesn't equate with speed or quality unless you have an emergency.

These days I have to have something really wrong before I venture a visit to the doctor, where I'm mostly asked if I've looked up my symptoms on the internet and diagnosed my own problem. And that's only after I've managed to get past the interrogation committee at reception who seem to believe we, the patients, are making it all up. Their attitude is that we're out to waste the doctor's time and we should pull ourselves together, take a paracetamol and get on with it—an effective way of dispensing with time-wasters, if nothing else.

In fairness, I'm told the system is very good when necessary, but I've yet to find out what they consider *is* necessary. Still, these are occasional irritations and they don't diminish my overall affection for my adopted country.

When I stop to think about it, I could easily write an entire book about my cultural adventures in the Netherlands, and perhaps I should one of these days. It's been a journey of discovery, for sure. But all things being equal, I'm pretty much okay with living here.

The Dutch have been good to me, this stray sort of South African English woman. While I didn't come here to chase any dreams, I have a life afloat many would envy; I've had a long, fulfilling teaching career; and I've made enduring friendships among the country's open-hearted, friendly people.

Leaving aside the disaster of the Covid-19 crisis and looking at the bigger picture, it is interesting to note that according to the World Happiness Reports, the Netherlands consistently scores higher than its neighbours in Belgium, Germany and the UK. The reports also claim it has the happiest children in the world. If that's anything to go by, it can't be bad, can it?

Books by Val Poore

Spontaneous decisions can take us in many directions, can't they? For Val Poore, one madcap idea took her from the UK to rural South Africa in 1981. Then twenty years later, another impulse landed her in the Netherlands where she became involved in a very different kind of world.

From South Africa's highlands to Holland's lowlands, Val's life changed from living on a remote KwaZulu farm to residing on a historic Dutch barge in the heart of Rotterdam. Where once she milked cows and picked lemons off a bush outside her door, she now spends her time fighting a war against rust on her piece of floating Dutch history.

Follow Val's unusual adventures in her six *'Ways'* memoirs, or travel with her on the canals of northern Europe in *Faring to France on a Shoe* and its sequel, *Faring Forth Again on the Shoe*.

For more about Val's books, please visit:
www.amazon.com/Valerie-Poore/e/B008LSV6CE
Or type B008LSV6CE in the search box on Amazon.

3

Waking up in Japan
TODD WASSEL

My first airplane ride ever in my life was at twenty-one. I still remember my hands sweating as I fumbled with my seatbelt, unsure how it worked. The passenger next to me, wearing the bemused smile of a frequent flyer, asked if I was okay. I nodded absently as I blocked everyone out. My eyes were glued on the view out of my precious window seat, eager not to miss a single treetop, passing cloud, or hidden arctic mountain.

The excitement kept me up the whole fifteen-hour, 7,000-mile trip from Boston to Osaka. As the first rays of a new day reached out, Mount Fuji filled the window. Alone, swimming in a sea of clouds, it towered over the other mountains, unable to reach the open skies. It was perfect. It was everything I dreamed Japan would be. It was the beginning of a new life I didn't know I had been searching for.

One year later, in the summer of 1999, a rickety train shook me awake as it fought against old uneven tracks. Far removed from the heavenly dreams of Mt Fuji, and the neon glow of city life in Osaka, I was on my way to a new home. A few short months ago I graduated from university and accepted my first job, as an assistant language teacher in a rural town in Shiga Prefecture. Perched on the northern edge of Japan's largest lake, Biwa, my new town had less than 5,000 people. I was the only foreigner living there. My head swam with images of rural Japan, walking through verdant green rice paddies, fishing on the shores of the lake, enjoying Shinto festivals in the mountains.

Hidden from me was the growing discontent in my soul. Something about the American blueprint made me tense up, avoid looking at the future. Go to school on the back of loans, get a job, get married, buy a house. Fill the house with so much stuff you scrape by every month just to pay for it. If you're lucky, piece together enough money over forty-five years to retire. I knew I would get caught some day, but I still tried to escape, if only for a few years. I needed to get 'it' out of my system. Only then could I settle down and be a good American. Little did I know 'it' would define my life for the next twenty years.

Brakes squealed as the train approached what passed for a

station in the countryside. A small wooden building provided the only way onto the station's platform. Overhead a corrugated iron awning protected the heads of five men, dressed in black suits, almost hidden in the evening dusk. They stood, backs straight, stern faces illuminated by the train's lights. My hands sweated as my excitement and nervousness grew. First impressions are important in Japan. I didn't want to make any mistakes. I juggled two duffle bags and a large bag of cookies. The bags would see me through my next few years. The cookies were a traditional offering, to show I understood the custom of gift giving, and that I was ready to fit in.

As I stepped off the train into the thick humidity of the Japanese summer, the five men regarded me. Faces set, there was no hint of welcome, and I was unsure if I had done something wrong. Self-doubt welled inside of me as we faced-off on the deserted platform.

I half fell, half bowed. *"Hajimemashite, Toddo-desu,"* I said too loudly. I thrust my hands outward as I offered the cookies.

Silence hung in the air. I kept my head down, hands stretched, waiting.

"I told you it was him," one man remarked in Japanese.

"But you never know!" another whispered.

"Somebody should say something," a third offered.

"How long do you think he will bow for?" the fourth wondered.

No one seemed to realize I understood what they were saying.

The fifth man stepped closer. "Hi, Toddo-san," he said in heavily accented English.

I looked up.

"Quickly, quickly, we eat." The man continued gesturing frantically.

Huh? I stood up and tried to open the cookies and a sudden burst of excitement poured out of everyone.

"What is he doing?"

"We will be late."

"Vice Principal, you need to make him understand."

This made me stop. Clearly, they didn't want the cookies.

"Excuse me, but I speak …"

The fifth man, who seemed to be the vice principal, turned and said "Come," in English. The other four men spun in unison and followed. They left me to gather my bags to keep up, half holding and half dragging as the cookies threatened to spill everywhere.

I approached a black taxi as the back door swung open on its own. The taxi driver, dressed in black with gleaming white gloves, opened the trunk for my bags. He hesitated to get his gloves dirty, so I pushed them in myself. I had never felt so far away from home, so foreign. How was this ever going to work?

The five men had their heads together. I was a sudden problem that needed to be fixed. They studied me, discussed again, seemed distressed, and then in an instant resolute.

"Do you eat rice?" the vice principal asked. He was the leader of the not-so-welcoming party.

"*Hai*," I began in Japanese. Before I could continue, the heads bobbed in unison and everyone started walking away.

I stood still, waiting for an explanation and unsure what to do.

"*Sumimasen* …" I tried.

The group looked back, stunned. "You, taxi," the vice said. Was this my first order from my new boss? Learning to do something with no idea what was happening is an important skill. I'd become an expert at it after six years in Japan.

The taxi door shut on its own, and we pulled out into a dark country lane. Alone in the back, I wondered what I had gotten myself into.

○෨☼ඣ○

Three days earlier I had arrived in Tokyo with over 1,000 new teachers on the Japan Exchange and Teaching (JET) Program for a few days of orientation. Set up in posh hotels in the center of the city, they prepped us for our assignments before sending us all over the country. Beyond the cultural classes, advice from current teachers on how to fit into your school, and a thin coating of teacher training, they taught us the most important rule of all: Every Situation is Different.

Some JETs would be in cities, some in the countryside. Some

schools had a history of JETs and knew how to use them, how to welcome them. Other schools were taking part in the program for the first time. I was still getting used to living abroad, but the rule would come to guide me over the next two decades. Nothing will be like you imagined, and you needed to stay relaxed and willing to adapt.

The taxi rolled to a gentle stop in front of an oasis of light in otherwise dark rice paddies stretching out as far as the lights illuminated. A curious blue squid was being chased around the building's sign by a crab and a fish. The men in black waited by the door, forming a tunnel of suited bows, the boss gesturing me inside. No one made any attempt to help with my bags as I struggled to pass through their narrow channel of politeness without knocking them over.

"*Irashaimase,*" a group of staff yelled as I walked into a conveyor belt sushi restaurant. Big grins broke out across the once stoic faces as they screamed at me from behind, "Welcome to our town," in their best English.

Plate after plate of glistening raw fish, nestled on top of beds of rice, zoomed past our table. The colors of each plate set the price, and you took what you wanted as it came by. The men in black turned out to be the vice principal, members of the local board of education, and the mayor's assistant. None of them spoke English, past the simple greetings. But it didn't matter once we sat down as they pushed a never-ending stream of raw fish in front of me.

Twenty minutes later, the food stopped. They demanded that I must be tired and ready to leave. I tried to speak and they shoved another plate of sushi in front of me. It seemed their plan was to keep me from talking with sushi. It was working.

"We have arranged a house for you," the vice principal began. "It is a gigantic house and you will be happy," he said in Japanese.

I tried to ask another question, but he raised his hand. "No, no, you don't have to say anything. We know how grateful you are for such a wonderful house. A house! No one your age lives in a house by themselves."

"Come," he demanded again as the rest of my welcoming

committee jumped to their feet and rushed out of the restaurant. They left me to struggle with my bags, as I tried my best to keep up with their pace. I didn't want to offend them by being too slow.

This time they put me into the vice principal's car, a small bright blue minivan that didn't match his stern manner, and we headed into the unknown. Barely a few minutes later they rushed me around a small grocery store. Thankfully, they let me leave my bags in the car.

"Here, have some butter," one man said.

Another man walked by, saw my butter, and shook his head. "You need to have bread with butter in the morning." I stayed silent.

All five agreed. I had everything I needed to stay alive for the next few days. They had done an outstanding job helping me to settle in.

All I had was butter and bread.

We got back into the car and drove around the dark town a couple of more times to make sure I was fully lost. We arrived at a run-down two-storey traditional house. Constructed only sixty years ago, it was an old house in an ancient country. The poor building materials were a mark of post-war poverty, when the imperative was to rehouse everyone as quickly as possible.

On the left-hand side was a small abandoned concrete block, the sign board long rusted away. In the back loomed an elementary school, closed now, abandoned by the children who'd grown up and moved away. On the right was a parking lot. It was chained off, just in case somebody thought to stop by, as if to remind them they were not welcome.

Only the vice principal and I remained of our original gang. The other four had taken the chance to sneak away.

I unlocked my new home with an oddly shaped key. Rather than a locking system, it was like a screw that released when I inserted the key and came out by unscrewing it. The front door slid open to the right. I stepped from the street right into the living room. Before I could find a light switch, I heard my new boss speaking.

"Well, I will leave you now," he said, still standing out in the street. "You have everything you need. We prepared everything." He sounded like he wanted me to sign an acknowledgement before releasing him from his duties. A warranty in case anyone thought to check if he did his job.

"*Sensei*," I called before he could disappear.

He paused, giving me a moment to ask a question.

"What time does work start tomorrow? Where …"

"Eight o'clock," he replied and jumped into his car, speeding away as if he had just committed a crime.

The welcome felt wrong. I wasn't going to push the issue as I didn't want to seem rude. I was too young to realize how weird it really was. I reassured myself that they were nice and were probably shy or worried about how I would be. Of course, they had failed to even tell me *where* the school was located. That would be tomorrow's adventure. For tonight, I was tired and ready to sleep.

I moved further into the house, searching for a light switch in the dark. I found a string and pulled on an overhead light. Click. Nothing. I pulled again. Nothing. I pulled again. One of the three circular florescent lights burst into light for a few seconds before falling into uneven flickering as it gasped its last days.

My beautiful dream burst as the old house came to life, covered in a layer of dust only disturbed by my own feet. Papers lay scattered all over the linoleum entrance way, tattered paper *shoji* doors leaned to the side in a failed attempt to divide the two woven tatami mat rooms apart. What the hell had happened here? It looked like a murder scene.

I pushed my way further into the house in search of a place to sleep. In the back corner, I found a rolled-out futon on the floor. In a moment of naive hope, on the border of jet-lagged mania, I thought, see, they are nice. They even rolled out my new bed like in a Japanese Inn.

As I got closer, the truth pushed me farther into the nightmare. Covered in dust, stains and smelling of mildew, I found where the murder must have taken place. I almost vomited. What had I gotten myself into?

Alone, far from home, I spent my first night feeling like a vagrant in my new home. Betting the dust was cleaner than the old futon, I slept on the bare tatami in my full clothes. I tried to remember that Every Situation was Different.

※※※※※

Things almost always look better in the morning. Not my new house. No one had lived in it for what looked like a year. No one had even stepped foot in it until I arrived last night.

I searched for a toaster for my bread. Nothing. I searched for a pan to toast it in. Nothing. So, I held the bread over the gas burner, singeing my fingers more than I succeeded at toasting the bread. I opened the drawer to get a knife to spread my butter. Nothing.

Welcome to the wonderful world of *Omote* and *Ura*. What is seen and unseen in Japan. While my hungry stomach didn't appreciate the lesson, as I look back this helped me to understand that not everything is what it seems in Japan. It reminded me to keep looking for the real meaning and not accept blindly the superficial niceties offered up.

The *omote* of everything is polite and by the book. It is the public image that everyone wants to convey. *Ura* is the opposite. It is the reality behind the public face. It is what people think, but do not let outsiders see. You know you are a full member of a group in Japan when they trust you enough to keep the *ura* a secret, and they stop presenting the *omote* version to you.

If you look carefully, hints of the *ura* are always there to see.

In my case, I was the unfortunate inheritor of an unpleasant situation. But to everyone else, my town was a success at hosting JETs. The town had welcomed JETs for five years straight. Of course, my town had also never kept a JET for over one year, let alone all the way to the third and final year allowed. In most cases, these teachers just didn't renew their contract. No one discussed why they didn't continue.

We never talked about the dirty house, or the lack of proper cleaning. I'm sure now that this was as much a part of the test as anything. Could they trust me not to point out difficult subjects? Could they trust me not to cause problems? It would be over a year later, after I signed up for another year in my crazy town, that my school trusted me with their secret.

No one ever mentioned the JET who preceded me. They avoided the topic when it came up, avoided me when I asked, or else just pretended that I didn't speak Japanese. Then, one day, during a late-night drinking party, held to celebrate me, the first JET to stay an extra year, it all came out.

The vice principal, drunk, was a close talker. As we listened to the other teachers bellow out Beatles' song after Beatles' song, he leaned in even closer.

"Toddo-san. Thank you. I thought we were in trouble after what happened to your predecessor," he slurred in Japanese.

Had someone murdered her after all? It had taken me almost a full month to clean the house so that no one would catch hepatitis, let alone want to visit me.

I leaned in closer, eager to hear the secret. He smelled like hair grease.

He leaned in closer, and we bumped heads. I tried to pull back, but he grabbed me.

"She just disappeared one day. One day she was teaching and the next day she was gone." He shrugged and took a long pull on the beer I poured him.

"No, no, no. You have it all wrong, *sensei*," a young woman yelled as she stumbled into us.

She was my Japanese supervisor, and one of two full-time Japanese teachers that taught English at the school.

He stood up and wobbled and said, "No, I can't hear this." And disappeared towards the Karaoke stage.

"He knows what happened," she said in English, not wanting the others to understand. "But he can't accept it. We'd all get in trouble if everyone knew. Except that is all in the past, now that you have stayed."

"I wasn't there," she added hastily.

I nodded, trying to reassure her. I wouldn't put her in with the offenders.

"It's true. One day she didn't come in. They all thought she was sick. She didn't speak Japanese, so she couldn't call. We thought it would be just a day or two. But after the first month, people stopped asking where she was."

I choked on my beer. "A month!" I yelled, not caring who heard.

She nodded. "But then another month passed. And then another. They debated calling the police. Should they enter her house? No, they couldn't invade her privacy. In the end, they got the mayor's office involved. All the teachers were called in, one by one, to find out what happened."

"What about the police?" I asked. I thought I knew where this was going.

She shook her head and looked around.

Had it just gotten quieter in here? Darker?

"No, they couldn't do that. Think what trouble it would cause …"

I was thinking about a poor woman dead in my apartment!

"They called each person in and asked what they knew. One by one, they claimed to know nothing. Only when they got to the office assistant did the truth come out."

The room was quiet now. I felt the eyes of the other teachers on me. Despite the English, they must have known what we were talking about. Was this a crazy initiation, and if I didn't pass, were they were preparing to kill me too?

"The office assistant showed them a fax that had come in three months ago. The cursive made it difficult to read. Since it was all in English, they figured it was a mistake. So, they filed it away. No one even thought to show it to the English teachers to translate!"

"What did it say?" I asked, more than ready to end the mystery.

"I quit. I'm moving to Osaka. Goodbye." She burst out laughing.

I joined her, all my unknown tension rushing out of my body in an instant. The bar grew brighter, and the teachers were as loud and cheerful as ever.

It turned out my predecessor hated living in the countryside. But she didn't have enough money to start all over. So, she quit by fax, and stole everything in the house to help her start up in Osaka. None of the teachers thought to check the apartment's silverware, toaster, etc. or to wonder about the futon. How bad could it have been after only three months? They had just locked the door, and waited for the next teacher to arrive, me, nine months later.

They were a sweet group of teachers. But if I died in the house, it would be at least three months until help arrived!

✿૭૦✿ஒ✿

I hope you enjoyed the first few days of me waking up and living the life I always wanted. Dreams never last through the night and never turn out the way we think they will. Go pursue your dreams, but know that in the end, life will entertain and fulfil you more than any dream ever could. It has kept me going around the world for over twenty years. Being fully awake is much more fun.

Walking in Circles
by Todd Wassel

Far from the lights of Tokyo. A 1,200-year-old pilgrimage. A life changed forever.

Guided by a wandering ascetic hiding from the Freemasons; naked Yakuza; a scam artist pilgrim; and a vengeful monk, *Walking in Circles* is a fun, inspirational travel memoir set in a Japan few outsiders ever get to see.

Award-winning writer Todd Wassel draws on over twenty years in Japan to retell his epic journey through the contradictions of a contemporary yet traditional Japan while trying to overcome the barriers to happiness modern life throws up.

Over half a decade after first landing in Japan Todd is lost. Convinced there is more to life, he risks everything to return to the one place he found answers years before: the ancient Shikoku Henro pilgrimage. Walking the 750-mile Henro path, sleeping outside each night, Todd is armed with only a Japanese map and the people he meets along the way.

**Find out more at Todd's website:
www.toddwassel.com**

4

An Unplanned Adventure in the Hills of Umbria
CLARE PEDRICK

People are always asking me what made me buy an old ruin on the top of a hill in a remote part of central Italy—and then give up my dream job, regular salary and comfortable lifestyle to go and live there. After all, I was only twenty-six at the time, entirely on my own, and after some quite daunting struggles, firmly established on a career path as a journalist, with Fleet Street beckoning tantalisingly in the middle distance. It is a question to which I still don't really have an answer, other than to say it was watching a video of chickens eating spaghetti that led me to take that first step, which would change the course of my entire life.

You see, I never really meant to buy the ruin at all—or anything else come to that. And I certainly had no intention of packing in the life I had taken such pains to create for myself, including the pretty pale blue Regency house I had bought near the Brighton seafront, and the strong ties I had already forged with my colleagues in the friendly newsroom at the local paper where I was a reporter. So if it hadn't been raining so hard that Sunday morning in November, I probably never would have pored over the overseas property section of the Sunday Times, after working my way through all the other parts of the newspaper. And if I hadn't happened to have a day off the following Monday, I might never have telephoned the number at the bottom of the small advertisement that finally caught my eye: *House for sale in hidden Umbria*. Then again, if the estate agency hadn't happened to be just a twenty-minute walk away, I might never have made the effort to go and see the man who had just set up the business of selling properties in Italy from his front room in neighbouring Hove. And if he hadn't sat me down with a cup of hot espresso and fiddled around with a video player to show me some flickering footage of chickens pecking at a small heap of cooked pasta in a cobbled piazza, I might never have been on a plane just two days later to buy an old house in a place that I barely knew how to pinpoint on a map.

Given the serendipitous start to my adventure, it could have all gone horribly wrong, and by rights, perhaps it should have, as I was totally unprepared for what lay ahead and had no game plan whatsoever. But for some strange reason that I have yet to fathom, the disaster that so many people saw looming on the horizon mysteriously failed to materialise. In many ways I would make a poor candidate for any reality TV show built around people's calamitous experiences buying property overseas, not that those really existed at the time. Mine is no syrupy tale of sunshine and happiness, for there were many hurdles to overcome along the way, but I can safely say that no one tried to rob me or cheat me—well no one who counted anyway—although nothing could probably have been easier, had they wanted to.

On the contrary, from the minute I stepped onto the train at Rome's Termini station and began my journey winding into the foothills of Umbria, with olive groves and rushing streams flashing by, and pale-coloured villages clinging to the mountains on either side, I felt strangely at home. Almost before the train had pulled out of the station, a family in the same carriage began plying me with food and drink as the mother unpacked endless parcels of salami, cheese and *frittata*—a type of omelette—all washed down with a glass of strong red wine poured by the father, and rounded off with a shot of dark coffee from a thermos. How different was this train journey from the other trip I took on a regular basis—generally to interview disgruntled commuters about delays on the Brighton-London Victoria line—and how extraordinary to be included in this seemingly impromptu family picnic, though this was by no means the last time I would be invited to join in such a ritual on an Italian train journey.

Following my arrival in Italy, finding the house that was to become my future home turned out to be extraordinarily quick and simple. The property in the advert had already been sold, I was told by Mirella, a well-built middle-aged lady who picked me up from my hotel in the town of Terni the next morning. She was the business partner of the estate agent in Hove, and in broken English explained that we were heading to see another house in the nearby town of Narni. I silently prayed it would be prettier than Terni, a largely industrial city based around a steelworks, much of whose heartland had been bombed to smithereens by British and American fighter planes during World War II. Narni was indeed a great deal lovelier, and the little stone house with wooden shutters that was currently for sale was in perfect condition and all ready to move into. But after a quick stop at a café in the local piazza for a drink and slice of pizza, Mirella had something else to show me.

This property was very different, she told me, as she drove deep into the Umbrian countryside, with scattered olive groves and a seeming endless vista of hills and valleys in every direction. It would certainly require extensive renovation, but it had something rather special about it.

I'm told that most people who buy a house take the trouble to get it checked out first, and see that there is no serious structural damage, or reason why they shouldn't invest their money in the property. When I fell in love with the old house that came into sight as we rounded the next bend, it took me less than ten minutes to make up my mind, before writing out a cheque on the spot. Perched by itself on a knoll just outside the miniscule village of San Massano, the house was magical, at least to my eyes. It was built in a warm-hued limestone, and bathed in the full glare of the morning sun it commanded uninterrupted views of rolling hills, with snow-capped mountains in the far distance. I knew that this house had to be mine, and bursting with excitement, I couldn't wait to tell my elder brother, calling him from the only telephone for miles around, which was located in the corner of the village shop.

Even the crackling phone line couldn't disguise the horror in his voice when he heard what I had done.

"What does the surveyor say? Presumably you've had the property checked out?" he said reasonably.

"I haven't got a surveyor," I answered.

"Well, what about a lawyer? Surely you've consulted one of those?"

"Er, no. I haven't."

"Well don't worry. We're still in time to stop this. We can get your deposit back if you only decided to buy the place this morning." My brother was trying to sound calm and reassuring.

"No we can't. I already paid the whole amount. And I don't want to pull out of the deal. It's the most beautiful place I've ever seen in my life."

In my defence, there wouldn't have been much point in having a surveyor inspect my new purchase, as there wasn't a great deal of it left standing. The old stone house I had rashly just bought was situated a stone's throw from a medieval hill village that was the oldest inhabited settlement in Umbria. It had hardly any roof, gaping holes in most of the stone floors and one entire section had disintegrated into a pile of rubble. There was no electricity or water source other than a nearby well, and the grounds were a mass of thick and twisted brambles that tore at the ankles of anyone bold enough to try to reach the front door, not that there was one.

The villagers I encountered in the following days appeared to be equally perplexed by my decision. This part of rural Italy is still very traditional and it was quite unthinkable that a young woman should even consider buying a house and doing it up, all on her own, without a family, or at least a husband. That's the question people asked me the whole time at first. "Where is your husband?" Or "What do your parents think of you coming over here, all alone?" In fact I had neither. My long-term relationship with my boyfriend had ended suddenly earlier that summer, and both my parents had died some years ago. Aside from my two brothers, I was quite alone in the world.

With hindsight, it's probably just as well I didn't think too carefully before plunging head first into my new life and all that it involved. There were some quite dramatic culture shocks in store, and even though I spoke Italian—I had studied it at school and university—I hadn't bargained for the local dialect, which, as in many Italian regions, is very broad here, especially among the older generation. It's not just a case of a strong accent; people actually use different words, which can make communication very difficult. Added to that was the fact that my vocabulary was entirely unsuited to terms linked to the building trade—I was quite capable of discussing Dante's imagery and symbolism, but completely at a loss when it came to talking about cesspits and sewerage systems. As I was soon to discover, the villagers in San Massano lived in a time warp, with women washing their clothes in the village piazza's public fountain. In England, I had owned a washing machine and a dishwasher, and lived in a house with central heating and double glazing, not to mention an electric blanket on my bed in winter. In my new home, I didn't even have a stove to cook on, but for the first few months at least, I had to rely on the system that local people had used for generations, cooking food over the open fire, boiling pasta in a cauldron that hung from a big iron hook.

I didn't move in straight away of course. But after returning to England, and my job in the newsroom, my thoughts were increasingly focused on the ruined hilltop house in a faraway part of southern Umbria. Blind as only a person in love can be, I would pull out a selection of well-thumbed photographs to show anyone who expressed the slightest interest. Only now can I understand the quizzical glances these elicited, since each photo clearly showed what was to all intents and purposes, little more than a wreck. Perilously, I dodged the eagle-eyed gaze of the news editor to make covert calls to Cesare, who would be taking care of the renovation in my absence, and enquire about the progress. Had the electricity been installed? What about the water? When would the plastering be starting? Was it time to start ordering the tiles for the bathroom? Would it all be ready for Christmas?

With unfailing good grace and courtesy, Cesare patiently did his best to explain to me that all the paperwork connected with the purchase would need to go through the myriad channels of the bureaucratic system before he could start any construction work.

"Perhaps you are forgetting that this is Italy," he said, vainly trying to manage my expectations. That would take weeks, maybe longer, so Christmas was unlikely, he warned. The owner of a small building firm, Cesare was Mirella's husband, a bear of a man with the gentlest disposition, who spent his spare time as a scout leader, and was regularly to be seen in his uniform, complete with dark blue corduroy shorts and a royal blue scarf and toggle. At every opportunity, Cesare would go out of his way to save me money. Hearing that I wanted to install a bath as well as a shower in the as yet non-existent bathroom, he sourced a nearly new bathtub from a ski chalet he had been renovating in the mountains, before his partner ran off with all the cash. Despite his own precarious financial situation, Cesare refused to accept any payment for the bathtub, and said that he and Mirella would be expecting me for dinner if I did decide to come for Christmas after all.

In fact I had thought of little else since I had signed the contract in Mirella's office that November day. Not only had I booked my flight, I had also sent out my younger brother Jamie as an advance party, with an old car packed with sheets, blankets, pots, pans and crockery I had bought in Brighton. Jamie was good with his hands and could start putting up shelves and building cupboards before my arrival. Perhaps we should organise a party and invite all the villagers? On I dreamed, oblivious to the stern gaze of the news editor from behind me, as my typewriter fell increasingly and suspiciously silent.

Most people probably associate Italy with a hot, sunny climate, but that Christmas was the coldest I have ever been. With no heating aside from the open fire, and the icy air seeping in through the rotten window frames and missing panes, the only way to get warm was to go outside and chop wood, then heat water over the open fire to cook a plate of pasta, all by the light of a candle as there was still no electricity. Going to bed involved putting on as many clothes as possible before diving under the freezing cold covers, the only source of warmth being a hot water bottle that we each filled from the cauldron over the fire. There was no bathroom either, so Jamie had used his considerable inventive skills to fashion an outdoor loo out of an old chair that he found in the cellar. After burning a hole in the middle of the seat with embers from the fire, he wrapped silver foil around the remaining ring and lashed an old stick to the backrest to hold a loo roll. The result became affectionately known as Space Bog, and would attract puzzled glances from anyone who approached the property for some time afterwards.

As things turned out, it was to be several months before all the paperwork and rubber stamps had been finalised, and the renovation work could finally go ahead. This was a rude awakening to the grindingly slow nature of Italian bureaucracy, but I was cushioned from the worst of its impacts—the interminable visits to local government offices and the filling out of never-ending forms—by Cesare, who uncomplainingly took charge of the administrative side of affairs, updating me on the sluggish progress in surreptitious phone calls made from the newsroom back in Brighton.

His was not the only help I received in those first difficult months. During one of the many table-groaning dinners to which I was invited at Cesare and Mirella's house during my frequent trips back and forth between England and Italy, I was introduced to a couple who were to become lifelong friends. Angela was originally English, the daughter of a wealthy Jewish family, though she had lived in Italy for a long time, after meeting Ercolino in Liverpool, where he was working as a waiter in a restaurant. Within six weeks of their first encounter they had eloped, and Angela had been disinherited by her father, who could not forgive her for marrying the son of a poor Italian family, who to add insult to injury, voted for the Communist Party.

It would be difficult to find a more unlikely couple, or a more devoted one, and in spite of the very modest circumstances in which they lived, they showed me the most extraordinary generosity from the outset. When not in San Massano, where they rented a tiny house in the village to spend weekends and summers, they lived in a small council house in Terni, together with Ercolino's mother, who quaffed several tumblers of wine with her lunch and dinner each day and gave me a toothless smack of a kiss on both cheeks every time I visited. I soon became the couple's unofficially adopted daughter, and spent many happy evenings in their kitchen down in Terni or up in San Massano, eating Ercolino's delicious *spaghetti alle vongole*—pasta with clams—and drinking wine he bought in five-litre flagons for a trifle from a little shop around the corner. Ercolino spoke English with a strange mix of Italian and Liverpudlian accents, and as the wine flowed his idioms became increasingly confused and profane.

"You drive me up the bloddy bend," he was fond of saying to me, with mock exasperation, in response to my many questions about what I considered to be curious facets of Italian life.

"Just heat your dinner and shut up, will you?" Another

endearing feature of his speech was putting aitches in the wrong places.

Time and time again, Angela and Ercolino helped me to negotiate the minefield that I was beginning to understand I had just walked into, paying my water and electricity bills on my behalf once these services had finally been connected, when I was back in Brighton. Incredibly, to someone like me, you couldn't settle any bill as a direct debit, but had to queue up at the post office on a certain day of the month, spending most of the morning to make the payment, and being sure to take along fistfuls of cash, since credit cards were not accepted. Frequently berating me as a "pain in the harse", Ercolino nevertheless took his role as my adoptive father very seriously, and on several occasions rescued me from the unwanted attentions of the many middle-aged lotharios who seemed to think that a young unaccompanied blond Englishwoman must be an easy catch.

Not everyone was kind to me though. Lecherous advances aside, on one occasion not long after I had bought the house I received an uninvited visit from a ginger-headed man with an aggressive manner and his equally hostile grown-up son, who threatened me with all sorts of unpleasant consequences if I refused to buy a piece of land adjoining my property. Outraged on my behalf, Ercolino and Cesare paid them a visit, ordering them to cease threatening the *signorina inglese*, and thankfully I heard no more from the unprepossessing duo. Ercolino and Cesare were old friends who had gone to school together, and when I heard about their mission I couldn't help smiling at the thought of the spectacle that must have greeted my aggressor when he opened the front door—Cesare's immense height and girth flanked by Ercolino's diminutive form, for he only came up to my shoulder.

Friendship, as I soon learned, is the key to everything in Italy. Quite apart from the social aspect, having people on your side can make all the difference in just about any setting. It can smooth your path through what can be difficult terrain even for those born and brought up in this country, let alone an outsider such as myself. I often wonder why I was shown such generosity by people who had no real reason to display such kindness, and certainly nothing to gain from it. The only answer I can come up with is that people felt sorry for me, as I was all on my own in a foreign country, and they wanted to protect me. Another possible reason is the quintessential *joie de vivre* that is still part and parcel of daily life, at least in this part of Italy. Where else would a team of builders who had just renovated your property throw a party in your honour, bringing food and wine and toasting your future happiness in the house? That day, with a feast set out on a long trestle table in my garden, is one of my most cherished memories. Before leaving, the chief builder presented me with a paper hat like the ones he and his crew used to cover their heads and protect them from falling dust and plaster as they worked. I had much admired these ingenious head coverings, which each builder would swiftly fashion out of a piece of old newspaper before starting work in the morning.

Life in Italy was not all about eating and drinking, however important these two pastimes were and continue to be in this country's daily life. I still had to make a living, as the renovations had quickly swallowed up all my savings, and I was determined to pursue my career as a journalist. By now I had taken the momentous decision to resign from my job at the newspaper in England, install tenants in my house in Brighton and move to Umbria full time. I had the princely sum of £50 left in my bank account, so this move clearly made no sense at all, but impetuously or bravely, depending on your perspective, I set off on the latest step in my uncharted adventure. I was helped by the fact that this, the mid-1980s, was a lively time news-wise in Italy, and I set about selling articles to foreign newspapers on a whole range of subjects, including culture, fashion, the mafia, skulduggery and machinations at the Vatican, and a dramatic terrorist attack at Rome's Fiumicino airport.

I soon managed to build up a network of newspaper contacts in locations that came to include England, the United States, Canada and Australia, but the business of communicating with them, not to mention sending my articles, was to prove extremely challenging. As in many parts of rural Italy, there was no telephone line except to the village shop. Speaking to news editors to pitch or discuss potential stories required walking up to the village, hoping the shopkeeper

Tito would already be awake (in the case of a call to Australia), or still be up (in the case of a call to North America), and trying to make him understand that I wanted to make a reverse charge call. This inevitably sent Tito into a whirl of confusion, as he failed to see how I could make a telephone call overseas and not pay for it, and was deeply concerned that the bill would somehow end up with him. However, the biggest hurdle came when I had to send the written article over to the newspaper, using my very basic Tandy laptop and an acoustic coupler. Realising that no amount of explanation would ever convince Tito that what I was doing was legitimate, I took to sneaking my equipment into the telephone cabin in a big shoulder bag, closing the door firmly, and talking loudly to invented characters on the other end of the phone as I waited for the signal and desperately rammed the acoustic coupler into the handset, praying that the connection would last long enough to send the piece. Often, the line would drop mid-way, and I would have to start all over again, with Tito shuffling about anxiously outside and intermittently calling out:

"Is everything all right *Signorina*? Are you sure that I'm not going to be charged for this long phone call?"

These days, sending an article—or anything else for that matter—is thankfully a great deal easier, though sadly Tito and his shop are both gone. The house is also very different from the old tumbledown wreck that caught my breath that first time I set eyes on it. Not only does it have a phone, including very passable wifi, it has a leakproof roof, central heating and even a swimming pool, which is an idyllic place to sit and watch the sun set over the rolling hills and see the fireflies that dance around in summer evenings, or scan the skies for shooting stars.

Since that first restoration, the entire house has been taken apart and reassembled brick by brick, and each room lined with wire cages, so that the structure will flex instead of collapsing in the event of an earthquake. That's another thing I omitted to inquire about when I first fell in love with the place on that November day. The village where my house is situated is in one of the most seismic areas of Italy, and you often feel tremors here, generally heralded by the sound of glasses rattling on the shelves. In the big 2016 earthquake that killed nearly 300 people in Amatrice, not so far from here as the crow flies, I was woken at three in the morning by a deafening roar and had the unnerving experience of feeling my cast iron four-poster bed literally march from one side of the room to the other as the building swayed dizzyingly. Miraculously, the only damage to the house when dawn finally broke after that long and sleepless night was some cracks in the mirror of a downstairs bathroom.

All things considered, perhaps it's just as well that I didn't ask if Umbria was in a high-risk earthquake zone, when I first watched that video of chickens scooping up a pile of spaghetti put out for them by an old woman in a pretty Umbrian hill village. Had it occurred to me to do so, or indeed to ask any of a number of sensible questions, I might never have bought the old ruin that was to become a much-loved home for me and the family I would go on to have. What is certain is that my life would have been different in very many ways. I recently took out Italian citizenship, though I am still English of course, and it was a proud moment when I was handed my huge, beautifully embossed certificate, which is now framed and hanging on the wall next to me as I write this in my study. The view from this room never fails to stop me in my tracks whatever I'm doing, and I just gaze into the rolling hills, which stretch forever and develop a mesmerising blue haze as the day wears on.

Of course, life is not always perfect here, but Italy is a country of great natural and architectural beauty, rich traditions and incredible human warmth, and I can't think of anywhere that I would rather live. Strangely, given its relative proximity to Rome, this part of southern Umbria is still off the beaten track, with daily life closely tied to the rhythms of the rural landscape. The winters can still be bitterly cold, just like that first one I spent here, when plunging temperatures killed hundreds of thousands of olive trees. But come March, you know that the first wild asparagus will soon be appearing on the hillsides, and local people will be out scouring for them, as will I, using sticks to push aside the undergrowth and ward off any errant vipers. Life goes on here much the way it has for generations, with seasonal rituals that often revolve round gathering food, and turning it into simple but delicious dishes.

My experience has confirmed a strong belief in the power of love, friendship and coincidences. I will never really understand what led me to the newspaper advert on that rainy Sunday morning in England, and I could never have imagined the overwhelming change it would make to almost every aspect of my life. But I'm extremely glad I didn't pay too much heed to the voice of reason. Sometimes, being reckless really can pay off, and at the end of the day, I suppose that's what my story is all about.

✧✿✧✿✧

For anyone who enjoys good food, Italy is of course a wonderful place to live. Umbria is known for a simple cuisine that is based on fresh ingredients, often sourced from the local countryside. My own favourite dish, which was taught to me by Ercolino, is *Strangozzi con asparagi*—Fresh pasta ribbons with wild asparagus. If you are lucky enough to be in Umbria in springtime, then you can find these on the hillsides or for sale at roadside stalls. If not, use cultivated asparagus instead, close your eyes and transport yourself to San Massano.

Ingredients for 4 people

- 2 wine glasses of extra virgin olive oil
- Small piece of chili pepper (optional)
- A big bunch of wild asparagus
- One large clove of peeled garlic
- 500 g fresh long pasta, such as *strangozzi* or *fettuccine*
- Salt and freshly ground black pepper if chili pepper is not used
- Freshly chopped parsley

Method

1. Crush the whole garlic clove by smashing it with a heavy knife blade (not by putting it through a garlic crusher as this makes the flavour too overpowering).
2. Take a saucepan and gently warm the garlic in the olive oil for a minute or two, taking care not to colour it.
3. Add a very small piece of chili pepper if liked, cut into tiny pieces.
4. Remove from the heat while you prepare the asparagus. The trick here is to use your fingers—not a knife—to snap off 2 cm pieces of the stalk, starting with the shoot at the top. As soon as it becomes more difficult to snap, discard the rest and move on to the next one.
5. Rinse and pat dry the asparagus pieces before adding them to the olive oil and simmering for 5 minutes over a low heat (parboil first if using cultivated asparagus).
6. Meanwhile, cook and drain the pasta.
7. Toss together with the asparagus mixture, adding salt and black pepper if chili pepper is not used, and sprinkling with parsley.
8. Serve with a crisp white wine such as Orvieto Classico.

Chickens Eat Pasta: Escape to Umbria
by Clare Pedrick

The tale of how Clare Pedrick came to buy an old stone house outside a tiny hamlet in the hills of southern Umbria is told in her book *Chickens Eat Pasta: Escape to Umbria*. It's a love story really, with the house itself, and with a man she later met there—a strange coincidence given that she was only the forty-third resident in the little hilltop village, where everyone knew everyone else, and most of them were related.

The story has a strong supporting cast of memorable characters, some of whom you have met briefly in this chapter. Without giving away too much, this is a story with a happy ending. The author and her husband are still married, with three children, who love the old house on the hill almost as much as she does.

The book is available in paperback or as an e-book. *Chickens Eat Pasta* has also been made into an audiobook, narrated by actor, author and artist Colleen MacMahon, who painted the watercolour for the book cover.

To purchase the book *Chickens Eat Pasta*, please visit:
www.amazon.com/dp/B012GZXOPY
Or type B012GZXOPY in the search box on Amazon.

Global Nomads
LINDA DECKER

When I was a child I dreamt of travel to distant lands. I have a vivid recollection of lying on my tummy on my bedroom floor in Scotland, with a large atlas open in front of me. I was probably about ten years old at the time. Poring over a map of the world (pre Google maps, pre internet). I was sad to work out that if I was lucky enough to go on a holiday every year for the rest of my life, I still wouldn't be able to visit all the countries I could see spread out in front of me, or get close to knowing or understanding what the geography and the people were like. I was a geography geek. So looking back, that is my earliest memory of a true longing to travel.

In fact, I didn't get on an aeroplane until August 1977 when, after unbearable nagging, my parents gave in and booked a family holiday in Malta. I can date this trip precisely, as I remember sitting round a swimming pool with my dad, who read the front page of a fellow holidaymaker's British newspaper. 'The King is Dead' the headline pronounced.

"Which king?" my dad mused.

It was of course the king of rock and roll himself, Elvis Presley, who had died at the tender age of forty-two.

Shortly after that holiday I began studying law at Strathclyde University in Glasgow, and on day one of freshers' week met a boy who was straight off the plane from Nairobi, Kenya. His parents were technically British, but had lived and worked abroad as expats for the whole of his life. We got chatting, started 'going out' immediately, and the rest is history.

Chris travelled home to Kenya for the university holidays, and I would join him there for a month or so after working for most of the summer in Glasgow, and saving some money. On one trip we flew together and booked a stop-over in Cairo, Egypt. We took in the pyramids, the Tutankhamun exhibition at the Cairo Museum (we were offered a mummy to buy) and we even made it to Aswan and the Temples of Abu Simbel. I contracted dysentery and after passing out, I was carried to the German Mission Hospital in Aswan on the shoulder of a tall Nubian gentleman.

"Do you speak German?" the head nurse enquired, hopeful of

the opportunity to converse in her native tongue when she spotted Chris's German surname in his passport.

"Sorry, sadly not," was Decker's disappointing reply.

We missed out on the Valley of the Kings and Queens as we were advised to fly straight to Chris's family home in Kenya when I was discharged. Chris had spent days sharing handfuls of sunflower seeds with expectant fathers, while I lay in bed on a drip surrounded by a sentry of covered Muslim women, dressed in black from head to foot. Their caring and curious eyes were all I could see whenever I opened mine.

After graduating, Chris resisted all offers of jobs overseas so that I could complete my legal training. For a person with a lust for travel my choice of career was not that wise or portable, even south of the border to England, due to the different legal systems.

We always knew we would move abroad one day; that had been discussed and agreed in the six years before we got married. So after completing his master's degree in water engineering, Chris looked to specialist consulting firms, with an international presence, for a job. Quite a specific brief, which was fulfilled when he was offered a place on a graduate trainee scheme within commuting distance of London (or so we thought). I felt like I'd won the lottery when I was offered a job with Linklaters and Paines, one of the leading international law firms to this day. Of course I had to write some exams for The Law Society of England and Wales to enable me to be admitted as a solicitor south of the border as well.

We both worked hard and had great friends we still see whenever possible, more than thirty years on. We ate out a lot, enjoyed seeing London shows and skied in Europe with our tribe most years. We travelled as much as possible, which was easy as we lived in West London, handy for Heathrow Airport.

One Christmas, we saved up our annual holiday entitlement and visited Chris's dad and his second wife Barbara (an American anthropologist) at their tented camp on the Tana river, Kenya. Barbara was researching endangered red colobus monkeys, which were falling out of the trees and dying for reasons that weren't obvious. The research project was being funded by the Coca Cola foundation through Emory University in Atlanta. Fred attended to the practical building and maintenance work around the camp, and the couple were instrumental in the founding of the Tana River nature reserve, which you can see on a map of Kenya today.

On arrival at camp, I was charmed that my practical father-in-law had spared no effort for our comfort. We had a detached tent, set up a short distance from the main action, for peace and privacy, but close enough to the river that we could hear the hippos cavorting and snorting.

My favourite touch was the luxury long drop toilet, which was just for our use. Fred had, with his usual ingenuity, cut the bottom out of a metal bucket, then carefully split a length of rubber hose and pressed it round the sharp rim to make for a very comfortable seat. The toilet itself was protected from view by woven screens, and there was a solar shower involving another bucket, which warmed water all day in the sun. Unfortunately there was no roof. I was always slightly nervous that a plane would fly overhead when I was attending to my ablutions.

That year, we ate barbecued lobster with garlic butter for Christmas dinner, having driven a four-hour round trip to the coastal town of Malindi for supplies. We also had Christmas cake with champagne, which we had brought to the African bush from London. Our four weeks in this remote paradise was an exciting experience, but not enough to kill the travel bug which was still under our skin.

After we returned home we settled back into our London lives. We got so comfortable that we had two daughters, Liberty and Amber. The new arrivals were the next major push for us to chase our dream of a life overseas.

We worked hard and enjoyed our jobs. I had long hours with a daily commute to the City of London. If I was working on a major transaction (takeovers and mergers were very popular in the 80s) I would sometimes work all night, travel home for a shower and clean clothes and head straight back into the office.

I worried that I didn't spend enough time with our girls or with

Chris. I also worried about a conversation I had with an American colleague at the office coffee machine.

"No one has ever had written on their tombstone 'I wish I'd spent more time in the office', Linda."

This really hit home, and so in January 1994 we put all our worldly goods into storage, having sold our family home and headed off for a posting in Brunei Darussalam, abode of peace. This was at the time when the Sultan of Brunei was the richest man in the world. Chris had been appointed Country Manager by his employers who specialised in water engineering consultancy work. We were surprised by his new title, one which may have upset the Sultan himself, had it come to his attention, as Country Manager was surely his role and his alone.

We had left a cold dark London in January and flown via Singapore to a tiny country whose oil and gas reserves made it the richest in the world per capita. It's now dropped to fifth place lagging behind Singapore, Luxembourg, Macau and Qatar.

As we swam in a warm pool under a dark blue velvet sky in the open air on a balmy January evening, we felt that we were finally realising our dream.

We could splash about in the South China Sea at sunset every weekday night if we wanted to, and collect driftwood for beach barbecues at the weekend. It was an idyllic life. We grew rambutan fruit in the garden. Our girls called them hairy strawberries, but their hard shell-like skins when peeled back revealed soft lychee-like fruit, sweet and aromatic. So sweet and aromatic that we were invaded by troupes of monkeys as the fruit ripened on the trees. This rambutan thievery was common and entertaining.

Of course the king of fruit in this part of the world is durian. It grows to the size of a watermelon, with thick spikey skin. When split open, large soft lobes of flesh are revealed, and the smell is revolting. It wasn't unusual to see a sign prohibiting durian being brought into a building or a hotel and many property leases banned them entirely. The experience of eating durian was colourfully described by a friend as eating the sweetest most delicious exotic fruit in the world while sitting on the smelliest toilet. Enough said. I couldn't resist trying it and I think it tastes a bit like sweet creamy fried onions. It wasn't the extreme eating experience I'd expected.

So we had time to enjoy our garden, which was full of tropical plants, fruit and flowers. I grew orchids outside and hung the pots on trees and around our veranda. When I say I grew them, I collected them and they grew themselves in the warm humid environment. The climate was perfect for orchids, not so much for humans at a steady thirty-three degrees for most of the year and close to 100% humidity.

Like the flowers, our children were thriving in their new environment. After a short delay, while their names were placed on waiting lists, Liberty started at the International School in the capital Bandar Seri Begawan, and Amber began nursery school. They made friends, as did we, and it really felt like we were not only chasing the dream, we were living the dream. We travelled to Singapore, Malaysia and Bali as often as we could for short holidays and enjoyed longer holidays in Australia, Hong Kong, Thailand, and Macau. This was all in addition to our annual leave trips back to the UK to spend time with family and friends.

I loved being with our girls every afternoon, swimming at the Royal Brunei Airlines Club and meeting up with friends. Gone were the frantic bath times and bedtimes, the highlight of the day in London, assuming I was able to get home.

But all good things come to an end, and when we had been in Brunei for five years we started casting the net for the next posting.

One day, as I was sitting on our veranda with Ann, my mother-in-law, who was visiting us at the time from the UK, Chris surprised us with a visit home at lunchtime. He was clutching a fax message which needed urgent attention. We had been asked to move to Amman in Jordan at very short notice, as a crisis in the water supply had arisen. Initially, I had serious concerns, not about moving to Jordan, but about moving to this part of the Middle East. Think Iraq (this was before the second Gulf war), Israel and Syria. I couldn't imagine this area being an 'abode of peace'. However, thoughts of the rose-red city of Petra and camping trips to Wadi Rum led us to accept the posting almost immediately.

By the time we reached Jordan, we really were living the life we wanted. Travelling and experiencing new countries and cultures and getting to know people in our host countries as well.

The geography was totally different to the lush tropics of the Far East, and we touched down in what is one of the most water starved countries in the world. You wouldn't guess that by looking at the colourful gardens. Mature plumbago plants crept over warm honey stone walls, bougainvillea brightened up many a beautiful old villa and it was possible to grow numerous familiar European garden staples. Amman is at 1,000 metres above sea level, so the climate is kind, even in the height of summer.

We were fortunate to find a beautiful villa, near the International School both girls would attend. When we arrived it was being rented by a family who were reassigned to a post in Beirut with the UN within days of us meeting them. The only condition attached to the transfer of the lease was that we should take on Tweety, their pet duck, and a large number of tortoises which wandered happily under the apricot trees, when they were not banging shells.

The tortoises were an easy yes, but Tweety was a bit more problematic, despite her clever party trick of untying children's shoelaces. I suffer from a debilitating fear of birds. On the other hand, there was a real shortage of lovely villas for rent and we needed somewhere to live. We were assured that Tweety never left her enclosure, which ran the whole width of the villa and took in the fruit trees. A lovely spot to peck away at vegetables and lay duck eggs.

On our first day in the new house Tweety was so happy to see her new family that she flew the coop, and free ranged round the garden. I was terrified and sprinted indoors.

"Catch the duck," I screamed through the open window to the children.

They were collapsing with laughter and not up to the speed of the bird who had made a break for freedom, or perhaps she was just excited to meet us.

Order was restored, eventually, and Tweety stayed with us for the five years of our posting to Amman. The tortoises multiplied (that's what all the banging was about), but it was a blessing as many friends wanted one or two to give to their children as pets. Our children had their special tortoises, named of course, who were under no circumstances to be given away.

We loved living in Jordan. The Jordanian people are the most friendly, hospitable people you might come across in a lifetime of travels, and we count it a privilege to be in touch with many of the friends we made there, both local and expats to this day.

Our children enjoyed horse riding and we walked in the wadis, searching for the beautiful but elusive black iris. Colourful spring flowers forced their way through the hard rocky ground stretching towards the sunshine. Some parts of the countryside were carpeted with them. Being so high above sea level, the winter rains, and sometimes snow, allowed the flowers to germinate and then bloom in abundance in the spring.

We all enjoyed weekends away, exploring Roman ruins, desert castles and ancient villages and towns. We drove to the Nabatean city of Petra often as it was a great place to walk and socialise. On one trip to Petra we joined a tennis party of friends from Amman. As we looked around at the entrants on the tennis ladder, we hoped there was no need for the services of the diplomatic community that weekend. Most were doing well in the tournament several hundred miles away from the office.

The biggest excitement of our time in Jordan was when we welcomed our son Morgan to the world. He was made in Jordan and born in Jordan, and is proud of that. We have returned to the land of his birth several times since moving on, and, on each occasion Morgan is received with a 'welcome home' greeting at immigration.

When we revisited Petra on one trip back we were surprised by how it had developed. A large visitor centre with a selection of gift shops had been built at the main gate. The other surprise was the entry cost, about thirty Jordanian dinar each (roughly £30), an increase from the seven dinars we had paid in the past. It is worth every penny and we handed over our passports without complaint. Photo ID was required before entry to this important archaeological site.

"That will be thirty dinar for Christian and Linda please. Morgan you go for free. You are Jordanian, welcome home."

I still look at the bright woven wool rugs from Madaba and think back to long lunches in a courtyard restaurant and craft centre, decorated with geraniums spilling out of jumbo-sized battered olive oil tins. Then there are the mosaics which we bought for the house we plan to build in Italy one day. My mantra during all our travels around the world is always, 'you never regret what you buy, only what you don't buy'.

In August each year Jordan hosts an international art festival in Jerash, a well-preserved Roman city. One of my favourite memories is of sitting in the amphitheatre, under the stars, watching the Russian Ballet perform Swan Lake.

Another vivid memory is of being press-ganged to play golf in a competition. I seem to remember it was for the Princess Muna al-Hussein cup. Princess Muna is the mother of King Abdullah ll of Jordan, and was the second wife of the late King Hussein of Jordan. She is British by birth. I love a game of golf, and despite playing the game on and off for nearly forty years I have never improved. I play with Chris, who is just as bad as me, although he would say differently.

When we were in Jordan, we had a mission to improve our game and were regular visitors to the only golf course in the country at the time, just outside Amman. We bought a patch of artificial grass which we attached securely to our golf bags. Every drive of the ball left from our patch of artificial grass, but very rarely landed straight on the green, or the brown as we called it. Each green, or brown, was a patch of oiled sand, raked to perfection. It would have been offensive to water a golf course in such a water-stressed country.

I played to my usual standard in the ladies tournament and after some time it was necessary to wave the first two players through. They were very good and had caught up with us. When I did eventually get back to the club house for lunch and presentations, one of the ladies I'd waved through came over for a chat and congratulated me on making it round the course. I must say in fairness, I narrowly missed out on a prize. I wasn't quite the worst player, but I was close. The lady giving the prizes was Princess Muna herself, the same friendly golfer I'd waved through and failed to recognise on the course and off in her sports gear.

We enjoyed our life in Jordan, where it was possible to find anything you might need, to buy a good cup of coffee and cake at a local café, to eat out and even order wine. It was a lovely change after the strict ban on alcohol being served in restaurants and hotels in Brunei. Amman was a great posting with a good social life and lots of opportunities to explore. I went on several day trips to Damascus, Syria and ate lunch at the famous Jabri house, bought hand-made glass, carpets and inlaid Syrian furniture, all used and treasured. We managed to ski in Lebanon after setting out in convoy and driving via the Bekaa Valley to the Faraya Mzaar ski resort just north of Beirut.

We travelled to the reefs of Aqaba and Sharm el-Sheikh for diving expeditions and had a fabulous trip to Istanbul. We even learned a bit of Arabic.

Despite the fact that we loved living in Jordan, we were all very excited when the opportunity came to move to Dubai. Schooling for our girls was an issue, and by the time we left Jordan, our older daughter Liberty had elected to go to boarding school in Scotland. We blame JK Rowling and the Harry Potter effect. Liberty said that she enjoyed being part of an 'international family' as she put it and rejected our offer to relocate back to the UK.

Several years later Amber, our younger daughter, didn't want to follow in her sister's footsteps to boarding school, so Dubai presented a great opportunity for her to continue her schooling and live at home. She was offered a place at Dubai College, a huge accolade and a great school.

The move went smoothly and, after a lot of searching, we found a perfect family home to rent on Jumeirah Islands. They weren't really islands at all, but due to clever excavation of sand, and the introduction of a lot of water, the developer had created an island-like environment. Our villa overlooked a small man-made lake, which was kept algae free and sweet smelling by the ingenuity of Dutch engineers.

Each villa had its own swimming pool, but the weather was so hot, entering the water was like floating in a bowl of warm soup. We counted ourselves lucky to have a pool at all.

It was so hot for most of the year in Dubai that we went from air-conditioned car, to air-conditioned car park, to an air-conditioned mall. That was where I discovered the phenomenon of mall walking. The Mall of the Emirates was so long, it was possible to join an organised group for early morning exercise indoors.

Having said that we all loved eating outside in our garden. In the hottest months (nearly all year round), we sat outside for a drink and a chat and jumped into the water to cool down, well maybe not cool down but as we emerged wet, our bodies felt cooler. We would then eat our main course and jump into the water again. You get the picture. It was odd to undress for dinner.

Weekend beach trips were restricted to early mornings as there was very little shade. I got into the habit of dropping the children at school and walking along the shore by the Burj al Arab, the world's first six-star hotel. It always made me smile when I looked up at the iconic sail shape and roof top helipad. I did feel a very long way from my hometown of Kirkintilloch in Scotland.

This was never more so than the night I dropped our girls off at Ski Dubai, a huge indoor ski slope in the Mall of the Emirates. I had taken Morgan, who was six at the time, for a drink while we waited for his sisters to finish their snowboard lesson. We were all totally shocked when Amber suffered a ruptured brain aneurysm at the beginning of the lesson. She was rushed to hospital but never regained consciousness.

We did chase our dream overseas, but when faced with the greatest tragedy of our lives we returned home to Scotland with Amber for her funeral. Later we scattered her ashes in her beloved Jordan.

We went back to Dubai for a further four years, but it was not the same. We were surrounded by caring friends, and a compassionate community, but I often felt deeply lonely, even when I was with people I loved.

We left Dubai when we were asked to return to Jordan. Chris's employers were advising on a mega project with the ambitious plan of connecting the Red Sea to the Dead Sea, and developing the port city of Aqaba. The level of the Dead Sea falls each year, and in my head this project could be summed up as 'Saving the Dead Sea'.

By the time we had packed up, sent our shipment back to Jordan, found a house and made the move, the Jordanian government had changed. Legitimate further questions were being raised about aspects of the environmental impact of the project. Suffice to say that it stalled and, after ten months of relative relaxation on the work front, and just enough time to completely unpack our boxes, Chris was asked to work in Ramallah in the Palestinian Occupied Territories.

We chose to live in Jerusalem as our permanent base, as we couldn't find a suitable school for Morgan in Ramallah. None taught the curriculum in English, for his age group. It was a relatively straight forward commute for Chris, or so we thought.

Our little piece of luck was to find a beautiful house on an Israeli moshav (agricultural village), convenient for school and Chris's Ramallah office. Houses for rent on the moshav were as rare as hen's teeth, so we counted ourselves lucky to find the perfect place to live. The house overlooked vineyards and had a large colourful garden. We enjoyed an abundance of fresh fruit and the novelty of passionfruit freshly plucked from our own vine. We also picked and cured our olives, good training for tending the four acres of olive terraces we had bought in Italy. That's another dream and another story.

When we arrived we had to wait for our furniture and assorted treasure to catch up with us. So we spent the first month in a comfortable fully furnished apartment in Ramallah, which Chris had been living in for a while. I had stayed behind in Amman with Morgan so that he could finish the school year.

Our bedroom window was very close to the local mosque minaret. The first call to prayer was around 4 a.m., followed by one at about 5 ish. I'm not sure of the exact timings but the second prayer (one of five a day) usually started just as I was drifting back to sleep.

The most obvious change to our lives was the increase in security. At that time I was trying to organise our move to Jerusalem and prepare for Morgan starting school. I needed to drive to and from Jerusalem, but before setting off I had to log our journey with security at Chris's office, and remember to tell them when I'd reached my destination. I wasn't used to sharing my every move, so this was challenging, until I got used to it.

Of course I had to pass through the security wall to get to Jerusalem. A relatively easy thing for me to do, as I had the luxury of a foreign passport. There is no such ease of passage for the average Palestinian, who needs to obtain permission in advance to cross into Israel.

By now you know that we had lived in the Far and Middle East, moving from one country to another every five years or so. The moves had been relatively easy and we all settled well into new adventures and challenges. It was only when we moved to Jerusalem that, for the first time in my life as a global nomad, I felt totally alien in my environment.

Looking back, I was spooked by the security checkpoints, the barrier wall and the number of weapons on display. Israel defends itself daily against possible attack, and the upshot of that is having to go through airport-style security checks when you visit a hospital, supermarket or museum. The risk of kidnap was at the forefront of my mind as Chris travelled between Jerusalem and Ramallah on a daily basis. This was something he brushed off and I grew used to with time. I spotted a tee shirt stretched across an ample belly in the leafy and affluent German Colony, while meeting up with a friend for coffee. 'Fat people are harder to kidnap' was the slogan. I was so pleased that I'd indulged in an almond croissant.

We enjoyed exploring the Old City of Jerusalem. It is a significant place for Christians, Jews and Muslims and has more fascinating religious sites than you could hope to see in a lifetime of pilgrimages.

We knew a bit about the Arab culture and Islam, but it was clear that we had a lot to uncover about Israel and the Jewish religion. I learned about different sorts of Jews and their ways of life, the holidays, the matchmakers and the kaleidoscope of people, nationalities and beliefs which make up modern-day Israel.

I also had an opportunity to get to know Israelis and Palestinians, Jerusalemites and Ramallahns, along with folk from Nablus, Jericho and Hebron. We enjoyed their food, family celebrations, culture and ways of life.

It was fascinating and I began to record what I was observing before it all became commonplace and normal, before I stopped noticing the differences. So, I started writing everything down. At first it was just for me, and then I thought I could share the thoughts and funny stories with family and friends.

But after a while my Jerusalem diary became a memoir, and then I was thrilled when it won the Scottish Association of Writers Non-Fiction Book of the Year in 2018. At a time when Israel and Palestine are hardly out of the international news, and there is little opportunity for either side to cross paths and get to understand how the other half lives, I was grateful that our very personal experiences on both sides of the security wall would be shared with a wider audience than I had ever imagined.

We left Jerusalem after five wonderful years, older and wiser. Our youngest, Morgan followed in the footsteps of his sister Liberty and started boarding school in Glenalmond, Scotland.

Chris and I took the opportunity to chase the next stage of our dream, which was an early retirement somewhere in the sun, warm and dry enough for olive trees to grow. Our dreams came true when we visited a small whitewashed mountain village in Andalucía, Spain and found our forever home. Casa Karibu (which means house of welcome in Swahili) has a framed sea view of the Mediterranean and on a clear day we can see all the way to the Rif mountains in Morocco. We enjoy eating figs while they are warm from the trees, and juicing our own oranges. We're surrounded by mango farms and regularly have to avoid driving over this favourite fruit of ours as they fall from the trees and bounce onto our track.

Life is good, with new adventures, friendships and another language to learn. We continue to follow our dreams and travel … I think we always will.

Bombs and Bougainvillea, An Expat in Jerusalem
by Linda Decker

The Decker family have been global nomads for over two decades, but it was not until they moved to Jerusalem that Linda felt alien in her new environment.

If they had foreseen the challenges of relocating to Israel and Palestine, they might have hesitated … they have no idea of the horrors in store. No idea that murders will take place on their doorstep. No idea they'll be so close to a fatal bombing, or that they'll adopt a dangerous dog. As they enjoy delicious local food and immerse themselves in different cultures, will the unspoilt countryside and friendships help them overcome the difficulties, or will they flee from an area which at times seems to have one wall, but two prisons?

Join them on their journey to better understanding of this highly volatile part of the world in Linda's award-winning travel memoir *Bombs and Bougainvillea, An Expat in Jerusalem.*

For more information please visit her website:
www.linda-decker.com

6

Finding the Dream
NICK ALBERT

"**A** pile of stones on ten acres, with an optional donkey," Lesley exclaimed, gleefully tapping the computer screen.

"Sounds delightful," I quipped, peeking cautiously through the doorway. "We should move in right away."

My wife was sitting in the office of our home, a newly renovated dormer bungalow a few miles east of Colchester, one of the oldest towns in England. She'd called me in from the garden to share yet another exciting find.

"Come and look," she said.

"How much this time?" I asked, dramatically rolling my eyes.

Aware the previous four properties had been outrageously over budget, Lesley folded her arms and play-acted the smug wife.

"It's only £40,000." Her blue eyes twinkled mischievously as she beckoned for me to come closer.

"Whatever are you looking at?" I asked, peering over her shoulder.

"I've found this wonderful website just bursting with reasonably priced properties," she gushed. "Many are exactly the kind of place we've always wanted. There's a crofter's cottage up in the hills, a quirky eco-house with a lake and a wood, an old farmhouse with a large vegetable garden, and—"

"A pile of stones with an optional donkey?" I suggested.

"On ten acres," Lesley added defensively.

I frowned. "Yesterday we were looking at small but well-kept houses within easy reach of a town and a golf course. When did stones and donkeys come onto our radar?"

"Since I found this website." She tapped the screen again. "The estate agent has won awards for being so honest."

"But presumably not from his competitors."

Lesley sniggered. After a tough few weeks, it was nice to hear her laughing again. In the month since my employer informed me they were downsizing for the eighth time in six years, Lesley and I had spent much of our time hunting for a better job or a smaller house. It was a two-pronged attack to solve a problem that had been keeping me awake for some time. Even with my generous salary and healthy bonuses, we had barely kept our heads above water during the five years it had taken to convert a large but neglected 1930s bungalow and a field of bramble, into a delightful modern home with a beautiful garden. Money was tight, so the prospect of redundancy couldn't have come at a worse time. Unfortunately, my employer wasn't the only firm making cuts. When it became clear the demand for over-paid, middle-aged mid-managers was practically zero, we'd switched to searching for a more affordable home.

"Have a look," Lesley said, pointing at the screen.

"Well, I guess it couldn't hurt," I sighed. Somewhere in my vivid imagination, fate threw his head back and laughed like a pantomime pirate at my naivety.

My wife edged sideways to make room. The picture on the computer showed a large field, overgrown with rushes and bramble, against a distant backdrop of rolling hills, silhouetted by an azure sky dotted with fluffy clouds. In the foreground, there was a large pile of mossy stones in the approximate shape of a house. Growing through what once may have been the roof was a mature ash tree. Standing to one side in a characteristically forlorn pose was the aforementioned donkey. The picture would have made an interesting painting but would do little to inspire the average homebuyer. Fortunately, Lesley and I are made of sterner stuff.

"Inter-est-ing." I sang the three syllables and wiggled my eyebrows. "And where is this quirky but enticing property situated?"

"Guess."

"Challenge accepted," I replied, rubbing my hands together.

As I stood back and scratched my chin, Romany, our rotund Lhasa apso, waddled into the room. Like a stiff-legged sheep, she peered at the desk in the hope of getting one of Lesley's digestive biscuits. Alas, the packet was empty. Undeterred, Romany lifted her front paws and balanced precariously on her bottom.

"It's too green to be Spain or Portugal," I said. "Anyway, the foliage looks wrong."

Lesley snorted. "As if you'd know!"

Although I'm always ready to lend a hand or do some heavy lifting, gardening and other green stuff are very much my wife's domain. She is a walking encyclopaedia of horticultural knowledge. I walk behind the lawnmower. Lesley knows the Latin name of every plant. I can only speak in tongues when I hit my thumb with a hammer. On the other hand, I have a good eye for detail. I pointed to one corner of the screen.

"That's gorse," I said proudly. "I've seen it on the golf course, but I don't think it grows in hot places like Spain."

"You're right," Lesley conceded. "It isn't in Spain or Portugal."

I smiled, but my moment of glory lasted but a few seconds.

"Although …" she added. "The species Genistas Lydia is a small flowering gorse which comes from the dry and sunny hillsides of southern France and northern Spain."

"Good to know," I said. Even though it wasn't. "That isn't France."

"Correct."

Romany's bum balancing act had deteriorated into a spasmodic wobble. I reached down and gave the old girl a fuss. Satisfied her work was done, she returned to the standard dog configuration, farted and waddled out of the room.

"You'll never guess." Lesley drew my attention back to the game.

"I think it's closer to home."

Lesley remained impassively silent.

Once we'd accepted the harsh reality that I was soon to be unemployed and unlikely to get another job with a similar salary, we had begun looking at other alternatives. Continuing our current lifestyle, but in a much smaller property, was an unpalatable thought. By far the most tempting idea was to sell our house, pay off the mortgage and buy a smallholding with whatever cash we had left. It was a scary plan in many ways, but the prospect of cutting up our credit cards and living a debt-free life was an appealing image.

I scratched my head thoughtfully. It made a squeaky sound. The once narrow footpath through thick wavy hair had long since become a broad highway of flesh. Male pattern baldness at its best.

Our guessing game resumed.

"We weren't keen on Wales and Scotland is too far away," I continued. "I think it's the Lake District!"

"No."

My shoulders slumped.

"I give up."

Lesley beamed triumphantly.

"It's Ireland!"

○ɷ○ʗ○

In retrospect, my inability to guess the donkey's secret location and the pile of stones was understandable. Ireland was a country we had never visited, we had no family connections there, and the climate was notoriously cool and damp. This last point was at odds with Lesley's preference for hot, dry weather and her desire to fill our garden with exotic sun-loving plants. Nevertheless, if a man's wife was enthusiastic about something, however quirky, he was obliged to appear interested—or so Lesley said.

Fortunately, the interweb thingy was awash with exciting and attractively priced Irish properties. With the troubles consigned to history, the country's economy was soaring like a hungry kestrel on a hot day. It seemed every newly affluent, upwardly mobile employee wanted to live near Dublin and own a holiday home in Bulgaria, regardless of the cost. In juxtaposition, rural house prices in Ireland were comparatively low, especially for the style of property we liked. For the first time, our idea to buy a smallholding and live debt-free seemed less like a wild dream and more of a practical possibility.

After some careful research, we decided to combine a fact-finding holiday with some window shopping for houses.

"We should make a list," I eagerly suggested.

Lesley rolled her eyes in exasperation.

"You and your lists!"

I pointed at the teetering pile of property details on my desk. Like children in a candy store, we had filled our basket with dozens of prospective houses, bungalows, cottages and plots of land with outline planning permission. It was no surprise my printer had run out of ink.

"If you want to see all of these properties, we'll need a month," I replied.

Lesley waved her hand dismissively.

"Go on, make your list." She paused for effect and sighed. "If you must."

I rubbed my hands in glee.

Whereas my dear wife is happy to navigate her way through life with all the pre-planning and directional stability of a butterfly on a windy day, I can scarcely function without a schedule and a list. Having an itemised to-do list, with different coloured headings, subheadings and a handy key in one corner, gives me great comfort. With Lesley's permission, I converted her vision of a relaxing holiday into a series of early starts and late finishes, interlaced with a precise schedule of property inspections. At best, we'd only have time to see twenty of the most exciting prospects, so many waifs and strays were discarded before the plan took shape. The pile of stones with an optional donkey didn't make the cut.

※※※※※

"What's the story?" the official asked.

"Excuse me?" I replied.

Lesley and I had just arrived at Shannon airport on the first day of our holiday. When we entered the arrivals hall, I had stopped to use the loo. It was the cleanest toilet I had ever seen in an airport. When I emerged, feeling relieved and wiping the water from my hands on the seat of my trousers, my wife was missing. Perhaps excited to visit Ireland without delay, Lesley had already passed through border control and was waiting somewhere off to my right. My flustered and impatient demeanour may well have raised a red flag as I handed over my passport. Sitting safe within a Perspex and wood-sided box, the border official wore a dark blue uniform with sergeant stripes on the arms and the word 'Garda' on a breast badge. His cool blue eyes quickly began to strip away my confidence and uncover some deep-seated feelings of guilt and inadequacy. Somehow I resisted the unnecessary urge to make a run for it.

"What's the story?" he asked again.

"Err," I stuttered, glancing over my shoulder at the queue of fellow travellers. "I haven't really got much of a story."

He looked at my passport photograph once more, tutted, and squinted at me suspiciously.

"That's not really my best side." I tried to sound confident but failed.

The Guard raised a quizzical eyebrow and waited for my response.

"Feck's sake!" an exasperated voice behind me cut in. "Yea man wants to know why you're here!"

"Oh!" I slapped my forehead as the penny dropped. "I'm here on holiday. My wife and I are looking at houses. We hope to move to Ireland."

"Ah, you're grand." The Guard smiled warmly, snapped my passport shut and handed it back. "Welcome to Ireland."

"Thank you," I replied, grinning self-consciously.

Passing through the sliding doors like an arriving gameshow contestant, I went in search of my wife. The terminal building was clean, spacious and surprisingly empty. Between the departure doors and arrivals desks was a small newsagent's shop. I found Lesley browsing for books. She was clutching a gardening magazine and a bar of chocolate.

"Do you need some euros, already?" I asked pointedly.

She nodded and grinned. I handed over one of the unfamiliar notes.

"How did you find a gardening magazine so quickly?"

"I'm like a magnet," Lesley joked. She pointed over my shoulder. "The car rental desk is over there. While I pay for these, you can do the paperwork."

"Yes, dear."

I know my place.

✧ℰ✧ℛ✧

Like time travellers who had stepped back into the 1960s, Lesley and I stared around in open-mouthed astonishment.

"It's 4 p.m. on a Monday afternoon, we're on the motorway, and there isn't another car in sight," I exclaimed.

That morning, the thirty-mile drive to Stansted airport had taken almost two hours.

"Not true," Lesley replied, pointing to a side road. "There's a car over there, though it looks rather old."

"Good grief. It's a vintage Morris Minor," I laughed. "This really is the 1960s!"

"It's so quiet and green. Really unspoiled." My wife smiled, her eyes twinkling in delight. "I love it."

"So far, so good," I agreed. "County Clare is certainly pushing all the right buttons."

Driving out of the airport complex had been straightforward. I'd found the signposts and roundabouts to be familiar and easy to use. Our little hire car was still the only vehicle on the two-lane motorway. The road was much the same as a British dual-carriageway, albeit in far better condition. The ground to our left was low-lying farmland, an endless succession of miniature grassy pastures, separated by stone walls and interspaced by the occasional stream. To our right, the terrain gradually rose to become a series of hills; the base gave way to bands of brown foliage and grey rock.

I pointed to the ramshackle remains of a building. A large bush grew from the top of one wall.

"That's the third castle ruin we've seen in under ten miles."

"According to that book I got, Ireland has around thirty thousand castles," Lesley said.

"If we buy a property, I wouldn't mind a bit of a project," I quipped. "But I'd draw the line at something that bad!"

Lesley grinned. She seemed to be smiling much more since Ireland came onto our radar.

"There's no litter, and I haven't seen any graffiti either," she whispered. "It really is quite beautiful and unspoiled."

I silently nodded in agreement.

✧෨✧ൃ✧

To avoid the commercial blandness of a faceless hotel chain, I had booked us into a homely B&B on the opposite side of Ennis, the county town of Clare. We traversed the town with hardly a pause for the rush-hour traffic and quickly found our destination. It wasn't until we were crunching our way across the icy car park that I spotted a problem.

"I think they've had a fire," I said, nodding towards the house.

"What do you mean?" Lesley asked.

"It's freezing out here, but all their windows are wide open."

"Perhaps someone burned the toast, and they're clearing the air of smoke," Lesley suggested.

Although there were no fire appliances in the car park or piles of charred furniture, clearly something was amiss. I was about to suggest we should turn on our heels and head to the nearest faceless hotel chain when the door burst open. Mary, a portly middle-aged blonde-haired woman, threw her arms wide and welcomed us into her home as if we were long-lost relatives.

"Oh, isn't it fierce mild today?" she asked.

Mary flapped her hands at her pinkish face as she led the way to our room. With our breath condensing into clouds of mist, I looked at my wife and grimaced. The interior of the house felt chillier than an industrial fridge. It seemed Mary was having another one of her hot flushes. For the remainder of our holiday, we lovingly referred to her as Mrs Menopause.

During our stay, Mary treated us like honoured guests, going above and beyond the required bed and breakfast with the loan of wellington boots and free late-night cups of tea, and even a plate of sandwiches when we returned late after a long day of house-hunting. Because of the chilling cold in our room, Lesley and I slept fully clothed, and even wore our hats in bed, but it was a small price to pay for Mary's kindness and hospitality.

Breakfast was a magnificent affair with eggs, sausages, black pudding, white pudding, mushrooms, baked beans, tomatoes, piles of thick buttery toast, and gallons of Barry's tea. It would have been a spectacular start to our day, had it been available when Lesley and I awoke at 7 a.m. Unfortunately, Mary considered this an ungodly hour and refused to serve any food before 9 a.m. Although this unexpectedly late start to each day left my schedule for the week becalmed and rudderless, Lesley and I were stoically accepting of the situation. Perhaps Ireland was rubbing off on us already.

My meticulously constructed plan may have been as battered as a heavyweight boxer hanging on the ropes and praying for the bell, but there was still hope. Over breakfast the following morning, I made a suggestion.

"We could buy sandwiches and eat in the car. That way, we wouldn't have to stop for lunch."

I used a buttery knife to indicate the hour-long breaks I'd built into our daily planner.

"Or, rather than stopping every half hour, you could pee into a bottle while you drive," Lesley replied, between bites of her toast. "That would save some time too."

I closed my eyes and did the sums.

"Not really. At best we'd only gain enough time to see half a house."

I looked at my wife. Her expression floated somewhere between exasperation and incredulity.

"Oh," I groaned. "You weren't serious."

Lesley reached over and patted my hand as if I were a naive child—which in many ways, I am.

"Nick, we're considering a move to Ireland in the hope of a better life, with less stress and more time. Perhaps we should start by relaxing a bit."

"You mean, go with the flow?" I asked, involuntarily stroking my chart. "I guess I could try."

"Good for you." My wife smiled and pushed the teapot towards me. "Now, have another cuppa."

I need not have fussed about my plan. It was destined to suffer a fatal blow.

The people trained to sell houses come by many names: property agent, house agent, realtor, estate agent, factor, broker and sometimes, something less polite. In Ireland, they are called auctioneers. Ours was Alan Sykes. Like me, Alan was an English eccentric. But while I barely repressed my bubbling unconventionality, Alan wore his quirky nonconformity as a badge of pride. He drove his rusty, clapped-out car very fast, played a tin whistle whenever he had a spare moment and, although we'd exchanged numerous emails and spoken on the phone that very morning, he had forgotten we had arranged a meeting. Moreover, he hadn't contacted any of the vendors whose homes we wanted to see. My carefully constructed schedule was now in total disarray. I could feel my stress and anger bubbling to the surface, and it could have boiled over, had Lesley not caught my eye. With a glance and a timely smile, my wife reminded me of our earlier conversation.

"Just go with the flow," she mouthed silently.

As I nodded in acceptance, I felt my heart slow and my blood pressure easing.

For an eccentric English auctioneer living in sleepy County Clare on the beautiful west coast of Ireland, Alan was acting more like a city trader in the panic of a stock market crash. In between bites of his sandwich, he typed emails, fielded multiple calls using two telephones, and examined the thick pile of property papers we had printed from his website and brought with us.

"Sorry about this. I've several clients from America and Germany who are trying to buy over the phone," Alan explained, between calls.

"Moving to Ireland seems very popular," Lesley said.

"Oh, they won't move here. They'll probably never visit either," Alan replied, disparagingly. "These people are land-banking. Property here is a great investment. At the moment it's comparatively cheap, but values are rising fast."

"So, this is a good time for us to buy?" I asked.

Our conversation was interrupted by the phone ringing once again. Whilst conducting his business with an American client, Alan sorted our property choices. Showing all the sensitivity of a callous door guard at a high-class nightclub refusing entrance to inappropriately attired guests, Alan laughed openly at some of our chosen properties and tutted at others. With a shake of his head, he tossed a handful of papers into the bin. Excusing himself momentarily from his conversation with a Texas millionaire, he shoved a sheet of paper into my hand.

"Most of those were dross. You wouldn't have liked them at all," he explained. "Go and see these people this afternoon. I'll let them know you're coming."

With that, Alan turned his back and continued with his telephone call. I politely tapped his shoulder.

"How do we find this place?" I whispered.

"Buy a map. You need ordnance survey map number 55," Alan replied, before dispatching us with a wave of his hand.

And so our property search began.

☙❧

"Are ye on yer holidays?" the barman asked.

It was the end of our first full day in Ireland and we were in an Ennis pub called Poet's Corner. Tired but pleased with our day, we were hungry for dinner.

"No," I replied, squinting at his name badge. "We're here looking at houses, Shane."

"Ah, you've family here den." Shane smiled and nodded.

"We've no family connection whatsoever," Lesley said. "Actually, it's our first visit here, but we've already fallen in love with the place."

"That's true," I added. "It's so reminiscent of England in the 1960s."

The barman nodded.

"I know what you mean."

Judging from Shane's dark wavy hair, slim waist, smooth complexion and lack of any facial hair, this kindly lad had probably been born in 1982 and was unlikely to know what England, or anywhere else looked like in the 1960s. However, as a newly relaxed visitor to this beautiful island, I chose not to mention this fact and instead watch the complicated process of producing the perfect pint of Guinness. With the glass tilted to forty-five degrees, it was slowly half-filled and left to settle. After a couple of minutes, it was safe for the procedure to continue. This was the most delicate stage. With all the care of someone trying to add bait to a rat trap, the dark fluid was eased into the glass until it was almost full. Then, as a final flourish, the last dribble of beer was used to draw a shamrock in the frothy head.

This was my first taste of the famous black stuff. I brought the glass to my lips, sniffed cautiously and took an experimental sip. For some reason, I had anticipated a thicker texture, but that thought dissolved from my mind as the flavour filled my pallet. Although the fluid was cold, it struck me as being warm and nutty. I imagined I was drinking a meal in a glass, full of goodness and bursting with vitamins and minerals.

"Delicious!" I smacked my lips.

"How's yer house-hunting going?" Shane asked.

"Too early to tell," I replied. "It's our first day."

"Me brudder's gora place for sale." Shane gave me a knowing wink. "I could get ye a good price."

"I'll bear that in mind," I said, noncommittedly. "Thank you for the beer."

"You're welcome." He nodded and moved to the other end of the bar.

I turned to my wife and chinked my glass with hers.

"Cheers. Here's to a better day of house-hunting tomorrow!"

Lesley smiled at the memory of our afternoon. Her eyes twinkled with glee.

"It was certainly interesting," she said. "It's so quaint we had to ask at the post office for directions. Imagine not having any postcodes. It really is like being in the 1960s."

"When I phoned Alan, he apologised for forgetting to give us the vendor's name. Apparently, rural houses are known by who the owner is, rather than the address. That's why we had so much trouble finding the place."

"Perhaps we'll have better luck tomorrow." Lesley tutted and rolled her eyes.

"It was a nice enough place, but I couldn't believe the mess inside. It looked like they'd been robbed!"

"So you said," Lesley groaned. "It was a good job that dear lady didn't hear you."

"Sorry. I guess my appropriateness filter was switched off again. I'll have to get it looked at." I shrugged apologetically. "It seems they don't follow those TV shows advising how to prepare your house for sale."

"That's for sure!" Lesley laughed. "Fancy suddenly adding twenty acres to the sale and doubling the price while we were walking around. You could have knocked me over with a feather."

"I'm sure it was just one of those one-off events." I reached over and patted my wife's hand. "Tomorrow, everything will be fine."

It wasn't fine, but it was interesting and funny.

✿✾✿ൟ✿

Lesley and I were attracted to County Clare by the beautiful scenery, the welcoming people and the relaxed lifestyle. From the spectacular Cliffs of Moher, 500 feet of iron-grey rock plunging vertically into the churning Atlantic Ocean, through the bare limestone and stunted trees of Burren national park, to the greens and gold of the Slieve Aughty mountains, Clare has a vista to please every taste. We prefer hills and forests to flat landscapes and beaches, so we gravitated towards houses in the east. By coincidence, we were following in the footsteps of many European immigrants who were every bit as eccentric as us. Their quirky, illogical homes were utterly unique and frequently delightfully appealing. After many frustrating weeks and several false starts, we finally found Glenmadrie. It was a semi-derelict, higgledy-piggledy farmhouse, with a few acres of land, a disused quarry, a small wood and views to die for.

If finding our dream house was difficult, buying it became a farcical comedy of administrative oafism, legal stubbornness and financial misogyny. Three months after our search began, I was out of work, and we'd just sold our house in England. We had done our best to move things along in Ireland, but emails, phone calls, persistence and patience can only do so much. I had no choice but to leave Lesley with her mother and move to County Clare, where I could be on hand to make things happen. It worked. One month later, Lesley and I began our new life at Glenmadrie.

That evening, we sat in front of the fire and relaxed for the first time in months.

"Ah, this is the life!" I sipped my beer and sighed in satisfaction.

Red-eyed and wheezing from the smoke occasionally billowing back down the chimney, Lesley pointed to the sagging ceiling.

"Enjoy the rest. Tomorrow, we'll have to start cleaning. This place is filthy."

"I quite like the way the cobwebs wave with each gust of wind," I quipped. "It's very calming."

The storm outside rattled the windows once more, forcing the wind through a hundred gaps in the stone walls. More smoke wafted into the room where it joined the shower of woodworm dust raining down on our heads.

"There's a lot to do here to make this house even halfway liveable," Lesley said. She began counting off on her fingers. "The floors are rotten, the chimney leaks, the electrics are dangerous, the—"

"I'll make a list," I cut in. "First thing tomorrow."

"This is a massive project. What if we can't get a builder?" she asked. "Alan said they're in short supply because of all the new houses being built."

"Then I'll do it myself," I replied firmly.

A battle raged across my wife's face as an expression of supportive confidence was chased by a look of incredulity. The latter beat the former by some margin.

"You?" she babbled. "How?"

"I guess I'll buy a book." I smiled and shrugged noncommittally.

After a minute, my wife sighed and patted my knee.

"I bought eggs at the village shop," she said. "Fresh from the chicken; they were still warm."

"Mmm. Fresh eggs for breakfast. I can hardly wait."

"Perhaps we could get some chickens?" Lesley asked, sleepily.

"I'll add it to the list. From now on, we can do whatever we want."

Romany grunted in her sleep and began chasing an imaginary rabbit. The pursuit wasn't going well. I gently nudged the little dog with my toe. Romany gave up the chase, sighed gratefully and softly farted.

"Shall we get another dog?" my wife asked, wrinkling her nose.

"Just one?" I snorted.

"Two would be better," she whispered.

I closed my eyes and allowed visions of the future to fill my mind.

"So, this is our new life," I mumbled. "DIY and fresh eggs."

"And dog beds," Lesley added.

"Fresh eggs and dog beds. It sounds heavenly."

And it is.

The Fresh Eggs and Dog Beds Series
by Nick Albert

Nick and Lesley Albert always had a yearning to leave the noise, stress and pollution of modern Britain behind and move to the countryside, where the living is good, the air sweet, and there is space for their dogs to run free. But their idea would have remained just a dream, had circumstances not forced their hands. Suddenly out of work and soon to be homeless, they set off in search of a new life in Ireland, a country they had never before visited.

Rural County Clare proved to be endlessly quirky but delightfully appealing. Although the driving was dicey and navigation difficult, they soon fell in love with the countryside, the culture and the people.

But as their adventure in Ireland began to unfold, not everything went according to plan. If finding their dream house was difficult, buying it seemed almost impossible, and that wasn't all. How would they cope with banks that didn't want customers, builders who didn't need work, or the complexed issue of where to buy some chickens?

Was 'Living the Dream' a possibility, or would it become a nightmare?

Fresh Eggs and Dog Beds, the bestselling comical memoir series from Nick Albert, is published by Ant Press and available at Amazon in print, Kindle and as an audiobook.

Visit Nick's website for more information:
www.nickalbertauthor.com

7

From Bench Life to French Life
BETH HASLAM

"Biff, come! *Biff!*" I yelled.

Ignoring me, off he galloped, a canine missile closing in on the man who had just come into view. Unfortunately, it was a direct hit. Biff had latched onto his trousers.

"Argh! You little swine!" roared Biff's target.

"Biff, leave!"

"Get it off me!" bellowed the man, bounding around.

"Sorry! But shaking your leg will only make him worse."

"Worse? *Worse?* I'm getting mauled here. Call the bloody thing off now!"

Biff was salivating like a rabid beast, making hideous noises. I grabbed his ruff, and gingerly started unpicking his teeth from the fabric. I tried pacifying the man.

"I'm awfully sorry. For some reason, he can't stand black trousers. I had no idea anyone else was about. Otherwise, I'd have kept him on the leash."

Furious, the man rolled up the material to examine his leg for signs of injury. Fortunately, there were none. I knew this because I was still grappling with Biff a hair's breadth from the man's shin.

"Luckily for you, I'm not bleeding. I've a good mind to report your dog to the police. It's a damned menace."

"Really, I do apologise, but I'm glad he hasn't marked you. It looks as though your trousers are fine too, although if you need me to replace them, that's no problem."

"Huh, they seem okay. But mark my words, if it so much as comes near me again I'll report you for having a dangerous dog."

The man stalked off.

I looked down at Biff, our middle-aged Norfolk Terrier, the size of a fat rabbit and the same colour. He gazed myopically back with a triumphant expression. For such a tiny dog, he was making a significant impact on the locals.

My husband, Jack, and I adopted Biff when my mum passed away. She had rescued him from a dreadful fate and asked if we would take care of him. As a passionate animal lover, of course, I agreed. In any case, it was the least I could do for my mum. But there was no doubt about it; the little chap did have issues.

For some reason, Biff hated black trousers. This wasn't a mild dislike; he was positively psychotic about them. Postmen, delivery men, businessmen, Biff didn't discriminate. If their trousers were black, they were all targets.

Luckily, as a small dog, despite trying his best, he rarely caused actual harm. This was just as well since, as a dedicated vigilante, it was impossible to stop that red haze misting his eyes when he spotted a perp. Despite this and his total lack of obedience, we adored him.

Sighing at our misadventure, I checked the lead and looked around for my other doggy companion.

"Sam? Come on, big lad, let's go."

Our black-tri Australian Shepherd was the apple of my eye. From the moment I saw the chubby two-month-old bundle of fun waddling towards me at the breeder, I was smitten. Now, in his middle years too, he had been by my side ever since the day I brought him home.

Sam had been observing from a safe distance. He wasn't stupid. Sam knew that anything could happen when his mate was in 'frenzy mode'. As he padded towards me, just to make the afternoon complete, the heavens opened. I could imagine what he was thinking.

That little rat! Every time we go for a walk, he finds someone to attack. No idea why, although I s'pose that bloke did look a bit shifty. And now mum's going to take us home. The only good thing is it's started raining. That should keep other walkers away, and I might get to play in a puddle. Rrresult!

It was a predictable end to the ramble. We reached our driveway, and my equally predictable husband working in the garage.

Let me try to describe him.

During his career moves, Jack took three IQ tests. He only saw one score, which was in the genius range. This level of super-intelligence is often accompanied by a quirk or two, and my husband has several. For example, Jack considers any more than four hours of sleep each night a decadent waste of time. He has the patience span of a gnat and is often horrifically grumpy.

Despite these tricky traits, in business, Jack was admired by the workforces he managed. Why? Because he listened to issues, rolled up his sleeves and solved problems, practical or otherwise. The niceties of tact were not requirements in those situations.

Sadly, in social settings, Jack's powers of diplomacy often desert him. His plain-speaking takes the term 'blunt' to a whole new level. I've tried for years to soften those edges, but with very little success.

Most importantly, though, beneath that rugged exterior lies a hugely capable, caring man with a heart of gold. And I should know. We've been together for over three decades.

During our full-time careers, we led a typical middle-class lifestyle. We enjoyed one, occasionally two, holidays abroad. But it was never in our thoughts that we would move from the UK.

From the moment the dubious decision to semi-retire was taken, Jack went into hyper-drive. The car was exiled to the drive and the double garage transformed into a mechanic's workshop. From here, he launched a portfolio of oily projects. Shelves now heaved with machines, and collections of tiny drawers appeared containing washers, screws, bolts and nails. Added to these were interesting metal items found on the road; an engineer's version of roadkill.

The workbenches groaned under the weight of important spare parts, and the ceiling sagged with ladders and a cornucopia of long metal implements. I knew from the clanks that he was in there somewhere. Stepping over several engine sections, I hailed him.

"We're back. I'm afraid it's happened again, another black trouser incident."

Jack appeared holding a smoking piece of metal.

"*Urgh*, you're soaking. Blasted weather! Was there much blood-letting?"

"No, but the man was fuming."

"I would be too, poor bloke. The little sod, can't we just put him down?" he said, fondly tousling Biff's head.

"*Jack*, how can you possibly say that? He just needs careful managing."

"Lord, if it's proper managing he needs, I doubt that one of *your* counselling sessions will do much good."

Jack was referring to my prior career in human resources. Being more of the 'pull yourself together' temperament, he never fully understood the welfare side of my job.

"That's not fair. Biff has deep-seated issues. He's evidently been traumatised. It's tricky as the area is becoming so popular now. I'm always coming across other folks."

"You're right. We're getting infested. It's spoiling what used to be a quiet little village."

"I'm sure you're becoming even more misanthropic these days."

I headed to the kitchen before Jack launched into his favourite monologue, justifying the merits of social selectivity.

I should have smelt a rat when I saw the trail of oily drips on the floor. They led to the kitchen sink. It was filled with filthy water and a can of some sort.

"Jack, what's going on in here?"

"Ah, yes, I should have warned you. That's the engine's blowby canister. It needed a good clean after I'd renewed the inlet valve stem seals."

"I don't have the first clue what you're talking about."

"Yep, looks as though I may have dripped a bit. Erm, sorry, I'll clean it up shortly."

"Okay, but I'm not sure our little house can cope with your new DIY projects. You need more space. We all do."

My mobile phone rang, mercifully interrupting Jack's reply.

"Hello Madam, it's Steve. Is there any chance you could chair a magistrate's criminal court tomorrow morning?"

"Hello Steve, yes, no problem at all."

"Lovely, we'll need you there at 9 a.m. to consider a search warrant before the bench business starts." (Bench, in this context, is the collective noun for three magistrates sitting in court session. It may seem a little weird, but it's better than some of the names we've been called.)

Some years earlier, my business career had been cut short by a serious car crash. Quite how I managed to break so many bones all in one go I shall never know, but I did. It took many attempts over an initial period of three years to put them back together again, during which period I eventually resigned from my job.

Now fit-ish, my time was chiefly spent looking after our dogs, gardening, and the usual domestic drudge. I also served as a magistrate (or Justice of the Peace; it's the same thing) in our regional area. I loved the work, which I found humbling, frustrating and rewarding in equal measure.

Jack, having overheard the conversation, grunted.

"That means I'll be left in charge of Fang and Fangetta again, I suppose?"

"Yep, it's only for the morning. Just leave them in the house to nap if they start getting under your feet."

○෨☼ଊ☼

I had served in court a lot recently. As a housework hater, it was a relief to be doing something productive. The garden was a boggy no-go zone, so aside from dog walks, which were becoming fraught with incidents, I was stymied.

Like all magistrates, when appointed, I underwent a lengthy training programme. With my previous experience in employment law, I had found it fascinating, and later trained as an adult court chairman.

I walked into the magistrates' retiring room, so-called because this is the place where justices retire to consider their verdicts. It doubles as a meeting room and, importantly, is stocked with supplies of tea and coffee.

Shortly after, my two colleague magistrates arrived. Known as wingers, they would sit either side of me in court. While every person's opinion is of equal value, during case hearings, theirs would be a non-speaking role. As chairman, my job would be to lead retiring room business and act as spokesman in court on behalf of the bench.

One of the magistrates was a great pal. A tough old retainer who had served for years, Ted was a factory foreman and called a spade a spade. The other magistrate, Sally, was new. This was her second criminal court session.

We were soon joined by David, our clerk for the day. Magistrates do not need formal legal qualifications because detailed advice on matters of law is provided by the clerk. Also known as legal advisors, clerks are trained solicitors or barristers.

David had worked at the court throughout his career. He knew the serial offenders and the tricks their solicitors used to con a bench into imposing a lighter sentence. His advice was always excellent.

"Morning, Your Honours, we have a steady caseload this morning with a few regulars, so you'll need to be on your toes."

"Okay, no problem, David," I said, handing out the wad of case documents. "And what about the search warrant?"

"Just the one, Madam, and you're in for a treat with it. It's that detective who is working on the Scotland Yard car thefts task force."

"Detective Roberts?" said Ted.

"Yes, Sir. They think they've tracked down another one of the suspects living in our area."

"I refused his last warrant. He'll be glad you're in charge today, Beth."

Detective Roberts had a pretty dim view of magistrates, and I understood why. In his opinion, our procedures got in the way of a speedy police operation. Like it or not, to protect potential innocents, he was stuck with us acting as a third-party safety valve and here's why.

If the police want to search a property, in many circumstances, they have to apply to the magistrates' court for a search warrant. It will only be granted if it is believed the police have reasonable grounds to suspect that an offence has been committed. And that the property needs to be searched as it may contain evidence that will be important to a case.

To help us make a judicial decision, we would work through a bespoke document and rely on David's advice when necessary.

Detective Roberts was called in.

A burly chap of strong character, he addressed us formally and outlined the background. Everything was in order until we reached the section that dealt with the address. Ted looked puzzled. I motioned for him to speak.

"This is my neck of the woods, detective. Are you sure that's the house?"

The detective gave him a cold stare.

"Yes, Sir, *definitely*. My team has had it under surveillance and strongly believe several stolen vehicles are stored there in a barn. They don't make mistakes."

"Hmm, I'm sure, but I don't reckon they wrote this warrant. Run that address by us one more time, would you?"

Detective Roberts, frowning, flipped through his notes and reeled off the address. Ted paused.

"I'm pretty sure there isn't one."

"One *what*, Sir?"

"A 188 Barnstaple Close."

The detective, visibly irritated, managed not to look at his watch. I asked David to double-check. Sure enough, the last property on that road was 180 Barnstaple Close. Having local knowledge often comes in handy for magistrates.

"It's just as well we looked. You could have been searching a field full of cows," smiled Ted.

Poor Detective Roberts, he wasn't having much luck with our bench. He had no option but to withdraw the warrant. It would be heard another day.

Our regular court business began at 10 a.m. Cases ran fairly efficiently until we got to Mr Henderson, a well-known drunk. The loveable rogue had been in and out of community programmes for as long as I had been serving. To date, none of them had worked.

On this occasion, he was charged with the theft of four whiskey bottles from the local supermarket. And, judging by his current demeanour, Mr Henderson's sources of alcohol had not dried up.

Following standard practice, David read out the charge and asked him to enter his plea to the offence. His solicitor, who had coached him through many similar cases, whispered hurriedly in his ear. Mr Henderson pootled over to the dock and propped himself against the lamp.

"*Not* guilty!"

His solicitor's eyebrows smacked against her hairline.

"No, *nooo*," she exclaimed. "Madam, Mr Henderson pleads guilty!"

"I bloody well don't. Oops, sorry, Yer Worshipses, but I ain't!"

Ted leaned towards me.

"Looks like he's been on the pop again," he murmured.

"You *are* guilty, Dan," the solicitor audibly hissed. "Just say the words!"

"Dunno what she's tawkin' about, I didn't steal nuffink."

This triggered a heated discussion between them.

Rather than lose the court decorum altogether, I quietly agreed with my colleagues that we should leave them to it.

"The court will retire," I announced.

This was the signal for all attendees to stand while we left the courtroom. It also stunned Mr Henderson into momentary silence, but only for a moment. The second the retiring room door closed behind us, we could hear him yelling at his solicitor.

Sally was looking shocked.

"Goodness, does this sort of thing often happen?"

"Not really," said Ted, "but with a character like Mr Henderson, anything goes. The last time he was here he fell out of the dock. Problem is, the poor fella's always drunk."

We discussed the situation and asked David to join us and give his legal opinion.

"The difficulty, Your Honours, is that the evidence against Mr Henderson is overwhelming."

"Possibly," I replied, "but we all know he must enter his own plea. It sounded as though he was being railroaded out there."

"Fair enough, his solicitor should know better. How do you want to proceed?"

David had a quiet word with Mr Henderson's solicitor about getting their game plan together. And if he were not fit to enter a plea, the case would have to be adjourned.

A short time later, we returned to the bench. Amazingly, all parties were still present and looking sheepish. David repeated his instruction for Mr Henderson to enter his plea.

"Sorry bowt that, Yer Worshipfuls, it is guilty achully. I jus' got misself a bit mixed up."

The case was heard, we sentenced Mr Henderson, and he shuffled off with his solicitor mouthing, "Sorry, Your Honours," on the way out.

Our penultimate case involved sentencing an offender who had already entered a guilty plea at a previous hearing. It was an either way case for an offence of ABH (assault occasioning actual bodily harm). This meant that the crime, if serious enough, could be heard by the crown court. A previous bench had decided the magistrates' powers of sentencing were sufficient, so had kept the case.

Further information about Mr Brown (the offender) and the crime had been ordered. We had already reviewed the pre-sentence report, and the contents weren't pretty.

Back in court, and Mr Brown confirmed his guilty plea from the dock. The prosecution lawyer summarised the case. Mr Brown had spent time in prison for a similar offence a few years ago. Since coming out, there had been sporadic instances of minor assault. The case before us was far more severe.

His version of events that he had been verbally provoked in a bar by another man had been accepted. It lessened his culpability, and there was no evidence of premeditation. However, what transpired was a reckless physical retaliation so brutal that he had to be hauled off the victim and restrained by a group of onlookers until the police arrived.

The terrified victim needed hospital treatment for injuries sustained during the assault and counselling afterwards. It seems that Mr Brown was not drunk. He just saw red. And this was not an isolated incident. The police had been called to several brawls recently where Mr Brown had been the centre of attention.

After hearing from both the prosecution and defence, I posed questions from the bench arising from our report reading. With no further information emerging, we retired to consider the verdict.

The evidence spoke for itself. Both the injuries the victim sustained and the violence of the attack aggravated Mr Brown's offence. We took each detail into account, including giving credit for his early guilty plea, and set them against a backcloth of Mr Brown's previous convictions and unchecked aggressive behaviour.

With a unanimous decision reached, I buzzed for David to join us and double-check our legal reasoning. As usual, his feedback was invaluable. Mr Brown would serve another custodial sentence.

We agreed on the detail and were good to go. So far, the sorry matter had been running smoothly. Famous last words …

The hearing resumed, and Mr Brown was returned to the dock. The doors at the back of court opened, and in came two brawny officers with jangly handcuffs. To an experienced criminal, this can only mean one thing.

I began the pronouncement, which for a custodial sentence is agonisingly long. The officers started clunking towards him as I reached the section that addressed his prison sentence. Mr Brown was pretty twitchy by now. He glanced at the officers, turned back and stared murderously at me.

Mr Brown exploded.

"Bugger you lot! I aren't going back to prison."

He clambered over the dock and landed on the lawyers' table. Papers flew as did his shocked solicitor, who had shoved his seat back and toppled off as it caught on the threadbare carpet.

I hit the panic button to alert the police next door.

Scenting freedom, Mr Brown leapt off the table and headed for the aisle between the public seating, towards the exit. Meanwhile, the officers, on the other side of the room, had been caught flat-footed.

As they tried to intervene, they were pinned back by a wave of terrified public onlookers, scared witless by the escapee.

"Retire, *now!*" snapped David.

I glanced at my colleagues, announced to nobody in particular that the court would rise, and we departed in a judicial flutter. By this stage, Sally was looking apprehensive.

"Are all criminal court hearings like this?"

"Only the fun days," Ted winked.

David joined us soon after. With judicial etiquette at a new low, we were bursting to know what happened.

"Thank you for retiring. He didn't seem to be heading in your direction, but it made sense to clear the bench just in case."

"Absolutely," I said. "Was he apprehended?"

"Yes, he didn't even make it out of the courtroom. Harold heard the shouting, ran in, knocked him over and hung on while the officers cuffed him."

"Brilliant!" laughed Ted, "I'd loved to have seen our seasoned security officer making that rugby tackle."

"That's very brave of Harold. We must thank him," I said. "And I don't suppose Mr Brown is a pushover."

"No, not at all," said David. "Harold did an impressive job considering he's retirement age. Mr Brown is cooling off in the cells now while they decide whether he should face further charges."

"Ah, we wondered what the banging below us was all about."

"Yes, he's not best pleased. I'm afraid we won't finish that case today, so I've processed it. We only have one more now."

We filed back into the reassembled court to hear the final case. Under the circumstances, and probably to Sally's relief, it was extremely tame. I concluded our business, and we returned to the retiring room.

I thanked Harold, who was looking a tad dishevelled and grinning like the Cheshire cat. We had a de-briefing with David and left, with poor Sally still looking shell-shocked. On my way out, I bumped into Steve, the listing clerk.

"Thanks very much for stepping in today, Madam. How did it go?"

"Fairly eventful, actually."

"So I hear. Anyway, I'm glad I've seen you. I've been checking rotas this morning, and I'm afraid we've been calling on you to serve too often. You'll be exceeding your permitted sittings, so we'll have to keep you strictly to the list. You won't be in court again for weeks."

✧৯✪ෘ✧

I drove home, brooding over how I was going to fill my time over winter. There was definitely something missing in our lives. I pulled up and picked my way through new lumps of discarded shrapnel on the drive. Jack was back in the garage, head under a car bonnet.

"Oh hello, hanged them all? Or have you introduced *la guillotine* to add spice to the process?"

"No, just routine stuff, well nearly. Where are the dogs?"

"They're inside. I got sick of them barking at every single person who walked past the house. It's bloody irritating, especially since they were getting under my feet with their mad dashes."

Sighing at Jack's frustration, I knew exactly what would cheer me up. I opened the door to a furball of delirious rapture. Sam and Biff cavorted around me like pups, behaving as though they hadn't seen me for six months.

After lunch, I took them out for a long walk. This time I kept Biff on the lead, just in case we had another black trouser incident. Most of the farmers' fields had either been ploughed or housed herds of frisky cattle. The last time we met them, they decided Biff was a football. Sticking to the lane was an easier option.

That evening we settled down with a drink. The dogs were sprawled in front of the fire, gently twitching in dreamland, Biff no doubt recounting his latest misdemeanour. I could see Jack was thoughtful.

"What's up?"

"I've got all these projects on the go, but I haven't sufficient space. It's extremely inefficient working in cramped conditions. Would you mind if I built another garden shed?"

"Jack, we have three already, and they're stuffed with your kit. The place'll start looking like a township."

"Alright, alright, but it is infuriating."

"I understand. I'm a bit fed up with being restricted too. What we need is a holiday."

"*Gaah!*" groaned my holiday-averse husband. "Why on earth do you think a holiday is the answer to everything?"

"I'm sure we'll feel better about things if we have a break."

"That's ridiculous logic. Nothing will have changed, I'll still have a space problem, and you'll still be moaning about the garden being too small, rotten weather, and not being able to take that canine serial killer out without getting sued."

"Yes, but ..."

"So the solution is self-evident."

"Is it?"

"Yes! We need a small second home with lots of workshop space in a dog-friendly environment."

"Ooh, I never thought of that. But I don't want to part with our nest."

Jack gave me a withering look.

"Nor do I. But I did say *second* home. We'll just have to budget appropriately. Let's get the specification sorted out first."

"Wow, how exciting, and don't forget enough land to enjoy wildlife-watching in peace."

"You and your animals!"

We started chatting through the UK options. That didn't take long. We dismissed them as too cold, too wet, or too expensive. As quickly as our idea had hatched, it started fizzling out. I began to feel despondent again.

"Oh, I don't know. Where else if nothing suits?"

"Well, it's becoming pretty clear. It'll have to be somewhere in Europe."

Amazingly, the decision came to us fairly quickly. We wanted somewhere close enough to keep an eye on the family. The location had to be within a sensible driving distance because of the dogs.

We didn't know much about the eastern countries, so ruled those out. This left Iberia, Germany, Italy and France. Jack had spent years working in Germany and announced that his personality and brand of humour didn't fit very well with the 'Fourth Reich'.

"Really, Jack? Let's be honest. If compatibility with the idiosyncrasies of your personality is a major criterion, then we'll have to include new planets on our list of possible locations."

"*Humph!*"

We both decided that Italy and its culture wasn't for us. Jack's fixation that he would end up eating pasta, bribing officials and pinching ladies' bottoms for the rest of his life confirmed it.

As keen golfers, we loved the idea of Portugal and Spain but didn't know enough about the inland areas or whether they had the temperate climate we sought.

Finally, the blindingly obvious occurred to me.

"How about France?"

"France?"

"Of course. We love it and have often said how closely the countryside resembles a big England."

"That's true. But don't think you're going to turn me into one of those snail-eating scarf-wearers."

"Jack, for someone who spent most of their life working in different countries, you can be horrifically parochial."

"Just thought I'd mention it."

"We can both get by in French, and I'm pretty sure Provence would be the best place to look because of its great climate."

"Alright, that sounds reasonable, and there's no doubt about it; land and property prices are much better."

"Great. So what next?"

"Why prevaricate? Decision made. You can start the research. You love that sort of thing."

"Okay, no problem, I'll produce a shortlist. I'll arrange things so we can spend two or three weeks on viewings. We'll have to bring the dogs with us, obviously."

"What? I do *not* believe you just said that!"

And so our French escapades began.

✿ೞ✿ೡ✿

I look back on it now and smile at how we thought buying a country home in France would be so simple. When we eventually set off with our two fat dogs, we had no idea it would become the adventure of our lives.

Surviving near-death experiences, dealing with disasters and negotiating with crazy aristocrats, we drove thousands of kilometres in search of the right property. Did we at times question the sanity of our decision? Oh yes. And did it take ages to find the house we sought? Absolutely. But we never gave up on chasing our dream.

Today, we are settled in a home we never expected to own. We're part of a rural community so small it's just a dot on the map. We are surrounded by our land, which is teeming with wildlife and an odd assortment of rescued animals.

Our mobile phones, office desks and criminal case judgements have traded places with the tools of rustic living. We're in a place where something ever so slightly strange happens every single day. Our lives have altered forever, and would we change a thing?

Not a chance!

Fat Dogs and French Estates
by Beth Haslam

Beth, her grouchy husband, Jack, and their two fat dogs set off to buy a country home in France. Blissfully naive, they have no idea what lies in store. Natural disasters, dog misadventures, and nightmarish property viewings. You name it; they battle with them all.

Do they find the perfect property? Or is their dream shattered? And how on earth have they ended up with so many rescued animals?

The answers lie in Beth's fun-filled memoir series as she shares tales from their remarkable lives in rural France.

Find out more about their adventures and the *Fat Dogs and French Estates* series of books on Beth's website:
www.bethhaslam.com

Mountain Dreams
ROY CLARK

I swung off the smooth tarmac road and freewheeled into the car park on my bike, imagining myself as a professional cyclist who'd just crossed the finish line on a stage of the Tour de France. I was hot and exhausted from my imaginary long solo breakaway but I felt ridiculously exhilarated too. Sadly, the podium hadn't been set up yet, nor were there any fans jostling to get my autograph, but I spotted our car, a rusty Polo estate parked in a corner, and glided over to it. I stepped off my bike, my legs behaving oddly, as though I'd been at sea for a year. My partner Justi, waiting in the driver's seat, turned in surprise.

"Gosh, I wasn't expecting to see you so soon," she commented, as I hoisted my bike carefully into the back.

"Well, the cycle track into Italy is mostly downhill, and the Austrian road is fantastic," I said, still buzzing from my ride.

I'd just cycled from our apartment in the north-west corner of Slovenia across the border into Italy, then across another border into Austria, in just under an hour. I felt smugly satisfied to have cycled in three countries in less time than it takes to commute five miles in a vehicle during rush hour on the M25. The route had taken me along a dedicated cycle track through the Upper Sava Valley, where bare limestone peaks pierced the blue sky to my left and sublime forested mountains rose impressively to my right. Just before the small market town of Tarvisio in Italy, I'd cut off the cycle track and joined a quiet main road that led into Austria, passing through an unmanned border and continuing past rolling meadows on smooth sun-warmed tarmac.

"Okay, let's go before the peloton arrive," I said to Justi, who shook her head and sighed, resigned to my lamentable daydreaming.

We drove into Villach, a large market town that straddles the river Drau, and headed to our favourite café, which overlooked the river and the old part of the town with its abundance of attractive Carinthian architecture. As we eagerly awaited our brick-sized creamy *Cremeschnitte* cake and coffee, we watched a pleasure boat cruising languidly along the river. Tourists sat happily on the lower decks taking photos and eating ice cream, while a jazz band on the top deck supplied some suitably mellow sounds.

It was Justi's turn for some exercise now; she headed back to the car to pick up her rollerblades and enjoy an hour of in-line skating along the idyllic riverside track. I walked over the bridge and up the bustling pedestrian road to visit a cycle shop where I was allowed to rummage through an Aladdin's cave storage room of used bike parts.

It had been another day in paradise for us both, but we felt no sadness to be leaving as the journey home was a joy itself. On leaving Villach we took the improbably steep Wurzenpass road that led back to Slovenia. The warm sun shone through a deep azure sky, and we wound the car windows down to enjoy the scent of pine resin and the sound of cowbells from the small pastures that dotted the green Karavanke hills. Relieved as always that our car had made it to the summit, we crossed into Slovenia and began the descent, cautiously rounding the tight hairpins.

As we turned a bend, the Julian Alps filled the view ahead, their immense vertical crags hanging like a vast pale curtain of pleated rock. The town of Kranjska Gora came into view, nestled comfortably on the valley floor. The ornate bell tower of its medieval church marked the centre of the settlement, while grassy slopes, which become the arena of World Championship downhill ski events each winter, rose steeply behind to the right.

Before we reached the valley floor, we turned into the driveway of the house where we rented our apartment. After stowing my bike under the wooden staircase that led to our rooms, I joined Justi on the balcony with a cold beer and we downed them contentedly as we looked out across a sea of meadows dotted with brightly coloured wild flowers. Hay had already been gathered from the season's first cut, and it hung drying on long wooden hayracks while the rasping chirp of crickets filled the air.

You might be wondering how we came to be living in the mountainous north-west of Slovenia, a stunningly beautiful area that also allowed us to hop into Italy to buy sun-dried tomatoes or to visit a festive market in an Austrian village. I often wondered myself, and even after many years I still couldn't believe our luck. The fortuitous circumstances of life that brought us here probably started in our early teenage years when both Justi and I discovered an awakening passion for the outdoors, but I'll start our story in the Highlands of Scotland.

⚜︎

Another squall of wind-driven sleet thrashed the sash windows that rattled noisily in their wooden frames. It was 6.30 a.m. on a pitch-black winter's morning, and I'd just brewed a pot of tea and lit the fire in the old cottage that Justi and I rented. She was about to have a telephone interview for a job that, if she was successful, would see us moving to a country we knew very little about and had never even visited before: Slovenia. However, the little we'd been able to find out about the ex-Yugoslavian territory had been more than enough to excite our imaginations.

Justi and I had met in Scotland, a country we had both been drawn to because of its magnificent landscape. I was from Liverpool and she had moved up from north Wales. Our love for the outdoors was what brought us together, and that same passion and drive was hopefully now leading us to the Julian Alps of Slovenia.

Justi had become disheartened with her career and her discontent had been compounded by a run of wet Highland summers. Searching for a happier outlook had led to this slightly bizarre moment of her attending an interview wearing her dressing gown. As she sat in the living room chatting on the phone with her potential new employer while huddled close to the fire, I eavesdropped from the kitchen. I could sense that the interview was going well and a buzz of excitement started to build in my gut; a new adventure was on the horizon.

Despite us both having just turned forty years old, neither of us held any predilection to settle down or be absorbed into a run-of-the-mill existence. Like many itinerant wanderers who live for the outdoors, I'd had no thoughts about careers, owning a home or putting money aside for a pension; the only thing that seemed relevant and worthwhile was the next outdoor adventure. Since arriving in Scotland I'd worked as a cook, shop assistant, barman, graveyard groundskeeper, ski-lift operator, forest worker and gardener. My spare time was spent walking, climbing, canoeing, cycling and socialising with like-minded outdoor people. Justi held a professional qualification and had come to work in the Highlands as a speech therapist, choosing to work part-time to increase her opportunities to get out into the hills.

Because of our 'irregular' lifestyles, neither of us owned a house nor had any savings. While our financial prospects may have been pessimistic, the benefits of such a lifestyle outweighed the negatives. We were living amidst Britain's finest mountains and lochs with endless options for outdoor adventures. It also meant that we could act on opportunities that came our way without the responsibilities that come with mortgages, loans and job contracts. We also didn't have any children, so when the chance of a new adventure in Slovenia came, it was a 'seize the day' moment, and we grabbed it with both hands.

It wasn't long before Justi was notified that she had passed the interview for the job as an English language teaching assistant in a Slovene state school. She was embarking on a totally new career, so new that she was still awaiting her certificate for her TEFL (Teaching English as a Foreign Language) course. The school she'd been assigned to was located in a town close to the Croatian border in eastern Slovenia. It was as far away from the Julian Alps as it's possible to be in Slovenia.

"That's a bit of a blow," I said, when Justi told me the news of her allocation. "Are there any hills in the area?"

More research showed the town was surrounded by steep forested hills, with a higher range known as the Pohorje Mountains just an hour's drive away. Nothing is really far away in Slovenia, though, as the country is only half the size of Switzerland.

"I'm sure we'll be able to nip over to the Julian Alps at weekends and during school breaks," I said, as I struggled to find information on a fledgling internet.

Our last few months in the Highlands were perhaps more exciting for me than Justi. I was giving up my work as a self-employed gardener, a job I loved, but one I believed I'd be able to rejuvenate should our experience in Slovenia not live up to our utopian imaginings. To me, it felt like we were about to embark on an extended holiday to a hiker's paradise in sunnier climes. Despite not having a work permit, I imagined that I would be able to find casual jobs like I'd always done before.

Justi understandably had more worrying concerns. She was ending a seventeen-year career and starting out on a completely new one that involved a fifty percent wage cut. Would she be able to do it? Would she enjoy it? What would she return to if life in Slovenia didn't live up to our dreams?

Any melancholy thoughts we had of leaving the rented cottage that lay in the shadow of Britain's highest mountain, Ben Nevis, were tempered by the prospect of discovering Slovenia's incredible landscapes. We eagerly read all we could find out about our new country. The steep limestone peaks of the Julian Alps were home to Slovenia's highest mountain, Triglav, and the country possessed an abundance of pristine emerald lakes and rivers and vast natural forests.

Having sold our unnecessary and unwanted belongings at several car boot sales, we loaded the things we held dear into our latest acquisition, bought for the move: an old Renault estate. This included bikes, skis, a heap of outdoor equipment and our faithful collie, Bryn. We turned the long overland drive into a three-week camping holiday and tried hard to eke out the £1200 we had managed to save.

Our journey took us into Belgium and across France, Lichtenstein, Switzerland and Austria before entering Slovenia.

Despite our frugal living we managed to visit many beautiful destinations along the way, such as the Lauterbrunnen valley in Switzerland. Before leaving Scotland we'd noticed that the Slovene tourist board were trying to increase visitor numbers with the catch phrase 'Slovenia – the Sunny Side of the Alps'. As we hiked along the spectacular Swiss mountain paths we wondered if our prospective new homeland could possibly match such natural beauty.

By the time we reached Slovenia, it was late September and our money had all but run out. What little we had left we exchanged for Slovene currency and for a very brief moment we felt well off; the euro was yet to be implemented in Slovenia and the *tolar* was still in use. At about 1,000 tolars to £3 sterling, our remaining £110 was transformed into a five-figure sum!

Our first few months in Slovenia brought us all the excitement and interest of living in a new country and becoming familiar with a different culture. Time stretched as each day was filled with new experiences, and we quickly felt as if it had been years since we left Scotland. There were challenges and obstacles, such as struggling with the language (Slovene) and the unfathomable bureaucracy that seemed to be a hangover from Slovenia's communist past. These tribulations were to be expected, but we hadn't bargained for the support and kindness of the Slovenes as we overcame the many daily dilemmas.

The rural countryside of eastern Slovenia, with its magnificent forests of tall beech trees and rolling hills, is undeniably beautiful and its citizens remarkable. Their generosity and sincerity meant lasting friendships were made and helped build a treasure trove of special memories. We were nonetheless still longing to discover Slovenia's best known mountain range—the Julian Alps. Our expectation that we would be able to travel easily at weekends to explore them was soon dashed when we realised that the travelling time and our precarious finances meant that frequent short trips were out of the question.

We did, however, manage a half-term holiday during our first winter in Slovenia. Having found a cheap room in the tourist town of Kranjska Gora, we spent four unforgettable days skiing and snowshoeing amongst Slovenia's rocky Alpine jewels. It made us even more determined to get to know this mountain paradise, but we could not envisage the means to make our dream a reality.

Our hopes weren't raised until near the end of Justi's one-year teaching contract, when we were reluctantly considering moving back to the UK. She was informed that she could renew her teaching contract for another school year, and could apply for a transfer to a different school. This exciting disclosure came with one cautionary caveat: there would be no choice in the school's location.

It is at moments like this that Justi's strong belief in allowing the 'universe' to take control of certain matters comes to the fore. She applied for a transfer, firmly placing our hopes in the laps of whatever gods were listening. While I struggle to accept such spiritual concepts, I was elated when two weeks later she was informed that in September she could start at a new school located right on the doorstep of the Triglav National Park in the heartland of the Julian Alps. This was how we came to be living our dream near the foot of a steep mountain road close to Kranjska Gora.

Having already experienced a year in Slovenia, we soon settled into our breathtaking new environment in the country's far northwest. Kranjska Gora and the Julian Alps received more international tourists and with its close proximity to the border, Italian and Austrian day trippers were the most frequent visitors. Although we missed our friends in the east, we enjoyed the more cosmopolitan and touristy feel of the area, and it meant that 'fitting in' came a little easier. English was more widely spoken, which both helped and hindered us in our efforts to learn the language. Whenever we attempted to speak Slovene, our foreign accents would always be detected.

"Ah so, you are English, what can I get you?" was the usual reply we'd hear from smiling waiters and bar staff.

While Justi enjoyed her role as 'professor' (the Slovene title for a teacher), I spent almost all my free time hiking and scrambling in the Julian Alps. Since moving to Slovenia my role had become one of 'house husband'. In between my trips into the hills, I did the shopping, cooked, kept the place clean and walked Bryn, while Justi brought in a wage from her teaching. While I struggled with feelings of guilt generated by my ingrained British 'Protestant work ethic', Justi had no such hang-ups with this arrangement.

In 2004 we persuaded a publisher that Justi and I could write a trekking guidebook to the area, and I began to record all my mountain trips meticulously. Writing the guidebook gave me a much-needed sense of purpose. Although the book only provided pocket money, it helped assuage the sense of anguish I harboured about not working or contributing anything to our meagre finances. During weekends and holidays Justi joined me and together we enjoyed many satisfying days wandering the superb marked trails through Slovenia's mountains and valleys. Within another few years, we were the authors of three mountain guidebooks about our adopted country on the Sunny Side of the Alps.

✥

In July 2016, President Putin was due to visit Kranjska Gora. It was a formal visit to commemorate the 100th anniversary of the deaths of the Russian WW1 prisoners who perished while constructing the Vršič pass road that climbed steeply above the town.

Security was high on the agenda and even the motorway was to be temporarily closed. Huge tailbacks were forecast, as German and Dutch holidaymakers passed through Slovenia on their annual pilgrimage to the Croatian coast. Police were to be positioned every few hundred metres along our valley, with orders to prevent people even crossing the road in the hours before the state visit.

"Let's escape all the fuss," said Justi, on the eve of Mr Putin's visit.

"What do you have in mind?" I asked, knowing that Justi would have a plan to escape the 'Russian invasion'.

"Let's pack our rucksacks and head off in the morning to go and do Ratitovec. We could relax and stay overnight in the hut at Soriška near the ski station."

Ratitovec is a friendly looking hill that lies on the eastern edge of a more rugged range of mountains. We had often talked about the possibility of hiking it but had never got around to actually organising a trip.

"Good idea, it'll be nice to get away and have a quiet weekend in the hills," I agreed.

Having recently spent a lot of time in the Julian Alps working (Ha!) on an updated version of one of our guidebooks, climbing Ratitovec sounded a much more leisurely proposition.

"I imagine we'll probably have the hill to ourselves, as it's really just an outlier from the more popular higher mountains," I commented as we pored over the map.

The next morning we took the bus into town, passing policemen and women already standing guard along the main road. It was only 10 a.m. and Mr Putin wasn't expected to land at the airport, eighty kilometres distant, until 2.30 p.m.

Arriving in the nearby town of Jesenice, we swapped the bus for a train to take us to Bohinjska Bistrica, where we'd begin our two-day hike. The elderly two-carriage train chugged leisurely through the hauntingly beautiful Slovene countryside. Emerging from a tunnel cut through the steep rocky hillside, we stopped briefly at Lake Bled station. The scene looked like an illustration from a book of fairytales. An attractive old church stood serenely on the lake's small island, while a medieval castle sat high above the bright blue water atop a vertical cliff-face. Leaving Bled, we entered another tunnel as the little train negotiated its tortuous way through the foothills of the Julian Alps. Each time we emerged from a tunnel, the bright sunlight illuminated small pastures and verdant forests that clung to the steep mountainsides. The sparkling waters of the Bistrica river meandered along the valley floor linking small villages and settlements with its silvery green thread. All too soon, our enchanting train ride was over and we arrived at Bohinska Bistrica.

Leaving the station, we walked past a massive timber yard where long rows of scented pine dried in the warm air. Attractive residential houses with well-kept vegetable gardens lined the opposite side. The road began to climb steeply and we left it to join a way-marked narrow path. The map showed the road making a long serpentine detour which our path avoided as it led us between stands of larch and pine and across open pastures. It wasn't long before we arrived at a settlement, where we stopped for a moment outside an ancient timber-framed building and stood under its shady eaves to drink some water. The village seemed almost deserted, but we could hear the nearby sound of overtaxed engines from the steep road we had left earlier.

We continued on between the tightly clustered houses and past an old church. At the far end of the village we picked up the way-marked path again and headed into the slightly cooler temperature of the verdant forest. At times the trees relented and we found ourselves in glades and small pastures, many of which contained a pretty habitation: a Slovene *vikend*. *Vikends* are weekend getaways, a place in nature beloved by Slovenes of all ages. Practically all of these small unique chalets have been built by family members and remain a place of pride and joy. As we skirted along the path close to an attractive wooden *vikend*, we saw a group of people cutting and raking the long meadow grass. A powerful-looking man noticed us and stopped working his scythe.

"Professor Carey?" he called over with a surprised look.

"Yes? ... Oh hello, Tomaž. Is this your *vikend*?" replied Justi, looking equally surprised but recognising him as one of her postgraduate students.

"Yes it belongs to my family. We are just about to finish work and have lunch ... please, you must join us!"

We were invited to sit at a large picnic bench under the shade of a tall tree. After friendly introductions, Tomaž's family members scurried back and forth from the *vikend* bringing plates of delicious food and bottles of homemade drinks to the table. Dried meats, cheeses and fresh-baked bread were followed by fruit pastries and doughnuts. All this was washed down with freshly pressed apple juice and shots of homemade pine and honey schnapps. Tomaž told us how the family *vikend* had been built by his grandparents and how his family still loved spending time there every summer and occasionally in winter too. Necessary tasks such as maintaining the building, cutting the meadow and chopping firewood for their winter visits were jobs they found relaxing, rather than tiresome chores.

Our planned hike to Ratitovec was met with smiles and nods of approval. As a nation, Slovenia has a long history when it comes to mountaineering, and the entire country is crisscrossed with waymarked hiking trails and conveniently sited huts. It isn't unusual to see three generations of a family, from small children kitted out with climbing helmets and harnesses to venerable grandparents, scrambling on the steepest rocky trails and secured routes in the Julian Alps.

After saying our goodbyes to Tomaž and his family we continued on the tranquil forest path until it eventually merged with the road a short distance from the ski area. Several cars passed by along with a number of athletic-looking runners with numbers pinned to their vests. As the ski station came into view it was clear that a well-organised mountain marathon event was in full swing. A large inflatable arch across the road marked the finish line and cars were parked in any space where a tent wasn't pitched. It was late afternoon and with the day's racing over, runners thronged the bar of the mountain hut. Not feeling hopeful, I asked a frazzled-looking barman what our chances were of getting a room for the night.

Shrugging his shoulders, he lifted his palms and gazed around the packed room while giving me an 'are you kidding me?' look.

"Okay, can we get some food and drink then?"

"Yes of course, there are tables outside and I'll bring you a menu."

I ordered two beers and went onto the veranda with Justi to find a table. It was too late to walk back down to town to catch the last train, but as we sat and pondered our seemingly hopeless predicament, the barman arrived with two cold beers, smiling.

"You are very lucky! A guest just phoned and cancelled their booking so you can have a room."

He then lifted our spirits even more (well, mine at least!) by proudly presenting the beers, saying, "This is from a local micro-brewery, it's IPA … I know you English like it."

Later that evening, after a fantastic dinner of goulash and *Štruklji* (fruit-filled dumplings smothered in fresh cream), we sat and relaxed on the balcony outside our room. The clinking of glasses and the busy hum from the bar continued for a few more hours but we were comfortable and content.

"I thought we were supposed to be getting away for a quiet weekend," Justi quipped.

"Well, I'm sure we'll have a quiet day on Ratitovec tomorrow," I said confidently.

The next morning we weaved our way between the remaining runners' tents and headed out on a narrow path, following a sign for our hill. It was another warm sunny day and the path climbed gently through the forest before gaining the long undulating ridge that led to the summit. The forest gave way to clumps of dwarf pine and an abundance of wildflowers embellished the cropped grass with a kaleidoscope of colour. Removing our boots we carried on barefoot for a short section, revelling in the sensation of the warm grass between our toes. About thirty minutes from the summit we were surprised to hear the sound of music (we weren't expecting this hill to be quite so alive) drifting in the air. The unmistakable refrain of oom-pah became louder and as we approached the hut that stood below the summit of Ratitovec, it was clear a party was in full swing.

The band, with its booming tuba accompanied by accordions and clarinets, supplied the soundtrack for a group of dancers wearing traditional costume. The men, in their exquisitely embroidered waistcoats, red silk epaulettes, knee-high leather boots and black *klobuk* hats waltzed with the ladies in their voluminous skirts and lace-edged petticoats and blouses. The busy hut staff conveyed trays of delicious food and cold beer to more than a hundred folk who sat around on picnic benches.

We ordered *jota* (thick bean stew with sauerkraut), salad and beer.

"Where did all these people come from?" I asked Justi, feeling baffled as we'd hardly seen a soul on the way up. Justi was also curious, and asked the waiter as he served us our food.

"Aha, you must have come from Soriška, no? Everyone here has walked from the village at this end of Ratitovec to celebrate the summer festival."

The atmosphere was warm and convivial but unfortunately we couldn't linger long; it was late afternoon and we had a train to catch.

We began our descent down the forested north side of the hill to the receding sound of the big brass tuba. Within a short distance we met a Slovene couple who were about our own age, and we were impressed to see they were barefoot on the tortuously rocky path. They put our fifteen-minute tiptoe through the tulips to shame when they told us they had walked up from the valley unshod in order to 'energise' their senses.

As we batted on down the path we began to feel more edgy than energised, wondering if we'd catch our train. After another hour of anxious descent our path exited the wood onto a gravel road—and did not continue on the opposite side. Checking the map it was clear that without the path as a short-cut we wouldn't reach the isolated train stop on the valley floor in time.

"That's the last train ... we might end up having to sleep in the forest," Justi said, sounding apprehensive. As I put the map away an ancient Lada jeep rumbled around the bend and screeched to a stop. The dust cleared and a bright-eyed elderly man wound his window down to greet us.

"Dober dan, kam greste?" ("Hello, where are you going?") After explaining our predicament, he smiled, telling us to jump in while assuring us we would catch our train. Introducing himself, Andraž grinned as he told us we had met the right man, as he had recently retired from his lifelong work on the railway. The old Lada rattled noisily as Andraž negotiated the sharp bends of the gravel road, until we emerged from the forest into a large meadow with several attractive *vikend* chalets; the jeep lurched to a juddering stop outside one of them.

"Come," said Andraž, smiling, "you must meet my friends."

Our noisy arrival had been noted and his friends were already opening the door, welcoming us into the tiny living room as Andraž explained about the 'English hikers'. As soon as we were seated at the dining table, a bottle of homemade *slivovica* (plum schnapps) was produced along with plates of *prsut* (air-dried ham), cheeses and fresh bread. Our hosts, a middle-aged Slovene couple, were warm and friendly, and it didn't seem to matter that our Slovene was poor and that they had no English. They were interested to hear how we had come to be living in Slovenia and Andraž helped to translate.

Feeling tipsy from the eye-wateringly strong schnapps, we said our goodbyes and piled back into the jeep. We didn't get far though, as within a hundred metres Andraž pulled up outside another *vikend* where a retired couple sat outside on the covered veranda.

"Come," said Andraž, "Meet my friends, Janez and Martina."

I exchanged a worried glance with Justi—we still felt anxious about catching our train, despite Andraž's assurances.

"When in Rome ..." Justi whispered, sounding resigned.

As Martina presented us with *brinovec* (juniper berry schnapps) and plates of homemade biscuits, Andraž informed us that his friend Janez was the undisputed European scything champion. While wondering if we were about to become victims of a bit of harmless Slovene leg-pulling, Janez nodded proudly and produced a glossy magazine. The centrefold was a picture of him in an Austrian field with a scythe in one hand and a large trophy in the other. With Andraž translating, Janez spoke about the noble art of scything. He described how an experienced user can cut hay much faster than someone using a mechanical strimmer. Sadly (or perhaps fortunately), just as a slightly inebriated Janez was about to give us a practical demonstration of his technique, Andraž declared that it was time we caught our train.

Our weekend away proved typical of many trips and experiences we'd enjoyed since seizing the day and moving to Slovenia.

Andraž tooted the Lada's horn and waved goodbye as the train pulled into the tiny station at the edge of the dark forest.

Books by Roy Clark

With their hearts ruling their heads, Roy and Justi drove to Slovenia with all their belongings and their faithful old collie in a battered estate car hoping to forge a new life in the shadow of the majestic Julian Alps.

It was a country they had never visited before and knew very little about.

To find out if they made their dreams a reality you can read Roy's humorous and moving account of his and Justi's adventures in *The Sunny Side of the Alps: From Scotland to Slovenia on a Shoestring*.

Roy is currently working on his second memoir, *The Sunny Side of the Alps Book 2 – Running a B&B in the Julian Alps of Slovenia*, which will be published in 2021.

To purchase the book *The Sunny Side of the Alps*, please visit:
www.smarturl.it/sunnyside1
Or type B0848R8479 in the search box on Amazon.

A Toilet Behind the Sofa (and other stories)
LISA ROSE WRIGHT

1. On living in a ruin

"No, turn around. It's behind you!"

We were gathered on our sunny terrace, drinking tea with our friends. A perfectly normal activity. Lauren had asked to use our toilet. A perfectly normal request. I had directed her carefully, "through the red door, up the stairs and turn left and left again into the living room."

She obviously hadn't taken in my instructions as the door knob behind us gave another determined rattle.

"No! It's behind you!" I repeated in my best pantomime voice.

This time there was silence for a beat. I imagined her turning round and … yes there it was, the gasp of surprise.

"Oh!"

I couldn't blame poor Lauren. After all, what the eye doesn't expect, the brain doesn't register. And not many eyes would expect a toilet in the living room—even if it was tucked neatly behind the sofa.

✧☙✧ଓ✧

A toilet behind the sofa was a big improvement on our 'facilities' when myself and my then partner, now husband, S, had moved to a ruin of an old stone farmhouse in beautiful green Galicia some twelve months earlier in August 2007.

The house, called *A Casa do Campo* or the country house, had been empty for twelve years when we bought it. Even before that, the facilities couldn't have been exactly modern.

There was a bathroom—of sorts.

A one metre by two metre 'cube' had been built in the upstairs hallway. In this cube, poured onto the wooden floor beneath it, was a concrete shower base. At least I always assumed it was for a shower. As there was no shower head or other indication of its use, it was impossible to tell. A shower head would, in any case, have been superfluous as there was no plughole nor waste pipe in the concrete tray. In fact a shower head would have been doubly superfluous as there was no water to the bathroom cube—at all.

There was a sink in the room which even had a waste pipe, the water from which cleverly ran into the toilet bowl thereby flushing it. Though, as I've previously mentioned, as there was no water to the bathroom this function was not entirely useful either.

I imagined an elderly Pegarto, the ex-owner, (who had a number of medical problems if the full set of x-rays we found in the house were anything to go by) heating his shower water in the nice warm kitchen downstairs then crossing the arctic hallway carrying two sloshing buckets. Up four steps he would go, wobbling due to his dodgy hip (x-ray number seven). At this point he would have to put the buckets down on the top step in order to force open the heavy, warped door to the upstairs rooms. An upstairs which, I may add, had no heating whatsoever when we bought the house.

Pegarto carries his, by now half-empty and rapidly cooling, buckets into the bathroom cube. He then bravely strips off and stands in the concrete tray (there is no seat) whilst splashing himself with the, now at best lukewarm, water.

No, I couldn't see that scenario playing out.

We didn't use that bathroom either. Instead we rigged up a very satisfactory shower outdoors. In summer it was much warmer outside than within our seventy-centimetre-thick stone walls. Toileting was another matter entirely. The toilet flushed to … well, let's not go there, though that apple tree did look healthy. We used the great outdoors, and enough said.

Living in a semi-derelict old house is not for everyone. Not only did we have no running water or bathroom facilities, we had little in the way of floors or ceilings. Most of those which remained were sodden and, in the case of the ceilings, hanging on by sheer will power. The rotten floorboards were lost somewhere in the barns below.

It was a hair-raising adventure and hindsight blunts the memories of those earlier hardships, but luckily I have a whole eight years' worth of letters home to my mum in England to boost my memories.

I have always been a big letter writer. From the first day I moved to London from my rural home in the English Midlands, I wrote home weekly. Mum, on the other hand, is a prize hoarder, for which I am eternally grateful—although carrying all those boxes of letters back here to Galicia when she came to join us six years ago was somewhat surreal.

Here's a snippet from a letter years later, when we had a real bathroom (with real running water) proving the bathroom demons had not forgotten me.

Dear Mum,
'Oh dear what can the matter be, Lisa's stuck in the lavatory.'
Sad but true. On Friday night I rushed to beat S to the bathroom. Pulled the door to and something went click. The door handle swivelled but the latch wouldn't open.
I tried hairgrips, scissors, tweezers and string (handy place to be stuck, a bathroom) but to no avail. S says he was tempted to leave me there as I had plenty of towels and a nice big bath to sleep in. He relented after I threatened to scream all night and threw a screwdriver through the open window to me. I took all the screws out of the lock but it still wouldn't open. Eventually I had to bend the lock and unscrew the back. Half an hour later I got to bed.
Pleased it wasn't you or S would've had to climb in the window to rescue you, Rapunzel style!
Glad you enjoyed your holiday. It's too hot here at the moment. I am mortaring the wall in the Big Barn. I need another jetwashing session in there. Last time I had chunks of granite in my hair and in my belly button, and I was soaked. It was great fun!
We rang CJ today to ask to borrow his jetwash for the barn walls. Couldn't get him on the landline. When we finally caught him on the mobile he said the landline isn't working. Seems at around midnight last night someone made off with 300 metres of telephone cable from alongside the main road. And no one saw anything. Amazing!
Love you tons and tons

2. On fitting in

The theft of the telephone cable caused total chaos for a couple of days in our tiny market town of Taboada (population 3,000) as none of the bank ATMs worked.

We rarely paid with cards when we first came to Galicia. Being an entirely rural area, cash was very much king. The one time we tried to pay with a debit card (because the ATM wasn't working, because the telephone cable had been stolen, see above) our friendly local construction yard owner blew the years of accumulated dust from the card machine before handing it to us. She could not make the thing work and eventually told us to come in the following day with the cash.

Galicians, or *Galegos* in their own language, prefer cash. They don't trust banks. It is said that when the euro was first introduced, car sales spiked as elderly *Galegos* rushed to spend their non-taxed pesetas from under their mattresses.

Even now the first of the month is a bad day to go to the bank. There will be long lines at the ATM as locals take out money. There are even longer lines at the bank tills as they pay it back in. You see, they just want to check and make sure the bank hasn't stolen it from them. Very sensible if you ask me!

The cable theft was a one-off. Honesty is highly prized here. In fact it's a given. The day we inadvertently drove away from the local petrol station without paying is engraved into my brain, because Luis was laughing so hard when we screeched back into the forecourt ten minutes later. He had no worries about us not paying. Bars of course never expect you to pay before drinking. It can even be pretty difficult to pay afterwards. Many a time we have stood at a bar, suddenly devoid of staff, waving a note around. We have learned though. The trick is to place the money on the counter, push it nonchalantly away from you, and turn aside. Eventually, like a timid mouse, the staff will appear to whisk it away. I am told that in Galicia it is considered bad form to ask for money, which is probably why our friendly local construction yard was owed a considerable amount of money by one particular British chap (who has thankfully since left) before they plucked up courage to approach the man and ask for their money.

We try to fit in and to understand our place here as ambassadors for our country.

One day our friend Luisa was telling me she had been chatting with another local and saying we were coming to help with the *matanza* (pig killing) the following day. The friend apparently said the English wouldn't do something like that whereupon Luisa explained it was us.

"Oh, *those* English," said the friend. "They're okay."

And that, from a *Galego*, is the highest praise we could possibly have.

Attending a *matanza* was a difficult decision. Luisa said we could buy a pig from her but only if we helped with its slaughter. Her pigs are raised in her *finca*, solely on beets, chestnuts, pumpkins and vegetables. They are as close to organic as can be without a 'certificate' and are slaughtered on site.

We weren't exactly madly keen, having read in books of alcohol-fuelled killing frenzies, but I felt, and still do, that if I was going to eat meat I should know not only where it comes from, but how it dies.

One of the ways to fit in here is to keep animals. We bought our first three hens the spring after we moved here, and at one time our flock had risen to seventeen. We also keep rabbits for meat. This is a difficult subject for many Brits but is considered the norm for most rural Galicians. Both S and I were vegetarian (and in my case vegan) for a number of years. I hate the way meat is mass-reared. Now we eat an omnivorous diet of almost exclusively local produce which I personally feel is the best for the planet, and for us.

Our first and all subsequent pig killings were quick, calm, and devoid of a single frenzy, alcohol-fuelled or otherwise. I have so much respect for our neighbours.

Living in a rural environment is not an easy life. Many of our neighbours work on the land from dawn until dusk. Tilling the land

and growing veg is another must-do rural occupation here. We wanted to be as self-sufficient as possible from the outset so tried to grow a wide range of vegetables. Some did better than others and I'm still learning. Watching the neighbours helps. They grow their veg in a very specific way and plant by the phases of the moon. This is a highly skilled pursuit as one has to check not just whether the moon is waxing or waning but the precise time of day according to the chart. I have to admit to not fitting in well enough to plant my onions at midnight in a howling gale.

My fitting in has been sorely tried when it comes to vegetable growing. Galicians are, generally, quite conservative when it comes to food. They grow what they know. My neighbours still consider root vegetables suitable only for the animals. My cherry tomatoes are too small, my shallots strange and as for mangetout, forget it.

One of the things we miss is our English real ale. One year, our friends Jayne and Richard told us of an exciting event. A beer festival in our local city of Lugo. Most continental beer is what we call lager—often fizzy and bitter, and not to our taste.

The festival was a disappointment in some ways. Virtually all the stalls were selling the usual range of lagers found in any bar, at inflated prices. There was just one stall selling international artisan beers so the four of us sat there sampling beers for a while.

That's how the TV crew found us—we were the only customers at that particular stall. They asked if we would do an interview.

"Do you like the festival?" asked the interviewer.

"I think the festival is a great idea but it would be nice to see more artisan stuff next time."

"What do you think of Spanish beer?"

"It's much stronger than most traditional English ale …"

He looked surprised. "Really?"

"Yes, and it's too cold!"

That got a laugh out of him. Funny, but Luis in the bar thinks it hilarious that we don't want our beer in an iced glass too. He asks if we always drink beer 'hot' in England.

Despite our English oddities, we seem to fit in well here. At one point we struggled to buy a drink when we went into town; so many of our neighbours, friends or total strangers wanted to buy. And that's a nice way to know you fit in.

✥❀✥❁

3. On festivals and food

The beer festival was one of many such events we have attended in Galicia. Most festivals are associated with a saint's day and almost all have food involved in some way. This can be as simple as a *parillada* or grill set up on the village square or the whole event can be food orientated. The eve of San Juan (St. John the Baptist) on 23rd June sees our town council grilling sardines for the whole population whilst Magosto around 10th November means chestnuts grilling in the town square.

Although most fiestas are associated with saints' days, there is more than a whiff of Celtic tradition too.

San Juan, for example, celebrates midsummer with elements of fire and water, feasting and pagan rites. Magosto is held around the time of the Celtic festival of Samhain, the end of summer and the preparation for winter. One of our town festivals, *a feira de caldo do óso* or pig bone stew fair, (much nicer than it sounds) coincides with *entroido* or the beginning of lent and the run up to Easter, or Eostre, the beginning of spring.

Each small parish has their own saint's day which will inevitably involve a fiesta and often a bank holiday locally. Often we can go shopping to our next town and find it closed for a saint's day. It can be quite taxing at times and I think that after fourteen years I could do a pretty good specialist subject on Mastermind of saints' days and which town celebrates each one.

My favourite festivals though are the food related ones.

In Galicia we have cheese festivals, octopus festivals, festivals for Padrón peppers and for bread (made in Céa, very famous locally). In our local town we have had tortilla festivals, tapas festivals and for a number of years, a paella festival.

I'm not sure who the patron saint of paella is but it was always a good 'do'.

Dear Mum,
Had a great time at the paella fiesta last night. We went to the swimming pool for our Friday night swim and sauna early as it was advertised at starting at 9 p.m. I knew even a giant paella wouldn't last long in Taboada.
Nothing much was happening when we arrived so we went into Bar Scala for a pre-paella drink. The priest Don Pepe came up and introduced us to his companion by saying, "These are the English. They live nearby and like wine." I'm not sure I'm completely happy with that label!
We went to look at the paella. The pan was about three feet across but they hadn't added the rice or fish yet so we went into Bar Gema for another drink. Pepe (son of the lady we bought the house from) came in. We bought him a drink but he insisted on buying us one back. The lady at the bar was frying eggy bread (*Torrijas*, delicious) so we were getting quite merry and rather full before we even started on the paella.
When we got back to the tent they were just dishing up the paella so we were the very first to be served! It was €5 a head for paella and a plastic armband. S found the bread and wine (free, no armband needed). Paco's friend brought a whole cheese which he insisted on serving to everyone. The gaita (bagpipe) band played and then the dancing started with the night's 'orchestra'. We sneaked off around 1.15 a.m.
Love you
xxx

Our paella festival was for *el día de papeiros*. I still have no idea what *papeiros* are. Our friend at the bar said it was a rude expression used for local people, which didn't help me at all. But the locals seem happy to be called thus, so it can't be too bad.

4. On language

When we first moved here, Mum was concerned we would forget how to speak English. That has obviously not happened, though there are certain words which I first learnt in Spanish that I struggle to translate back into English. And I have caught myself pronouncing common words the Spanish way such as *'riber'* instead of river.

Unless you are one of those clever or lucky folk who are bilingual, language is always going to be a sticking point for emigrants. And we have been no exception.

Many Galicians have been forced to emigrate at one time or another for work. Galicia has always been a poor area of Spain. As a *Galego* friend once said of our local province, "All we have to export is wood and milk—and no one wants either". A bit extreme but sadly true. Those Galicians who have emigrated and returned to their homeland understand how difficult it can be to settle in a foreign land. These folk often speak a smattering of a second language and I am still surprised to occasionally be addressed in German, French or even Italian in a misguided attempt to communicate—though rarely in English. Those *Galegos* who have stayed in their homeland their whole lives are mightily impressed with anyone who has emigrated from their own. Both groups are more than willing to take the time to help understand our still bizarre attempts at their language.

Mum arrived here in 2015 to live, in a house we bought in the same tiny village. She tried her very best to learn the language but struggled to remember most of the words. Her vocabulary is still pretty much limited to *vino* and *brandy*, *hola* (which she uses interchangeably for hello and goodbye) and her 'naughty snake', the *Galego* for goodnight—*boa noite*.

Mum is, however, the master of interesting mime.

One day she went into the supermarket for eggs for me. A rare event but all our hens had gone on strike and I had a party coming up. I, meanwhile, did some shopping of my own.

There was a cheer as I entered the supermarket some little while later. Not, I have to admit, my usual welcome though the girls are always friendly.

Two of those assistants hustled over dragging a frustrated looking mother.

"What does she want?" asked one, imploringly.

I looked at Mum.

"They don't understand me," she pouted. "Eggs!"

"Ex?" chorused the assistants.

"*Huevos*," I said.

Light bulbs pinged in quick succession.

"I couldn't find them," explained Mum, forming her thumb and forefinger into a circle and waving her hand around chanting, "Eggs! Eggs!"

I stared at Mum's uncanny ability to find the least explanative mime possible in any given situation.

"Why not 'cluck, cluck' and pretend you are laying an egg?" I asked, fascinated.

Actually most of Mum's mimes are variations on the 'eggs' theme. Her 'mayonnaise' mime—a hand, palm downwards, waved in a circle, was so well known in our local market town that the waitress would ask if we wanted the stuff by using Mum's mime.

What a claim to fame to have!

Galicia is on the very far edge of Spain, a world away from the Mediterranean costas and English tourism and a whole language away from Castilian Spanish.

When we first decided to move here we went to evening classes to try and learn some Spanish. Our teacher was friendly with a marked Lancashire accent which carried on into his Spanish. Still, we did the course and felt we were ready to tackle the language with real Spaniards.

What we got of course were real Galicians with their very own language. Galician bears a striking resemblance to Portuguese with its diphthongs and its shushing sounds. In fact a room full of Galicians talking at full volume sounds like a room full of waves lapping over a pebbled shore.

It doesn't help that most male Galicians over the age of sixty never seem to open their mouths at all to speak. One chap always spoke around the large cigar he had permanently clamped in his teeth. When the smoking ban came in, he swapped the cigar for a toothpick. It didn't make his speech any clearer. One day he stopped me, obviously wanting to ask a question. As hard as I tried, I had no idea at all what he wanted. Luckily his son was nearby and he 'translated' using recognisable Spanish words. It turns out Pepe was asking us if the car abandoned at the top of the road was ours. Why did he think this? Because it had a British registration. We were 'The English' and therefore had to know who owned it if we didn't.

✿ຉ✿ଊ✿

5. On Galicia and the weather

Galicia is the most remote of Spain's seventeen autonomous communities, with a land area of 29,574 square kilometres (11,419 square miles), a population of 2.7 million, and a coastline of 1,498 kilometres (930 miles). It is green and beautiful: full of mystery and mists, Celtic music and Celtic legends. As one of the seven Celtic nations (along with Scotland, Ireland, Wales, The Isle of Man, Cornwall and Brittany) Galicia has more in common with its northern cousins than with the rest of Spain.

Galicia's beaches are wild, backed by sand dunes and fronted by the Atlantic to the west or the Cantabrian Sea to the north. Its people are, to a great extent, rural farmers. They live off the land, often at a subsistence level, growing their own vegetables, pigs and chickens to eat or sell at the local markets.

There is a fierce pride here, at the end of the world. A pride undiminished by General Franco's dictatorship and banning of the Galician language. (Franco was, interestingly, a Galician, as was Fidel Castro of Cuba. I've often thought it must be something in the water here.)

Galicia also has some of the most erratic weather in the Iberian Peninsula.

I've written a lot about the Galician weather over the years. It seems to be as much an obsession with *Galegos* as with the English, which means we fit right in.

Most conversations with our neighbours begin with, "Isn't it hot, cold, humid, dry?" or variations on the above. These comments are often accompanied by, "It didn't used to be this hot, cold, humid, dry when I was a child."

Most foreigners who have heard of Galicia tend to start a conversation with us in the same way … "It always rains there doesn't it?"

For the record. It does not always rain in Galicia. We often see the sun two or three days a year. Only joking. In the interior we tend to have hot, dry summers and mild, wet winters. Certainly it is much warmer, and drier, than the north-west of England where I briefly lived. What we do have though is high humidity—constantly. Galicia has many rivers and many valleys. The mighty Miño and the deep and forbidding Sil affect the weather patterns locally. We often have morning mists in the summer, and boy are we grateful for them to water our plants and work outdoors before the heat arrives.

Oddly, it's not only foreigners who think it always rains in Galicia.

We were on our very first pensioner holiday here in Spain and were chatting to a pleasant couple from Tarragona. "Oh, Galicia. Beautiful spot, pity it always rains there, isn't it?" she said.

But it works both ways.

On that first pensioner holiday, we were on a plane full of elderly *Galegos*, coming in to land at Alicante airport.

As we descended I heard,

"Where are all the trees?"

"It's so brown."

"Where's the greenery?"

"I want to go home!"

✿ဢ✿ଓ✿

6. On age and emigrating

We are now eligible for those pensioner holidays (well, S is, I get to go along as his 'carer', still being well under retirement age) but when we first came to Galicia, S was a mere 58 years old and I was a babe of 42. We were younger than most silver-haired émigrés looking for sunshine, and of course we wouldn't have chosen Galicia had we been looking solely for sunshine and G&Ts by the pool.

We were, however, too old to easily get a job here.

When we first started to look at houses, our idea was simple—buy somewhere with enough land to be self-sufficient (my trusty self-sufficiency book suggested three hectares was the correct amount) with a house on it—needing renovation was fine—and near to a town. We are both DIYers and felt we could tackle most jobs given time and a good book.

Our initial plan was to continue working in the UK, as newt catchers, whilst renovating the house during our down-time in winter, when our charges are generally asleep.

Things didn't quite work out like that.

By the time we met Mark, an English estate agent, we felt we knew what we were looking for. We also realised that renovating a house and a sizeable patch of land whilst dashing back and forth to England was never going to be practical.

The decision to relocate lock, stock, and kettle was not a difficult one when we came down to it. Our hearts were already in Galicia and we reckoned that with the money we would get from selling each of our homes in the UK plus our normally frugal spending habits we could afford to move full time.

Of course our 'retirement' came with a fistful of problems and more work than I had done in years, but we have been here for fourteen years now and I really can't imagine living anywhere else.

I've often wondered what makes one person decide to up sticks whilst another not. There are obviously commitments, jobs, and money to take into account but when it comes down to it, I think we would have moved regardless of our circumstances.

I've always loved travelling and exploring new places. I think new cultures and trying to speak a new language keep me young. I remember at school, long before I had ever even been across the Channel, a teacher came back from holiday in North Africa carrying a box full of food for us to try. I can still remember the taste of the falafel and exotic treats he brought in. They were the most incredible things I had ever eaten. Maybe that teacher inspired me? Or maybe it was in my genes.

Mum was eighty-three and eleven months when she came here to live. She had lived in the same house for sixty-three years until, in June 2015, she upped sticks and moved to Galicia. A short time later both my siblings upped and moved abroad too. Inspired themselves by Mum maybe, but I don't think any of us has ever regretted our decisions. I know Mum hasn't.

☼ඐ☼ଓ☼

7. On staying put

Other emigrants have come and gone since we have been here, for a variety of reasons. Missing family and friends is always a big one for people, as is missing English food. Then there are the day-to-day difficulties of making oneself understood in a language in which you will never be fluent. I think there is a mindset to moving abroad successfully. We have, over the years, become more Galician in our thinking, eating, and socialising. Those of our friends who have stayed have the same mindset: to fit in and accept the country for what it is, warts and all.

Many of our *Galego* friends cannot imagine that we are not homesick. Homesickness for Galician émigrés can be so severe it has its own word, *morriña*, which I'm told is far more than a simple homesickness.

One year we went to the UK for a fortnight to visit Mum. We stopped for fuel at our local service station before we left and said we were off to England. This obviously translated as leaving for good as our neighbours and friends were amazed to see us back just fourteen days later. Our gas delivery man didn't visit at all until we had to eventually ring him.

"Oh, but I thought you had left," he said.

He still forgets us occasionally if he thinks we have been away a while.

With the spectre of Brexit having loomed and sadly happened, again people have asked us if we are leaving.

Mum's answer, I think, speaks for us all.

"I'm not going back. If they throw me out I'll just go and hide somewhere. I don't want to go back."

So that's a no then.

After all we have everything we need here in Galicia. We have peace and acres of countryside, relatively low Covid numbers, friends and fiestas. We even have a flushing toilet, which is not hiding behind a sofa.

The Writing Home Series
by Lisa Rose Wright

Have you ever wanted to leave the rat race, move abroad and live the good life somewhere green and bountiful?

Lisa and her partner, the enigmatic S, did just that. In 2007 they left their jobs as newt catchers and their native English shores for beautiful green Galicia, in the remote north-west of Spain—a land of mystery and mists, Celtic music and Celtic legends, and a language of its very own.

Follow one couple's love affair with this unspoilt region as Lisa and S set to work to self-renovate a derelict farmhouse, whilst trying to become self-sufficient and learn more about this untamed part of the Iberian Peninsula.

Their story unfolds through Lisa's letters to her mum, making this truly a series to write home about.

Book 3 in the series, *Chestnut, Cherry & Kiwi Fruit Sponge* will be published in 2021.

**For information on Lisa's books and how to get her short story prequel *Camino* for free go to her website:
www.lisarosewright.wixsite.com/author**

10

"You lived where?"
LUCINDA E CLARKE

I shouldn't be here in this book because when I moved from country to country to country, I wasn't chasing a dream but escaping a nightmare.

In the early 1970s I fled from my narcissistic parent and compounded my problems by marrying a Walter Mitty clone, a charismatic dreamer with unrealistic ambitions, and for over two decades we moved country six times, often one step ahead of the law.

I'm the progeny of colonial stock. My mother was born in China to descendants of early missionaries who rapidly lost their religious zeal, set up a newspaper company and created a mega-rich empire. So, maybe travel is in my blood? I've always wanted to see what was over the next hill and I still can't decide if it's a blessing or a curse. Despite all the trauma, and I only mention a fraction in this story, I've led a rollercoaster life and have no regrets.

We began small, moving from England to a croft in the wilds of Scotland, our first disaster. It was impossible to dig and plant in sub-zero soil, so we abandoned the cabbages and tomatoes and attempted small animal and puppy breeding. A swathe of an unpronounceable disease wiped out all the small creatures in two weeks, and one Cairn Terrier broke out and savaged the chickens on the adjoining farm before eyeing up their sheep. We put the whole adventure down to inexperience and moved on to disaster number two.

We landed in Nairobi, Kenya, where I was expecting to live with other company wives while husbands were busy working far away for weeks, desecrating the countryside in the neighbouring country.

I never met any of the other wives. I was abandoned twenty-five kilometres outside the city in a bungalow owned by a local landlord who liked crinkly handshakes. I did have a nine-week-old baby—did I mention I had also been busy breeding?—and an ayah (housemaid by any other name).

I discovered that everyone liked crinkly greetings and I quickly ran out of the little money I had. To add to my woes, the baby got sick, the gardener the landlord insisted I employ was perpetually drunk, and a leopard was visiting the garden at night. Even the monkeys swiped the bananas I'd watched ripening outside the bedroom window.

I thought things couldn't get any worse, but they did. Husband was imprisoned in Tanzania along with the rest of the crew for prospecting too close to the Chinese enclave and when he was finally released and returned on leave, a couple of his friends were arrested when they arrived back in Nairobi.

'It was a tad suspicious' immigration announced *'to declare that $20 a month salary was acceptable for expatriates'*, and, further, they cruelly suggested, *'it was a tax dodge'*.

Husband refused to return to work and after a long wrangle with the company we were forced to fly home after less than a year.

We touched down in Heathrow to two inches of snow desperate to escape again and a couple of months later he was on his way to Libya with promises to fly me over in a few weeks. (Yes, that's the one in North Africa with Colonel Gadaffi in charge).

This was our third disaster but that came nearly six years later. I became familiar with men holding hands, spitting and urinating in the street, the absence of women, the insane driving and the sand; there was always the sand.

For me as a married expat the best thing about Libya was that I could drive, and as long as I dressed modestly, I didn't have to wear the full burka or cover my face. Since my ex was working for a Libyan family, and not an overseas contractor, I was never harassed or groped. My only unpleasant experience was the day I went to buy a seven-inch, pink zip for the dress I was making—I had to make all our clothes as the merchandise was just too awful to contemplate. It was even difficult to find material that didn't glow in the dark. How was I to know that a *'zip'* was the Arabic slang for what most men hold most dear in all the world? The shopkeeper went ballistic and left the building, leaving me in tears.

Shopping in the meat market was a nightmare as I scooted the pushchair around the broken and bleeding carcases of mostly goats and camels. The heat, the smell and total absence of hygiene defy words. I eventually found an Egyptian butcher and for five years we only ate beef fillet. Did you know there are 250 ways to cook a dead cow? Today, I can only remember 247 of them.

All children need a pet, right? So, seeing some really cute

bunnies in the market, my young daughter cried out for a bugger—apologies, my eldest couldn't pronounce 'n' but had no trouble with 'g'. *What harm could it do?* I asked myself as the seller, sitting cross-legged on the ground, grabbed it by the ears and slung it on the scales. *Interesting way to charge for a pet by weight,* I thought before lunging forward in time to stop him lopping its head off with a cleaver. So now, I was piloting a pushchair around piles of offal on the floor while struggling to control a wriggling rabbit in a plastic bag. A couple of years later, when poor Bugger became ill, the vet was confused. Why pay big bucks for treatment only to toss the patient into a pot or a pie a few days later?

As I rounded the corner from the meat market I barrelled into a particularly excited crowd, who, as I was a woman, parted like the Red Sea until I stood at the front. To my horror I was forced to witness a public execution, gruesome at the least, and all I could do was wave the plastic bag in front of my infant to shut out the view. I foresaw lifelong trauma in my offspring.

Few women did their own shopping, and at first it was amusing to observe men buying intimate feminine products, but in every establishment, I was waved to the front of the queue. The bakery was a little dangerous though, as they slid out the red-hot trays holding the flat bread loaves skidding over the floor and missing my toes by millimetres.

We were only in Tripoli for a month before we were sent east to Benghazi, the second city. Rules were a little more relaxed and there was a tight-knit community of around two hundred foreigners.

Within a month of arriving, I was teaching at the local International School, and a month after that, working on the local radio station four early evenings a week.

I could write a book about my time with the *English Language Service of the Libyan Arab Jamahiriya broadcasting on 94.5 FM.* I first worked as a continuity presenter, introducing programmes from my hastily scribbled links, and cueing the engineer on the other side of the glass before sloping off for a fag and a coffee in the production office.

This worked fine, unless the air went dead. Then I'd race to the control room to discover why we were broadcasting an unexciting, loud, white hiss. Sometimes the engineer had fallen asleep, was prostrate on the floor saying his prayers; at others, he was as high as a kite or not there at all. I became an expert at splicing the spinning tape with a roll of Sellotape I kept in my pocket, often while straddling the prone engineer in the most unprofessional way. If anyone had seen, I would have been hauled off and locked up for indecency.

I only apologised for the break in transmission once and was soundly castigated for lowering the professionalism of the radio station.

There were more disasters when the tapes scheduled to play didn't arrive from Tripoli. "What do I do?" I asked trembling. There were four, long hours to fill. The reply was a shrug and the word 'music'. We were going live in two minutes so I raced to the record library and pulled an armful of LPs off the shelves. Just as I was about to exit, the notice pinned to the door listed all the banned artists under 'DO NOT PLAY'. You're ahead of me here, right? Every album I was clutching was from a 'non persona' group; they had played in Israel, had a relative in Israel or been seen in public drinking Coca Cola, a banned American abomination.

I dropped the lot and started again, choosing artists I'd never heard of. I dumped the records in the control room, and carted the covers into the studio. And while indicating which tracks to play, I read the information off the cardboard sleeve. Hardly scintillating I admit.

The station chief decided to up the game with book readings. He called me into his office, waved a copy of *The Old Man and the Sea* and instructed me to narrate it live on air.

Yes, I know it's a classic, but it's hardly fun is it? A desperate old man who after eighty-four luckless days catches a huge fish only to have it eaten before he returns to shore.

By week four, my friends were begging me to precis it, or leave out chunks and find something more cheerful. Bravely I ploughed on wondering if anyone would ever speak to me again.

They did but then I put all my friendships at risk by inviting them on air to take part in 'Top of Benghazi' a take on 'Top of the Form', a popular radio quiz for school children. I'd discovered an old book of questions from the show in the English bookshop and thought it might be fun.

I think the idea was excellent but the questions were a tad difficult for my contestants, and to be honest I didn't know many of the answers either. When, at the end of each episode I was reading scores ranging from '*W has yet to score, to X has two points*', it became more and more difficult to recruit anyone willing to come on the show.

The one exception was an over-bearing, over-bright, over-confident American student studying at the Garyounis University. He knew all the answers to every question; yes, all of them no matter what subject. That first series was pre-recorded, (for obvious reasons there was never a second series), and we had a stand-up fight when he told me the chemical composition for the lead in pencils and I insisted the answer was graphite. Why he couldn't call it graphite I have no idea but insisted it was carbon. He won. In fact, he won the whole series and then made a terrible fuss when I handed him his prize, a partly chewed ruler the dog had filched and gnawed in half.

I turned off the mic as I explained it wasn't his real prize. I would be purchasing that the next day, but as we were on air, the listeners couldn't see us so could he just drool over the beautiful pen I wasn't handing him?

He didn't get it and stormed off bellowing to all who would listen that he'd been cheated. And even when I tracked him down the next day, the morality police a car behind while I parked up by the student quarters, he swiped the pen out of my hand with very bad grace.

My worst day on the radio was 1 September 1979, the anniversary of the day Colonel Gaddafi took control of Libya in a bloodless coup by occupying the radio stations and telling everyone to stay indoors. It's understandable then he was a little twitchy about radio broadcasts.

I was lying on the beach in the 'Foreigners Enclosure' when I heard gunshots coming from the port. I'd heard our leader was visiting to inspect the navy, which at the time I believe consisted of one sixteen-foot gun boat. I had no idea it was an assassination attempt so as I blithely drove into the station, my car was surrounded by five sloppily dressed soldiers wielding bayonets. I had little choice but to get out of the car, and the whole bunch of us walked into the production office as they eyed me collect the tapes, note the titles and scribble my cues.

They stood to attention, silent and menacing.

I began to sweat, despite the overhead fans. I tried a little conversation, but it was evident none of them spoke a word of English. What were they hoping to prevent? If I criticised their beloved leader or called for a revolution on air, would they be any the wiser? Not that I had any intentions of doing that but how would they know?

Hands trembling, legs like rubber bands and with sweat pouring from every pore, I delivered the tapes to the terrified controller who was similarly guarded by two more armed soldiers and took my place in the studio.

By now the perspiration running down my face and dripping off my nose was obliterating the script which became dangerously soggy. In this instance I was not in the right frame of mind to ad-lib.

A couple of hours later, I introduced a half-hour drama from the BBC, so old even the jokes were out of date, and raced for the loo. They followed me. I mean they were right behind me even into the washroom itself. I slammed the cubicle door shut and fumed. This was beyond the height of disrespect, but I dared not question them. It was an effort to keep my face neutral as I washed my hands and returned to huddle on my chair in the studio.

I may have betrayed my feelings just a little, for one particularly unfriendly specimen then placed the fixed bayonet at the end of his long and lethal-looking gun and rested it on my shoulder. I could feel the point of it pricking the skin on my neck. I froze. My next introduction came out staccato as by now the tears were fighting for space with the sweat running down every part of my body.

It was time for the news, sent down the wires from Tripoli the capital. When I first worked at the station, we read the evening news, but as time went by and the diatribes grew more extreme, we refused to broadcast information such as *'the lying, cheating bastards in Washington'*, and *'the power hungry and destructive oligarchs in Westminster'* was a step too far, so we all refused to cooperate. Broadcasting hate speech about our countries of origin was asking too much.

I sat rigid as the news began. Were these the last words I was to hear before they ran me through? I noticed with horror that the blade on one of the other bayonets was rusty, or was that dried blood?

Almost five hours after arriving I stumbled out into the warm twilight, the cool breeze on my skin, the tears still rolling down my face, and climbed into my car.

"Why," my friends asked, "had I not sounded my usual bouncy self tonight? Was I going down with something?"

I had one other dice with death when I foolishly faced a hail of bullets attempting to save our dogs. Husband had left the garden gates open while returning the babysitter and the local animal brigade were driving along shooting the feral dogs. I ran out screaming at them to leave our pets alone.

They ignored me, aimed into the garden, shot one and injured the other. With a smile, one guy jumped out, grabbed Samantha by her back legs and flung her body into the forty-five-gallon waste bin by the gate. Rebecca fled but she was a basket case afterwards and for the safety of the children, we sent her to live at the workshop.

I was so lucky my friends forgave me for making public fools of them on air, since we were a close-knit group in a foreign land with no access to family and the outside world. In those early days, the mid to late 70s, you could not pick up a phone and call home; only the offices had telecoms, and there was no internet, Zoom, Skype, Facebook, WhatsApp and so on. Letters would take months to arrive, if at all, and it was puzzling to read, *'I hope your cold is better'*, when you'd forgotten ever having one.

Every family invested in top-of-the-range radios to keep in touch with the world outside Libyan borders. Friends and family were not permitted to visit; you had to be invited by an important Libyan citizen and that didn't happen.

On a lighter note, while we worked hard, we also played hard and we kept ourselves busy, very busy. The entertainment scene was hectic; the darts league was contested with more fervour than a mere football world cup. There were dinner parties; I never offered less than five courses. Those were the days when I could fling together a banquet for twelve, hold down a full-time job teaching, entertain the occasional overseas company visitor, nurture and care for two toddlers and broadcast four early evenings a week, live on radio.

We had events more familiar to the Victorians, with beetle drives, whist drives and 'stand up and entertain us' slots. There was also a very active underground drama group that put on amazing plays. Guards were placed outside on the lookout for the morality police who patrolled the areas where the wild expats were known to congregate. Theatre was strictly against the law.

Eating out was not on the cards. No one could name a restaurant or a hotel dining room which didn't serve up food poisoning with every meal, although to be fair, they didn't charge any extra for this.

Besides the illicit theatre performances, the booze making was also underground. New arrivals were greeted with a jar of *mash*, to which you added fifty litres of water and several tins of Biomalt to make home-brewed beer. I'm sure the pharmacies realised what we were up to as one tin of the malt would last a family several months and we bought them up a dozen at a time.

The whole concoction was poured into huge dustbins set up on bricks with nightlights below in winter and left until the hydrometer gave the correct reading. It was then bottled in thick glass bottles which originally held Benglashia sparkling water, with a spoonful of sugar and left for another couple of weeks. The result was lethal, even when carefully decanted. We, like all the other families, brewed up approximately fifty litres of the stuff every week.

But our alcoholic adventures did not stop there. We trod fresh grapes and bottled the juice with sugar and water, not exactly cabernet sauvignon, but after the first batch I revolted. Not because of the taste, but because we'd used red grapes and it didn't occur to me, as my legs worked like pistons up and down in the dustbin squashing the fruit, with a fag in one hand and a book in the other, that my legs would turn bright pink and it didn't wash off. After that, I would only cooperate if we were making white wine.

Other Europeans were more inventive and produced old Johnny Walker bottles of pure alcohol, if I remember correctly 150% proof. Cut back with water you could then manufacture crème de cacao, a form of Baileys, Tia Maria and a woodchip whisky, though drain cleaner tasted fractionally better. The biggest failure was the gin with juniper berries; that never worked out.

Many a happy hour I spent with my sewing needles threading string through oranges to suspend them over pure alcohol sealed in Kilner jars. I even managed to fool one overseas business manager from France who wanted to know how we'd managed to smuggle a bottle of Cointreau into a dry country.

Of course, my ex had to go one further and purchase a still despite my begging him not to. To my horror, he set up this enormous metal contraption in our utility room, rusty tubes filled with marbles which belted out steam and made a heck of a racket.

I finally got my way one night during a party in full swing when some locals banged on our gates demanding to be allowed to join in the fun. We refused of course so they then declared they were off to collect the police as they were convinced that we had illicit drink on the premises. Really?

Never have I seen fifty people sober up as quickly as some rushed to pour gallons of booze down every sink and drain, while others attacked the baked ground in the back garden to dig a hole large enough to bury the enormous still. I wonder if it's still there?

Every time we flew back to Benghazi off leave, we broke the law. Checking into our usual Heathrow hotel the night before the flight we'd hand over our newspaper-wrapped package, which was quickly taken down to their deep freeze. Next day we'd pack it on the base of the carrycot then add mattress and baby, leaving about an inch of free board. When the youngest was too large for the carrycot, we used those Cozy-Toes papoose bags with the infant scrunched up in the top third, feet resting on the frozen newspaper.

We were smuggling of course. Bacon, how we missed our pork products, and as each friend returned from leave we all waited with bated breath to see who would be invited for breakfast to gaze in wonder at the single rasher on the plate.

When we landed in London we'd rush to the nearest café and order bacon sandwiches and fresh milk and make ourselves totally sick as a result. Shopping was a nightmare back in Europe as I dithered in supermarkets, overwhelmed by the choice and variety, I couldn't decide which brand to buy. In Libya there was no choice at all: one kind of cheese, one brand of powdered milk and one cut of meat.

I was sad for a German friend we met at customs in Benghazi, declaring his beef sausages. No dice, the officer produced the tongs and removed them despite his protests they did not contain pork, while his colleague caressed our new dart board before waving us through. To my horror, I later discovered it was made from pig bristle.

One quiet afternoon, during siesta there was a banging on our outside gates. A quick aside here. When we were first moved to Benghazi, we were given a ginormous apartment on the ninth floor of a very smart building. This was fine, until the day I found my adventurous two-year-old dangling out of one of the windows eyeing the spiked railings below. We were hastily relocated to a villa belonging to the Libyans my ex worked for that had previously been the home for the British Consul. If the apartment was large, the new residence was super mansion size, with an all-round front and back garden and a back terrace larger than a tennis court.

Back to the banging on our front gate which revealed a delegation from the British Embassy from Tripoli—they had withdrawn from the second city just after we'd arrived. Our visitors requested that we host Her Majesty's Birthday Celebrations that year. Regulations were more relaxed outside the capital and it would also give the second city expatriates a day out.

We were thrilled and promptly agreed. Work groups gathered to paint the walls and clear up the garden; no grass you understand, just prickly undergrowth and sand as there was never spare water for irrigating. The kitchens at the university baked an enormous cake. Along with piles of goodies, the embassy sent posters and pictures and the villa disappeared under swathes of red, blue and white bunting.

The sewing machines were over-worked, and on the day, we rescued our tortoises and favourite chameleon and left them in the bedroom in case they were inadvertently crushed to death.

To save the time and effort of painting the whole villa, we wrenched open a never-before-used side gate for the guests.

We stood and waited for the Ambassador and wife and waited and waited and waited. You know that feeling wondering if you got the date wrong? No, other ambassadors and consulate officials arrived from every Christian country in Libya.

We had no option but to welcome them personally, shaking hands, as we mumbled that we were so sorry the British Ambassador's plane must have been delayed, but any moment …?

We were unaware that the Rolls Royce, the only one in Benghazi, had not been used for quite some time and on the great day refused to start. In desperation the chauffeur used his own car, a battered and dented Fiat 500 to collect them from the airport.

In the excitement no one had told him we were using the side entrance and he spent frustrating minutes hammering on the main gate. At last, someone let them in and without thinking led them around the side of the villa where all the spiky brush undergrowth we had cleared from the back garden below the terrace was piled up. It made short work of the tights worn by the Ambassador's wife, and his trousers seriously needed a clothes brush. After helping them clean up, I was happy to hand over the host duties to them.

It was a stunning occasion. The cake was cut, the speakers belted out patriotic marches and the drink was imbibed in large quantities. Since Libya was a dry country it was not possible to serve any alcohol to the couple of hundred honoured guests, so we bought in crates and crates of red and white grape juice. As the music played, the chatter flowed, the nibbles got nibbled, and the twinkly lights twinkled and people got drunk. I promise this is true. Guests constantly waylaid me commenting on how brave we were serving wine and did I brew it all myself?

Two weeks later came one of those moments when life tells you that you are special—for a very brief time of course.

We had a visit from the French Embassy with an invite to the Bastille Day celebrations. They would like twelve British citizens to attend. Would we compile a list?

What power! Who did we like best? Who had lived here the longest? Who, on the other hand, had upset us? Their name was off the list. Today I can't even remember the event but it was another highlight in our frenetic social life.

Since my husband was working directly for a Libyan family related to the deposed king, we were not fixed to an annual contract and we may well have stayed for longer. We were making shedloads of money. Until the day my ex got extra drunk and ran over a Libyan in the new company Land Cruiser. The police were called, and he was escorted to our villa so he could explain they were arresting him. I called a neighbour to watch the children and drove behind them to the police station.

I didn't sleep that night. We all knew of cases where expats had disappeared after imprisonment, never to be seen again.

The following morning, I dropped the children off and returned to the police station armed with cigarettes, food and coffee. They denied all knowledge of him. I drove to every police station in the city and they all said the same thing. He had vanished into thin air.

In desperation I went to his place of work, the first time ever, and was kept waiting for three hours. I choked back the tears as I told the story. His boss sent me away.

For days I tried to carry on as best I could. My nerves were in shreds, the children beyond fractious and my friends rallied around and did what they could. I didn't expect to see my husband again and I had no idea what to do; by law I couldn't even leave Libya without my husband's permission.

On day five, my ex was dropped on the doorstep clutching airline tickets. We were to leave the country within seven days. Now, I've moved house many times, but we had five years' worth of personal and household possessions and could only take the usual plane luggage.

We sent out the word, drove to local markets and practically gave away three cars, two yachts, Persian carpets and tons of toys, household goods and clothing.

Each day my ex went to the bank to deposit money from the sale, before it dawned on him it was going nowhere as the tellers ripped up the deposit slips. Desperate, he appealed to his boss and the night before we flew out, they took him into the bank via the back door and handed him a huge pile of dirty, greasy, slimy, Libyan currency notes.

That night we wondered how we were going to smuggle them out, it was highly illegal to remove money this way. The only answer was to stuff it all in my bra. I still shudder today when I remember how it felt and I could have given Pamela Anderson or Barbara Windsor a run for their money.

We stood in line to pass through onto the apron, the plane shimmering through the sweat pouring into my eyes. It was then I saw the new metal detector. Would it measure the metal strips in the money? I went cold and told my husband to take the children and the pushchair through first. It would either blow the contraption up, or, like most things, prove it wasn't working.

I hung back and waited until the rest of the family were climbing the boarding stairs before I barrelled through and raced for dear life across the baking tarmac. I didn't care Libyan Arab Airways had crammed three people into two seats in several rows; I was on and nothing was going to drag me off.

The final horror after we landed at Heathrow was to discover that my ex had not repatriated a single cent to the UK in the almost six years we spent in Libya. From millionaire status we were almost broke and all we could do was to pick ourselves up and start over.

A few years later, we were invited to a reception at the Libyan Embassy in Johannesburg. Were we still *persona non grata*? We didn't go—just in case.

Books by Lucinda E Clarke

After thirty years writing professionally for every conceivable outlet, Lucinda believes an author can write on any topic and any subject.

This led her to describe herself as a schizophrenic, hopping from one genre to the next as the mood takes her. The three award-winning memoirs cover her personal, abusive and globe-trotting life—and her career writing and producing programmes for radio and TV. Her knowledge and love of Africa gave birth to the *Amie in Africa Series* where she threw a young, suburban newlywed into Africa before abandoning her in the middle of a bloody civil war. There followed four more books in the series.

Next, she exercised her cruel talents on Leah in *A Year in the Life of… Series*, four psychological thrillers in an urban setting.

She has two traditionally published books and independently—by choice—launched a further sixteen.

For more information, visit her website:
www.lucindaeclarke.com

From the Garden of England to the Foothills of the French Pyrenees
NIKKI MCARTHUR

Hello, let me introduce myself. My name is Nikki McArthur. I currently live in a huge watermill in the picturesque countryside of the Haute-Garonne, an hour south-west of Toulouse, France and just an hour from the border with Spain. I have five children aged from thirty down to teens and my husband Gary and I have been happily married (well largely) for over thirty years.

Since moving to France in 2004 when we were both in our thirties, we have renovated a large portion of our 1200 m² watermill and transformed our five-acre property. I've given birth to two of our five children here and we've started several businesses. We opened a garden centre, created a successful landscape gardening business specialising in natural swimming ponds and a holiday rental business. We have hosted dozens of students teaching English and I work also as a freelance editor/proof-reader. For several years we ran a charity helping refugees. We coordinated the collection of food, clothing, hygiene products and medical aid (including an ambulance) for six containers loaded from our home and shipped to war-torn Syria. We are privileged to have met some wonderfully kind and caring people in the process. Last, but by no means least, I'm an author. You may ask how we managed to fit all this in—the truth is it has been hard at times, but we wouldn't have it any other way. Well ... maybe just a little.

One of the most common questions everyone asks is, "Why did you move to France?" and it's not easy to answer in a sentence. Our experiences in France have been vastly different to the UK ... it feels now as though it was another life and in many ways it was.

When I was young, you may be surprised to learn that French was one of my least favourite subjects. I only chose it as an 'O' level option because I had the choice of French or geography. I didn't like the geography teacher as he was more than a little scary, so that was the only reason I chose to study French. I wasn't motivated to learn; why on earth did I need to speak French? And I barely managed to scrape a C grade. Oh, if only I'd known that twenty years later I'd be taking up residence there, maybe, just maybe I'd have put in a little more effort.

You may have concluded that living in France had not always

been my dream. In fact, in the early days of our relationship when I was just eighteen and Gary four years my senior, we dreamed of moving somewhere very different. It all started back in 1985. Let me share with you a few of the relevant times in my life so far that have led to where I find myself today.

✧✿✧✿

July 1985 – Where it all began

I had just come back from the most fantastic holiday ever with my new boyfriend, Gary. We'd met on a blind date a few months earlier and we'd hit it off immediately. We booked a last-minute cheap package deal to Crete—neither of us had ever been to Greece before.

When we arrived on the island the strength of the sun hit us as we got off the plane—it was such a wonderful feeling. The journey from the airport to the resort had us hooked—all the olive trees and agaves, wild rosemary, brightly coloured pink and red climbing bougainvilleas over whitewashed houses picked out against the crisp blue Mediterranean sky. The airport bus wove its way along the small mountain roads and as we turned a corner on another death-defying hairpin bend, the view almost took our breath away. Sheer rocks plunged dramatically to the coast and we were treated to our first glimpse of the shimmering Mediterranean Sea. It was love at first sight—it felt so natural to be there, like we had found our home.

By contrast, our accommodation in the town of Chania was shabby—it was a basic room above a café, with communal showers and toilets shared between six rooms. The toilets were constantly blocked and overflowing due to the tourists putting paper down them (when the sign quite clearly said not to). But it didn't bother us. We were young and it was just a place to rest our heads—there was so much outside the door to discover and explore. We had a small balcony that looked out onto the bustling street below. We enjoyed just sitting there sometimes, watching the world go by and soaking up the atmosphere.

On one such morning, Gary was sitting on the balcony as I got ready for the day. Whilst packing the bag for the beach, I heard a terrifyingly loud buzzing sound. I looked up and saw the most enormous insect heading towards me. I ran to the balcony screaming.

"Gary! Help! It's massive and it's going to sting me!"

Gary sighed when he saw what it was. "Don't panic, it's only a hornet. It won't hurt you."

"Please get rid of it for me. I can't go back in if it's still there." I'm embarrassed at what a wimp I was back then.

Sorry to say it, but Gary did what I asked and came back to join me on the balcony with his flip-flop in his hand. He scraped the poor squashed insect onto the railings and then flicked it over the edge. We leaned over the balcony and watched in horror as it plopped, then slowly sank into the froth of a small espresso coffee sitting on a table outside the bar below us. We exchanged a wide-eyed glance, quickly slunk away from the edge of the balcony and crept back inside our room giggling—we didn't wait around to see what happened next!

We loved Chania, it was full of interesting shops and cafés, and the harbour was so beautiful—particularly at night when the lights of the restaurants and bars reflected across the water. It was truly magical. We spent most of our days on the beach and our evenings eating, drinking and wandering in and out of shops buying souvenirs for just about everyone we knew. We got a bit carried away and I don't think our families were quite so enthusiastic about the Grecian vases and lacquered coffee cups we bought them.

We enjoyed the holiday so much it got us thinking ... why couldn't we have this life all the time? Instead of working nine to five to pay for a holiday just a week or two a year, why couldn't we live somewhere like that permanently? However, we didn't know how we could do it at the time. I was still living at home and commuting to London every day and Gary rented a house and worked as an assistant manager of a garden centre. We had no savings and so we felt we had to wait until we had enough money to make a new life in Greece. This was the moment we started chasing the dream.

Less than a year later, Gary accepted a new job in Surrey and we moved in together. Unfortunately, we suffered a catalogue of disasters which would have been enough to put most people off, but we picked ourselves up and started over again in a new town. After a shaky start, things began falling into place. Gary was offered a partnership in a landscape gardening business and life started to quickly improve for us. We managed to scrape together the money to buy a run-down flat, did it up and made a tidy profit as the property prices had started to soar. We then bought a little cottage in the Kent countryside. It wasn't Greece, but for us at the time, it was the next best thing.

Fast forward to May 1988. We had just got back from the most wonderful honeymoon on the Greek island of Zante. Gary's business partner had a friend who owned a villa there in the hills overlooking the fishing village of Lagana. The village was small and simple, with a couple of bars and a beautiful beach. It's totally changed now as we found when we visited it again ten years later, but back then it was quiet and unspoilt. It was a fantastic holiday, with lots of very fond memories. We got to know the locals well. Our villa was up a dirt track and at the end of it was a taverna called 'Dennis'. We ate there most nights and were overwhelmed by the kindness and hospitality of the owner and the locals who frequented it. Dennis took us back to his home one day and invited us to attempt to milk his goats. Gary seemed to have the knack, but I just couldn't get the hang of it—it's much harder than it looks! Another of the locals, Stephano, invited us to his house for lunch. It was so kind of him—he could speak hardly a word of English and we could only speak a few words of Greek, but he shared what little he had with us and offered for us to stay in his little house the next time we visited. Everyone seemed so laid back and had time for others—it was a refreshing difference to the life back home in the UK. This holiday helped to renew our resolve to move to Greece one day.

In 1990, the birth of our first son Max made our rosy lives complete, but just a few months later the UK was hit by a financial recession and our perfect life started to fall apart. Interest rates soared, our mortgage payments doubled and our income was diminishing at an even faster rate. We decided it was time to get out while we still could. We put our house on the market intending to follow our dream to live in Greece. Unfortunately, our timing was wrong; the housing market had plummeted and we couldn't sell the house. It was not meant to be at that time and looking back I know we were not ready for the move then.

The recession hit us hard. We eventually lost our business and soon after our little cottage too. I was only in my mid-twenties, but it felt as though our lives were over. Job-hunting proved difficult for Gary because although he had many years of experience and knowledge in horticulture, he had no formal qualification to prove it. We had to pick ourselves up and start again from scratch and had no choice but to stay in the UK. So, at thirty, Gary started studying full time for a BSc degree in Landscape Management. It wasn't easy for him to be a full-time student with a wife and, by this time, two small children to support. He studied four days a week and worked the other three days gardening. I took on different jobs to supplement our income too, typing from home. Gary studied hard and worked hard and I supported him all I could with typing up his assignments, often staying up till the early hours of the morning printing out his projects on an old dot matrix printer. It often took hours to print and I had to sit and watch it, as every so often the paper would get jammed and I'd have to stop the printer and realign it or the whole thing would be ruined and we'd have to start again.

Once Gary finished his studies he was offered a full-time job working for the college he studied at as a lecturer in horticulture. Then as the children got older I started working part-time too and life started to look up for us again.

In 2000 we bought my parents' guesthouse in Westgate-on-Sea and we ran it between us whilst Gary worked as a freelance lecturer and I worked as a part-time IT trainer. We spent a lot of time and money doing up the building inside and out and promoting and developing the business. Our sons were a little older by then (seven and eleven) and so much easier to manage. Max even started helping with the breakfasts and washing-up for pocket money. It was a better life, as we lived close to the sea and the boys had lovely summers on the beach (despite the weather). But it was hard and we worked far more than we played. Our social life was limited to talking to guests and we hardly ever went out. We seemed to live to work rather than work to live. Our dream of moving abroad had been gradually pushed to the background. We had decided it was difficult to move our sons when they were settled, so perhaps it would be better to wait until they'd both left home.

However, in 2002 life took another unexpected turn when we welcomed our third son into the world. It was during the first year of Tom's life that we started to think that we really couldn't wait another eighteen years or so until he left home to move abroad. We decided it had to be now or never. At the same time, the value of our property had significantly increased to a position where we had enough equity to buy a sizeable property without a mortgage abroad, or a two-bed semi in south-east England. There was no competition. We weren't happy with the way things were going in England: the crime, the youth culture, the politics. We felt we were stagnating and needed a new way of life—life is too short and we felt we weren't making the most of it.

We started to look at moving to our favourite Greek island of Crete, but unfortunately at that time, it seemed difficult with the ages of our children. Max was at a critical time in his education. He was doing well at the private secondary school he'd won a scholarship to attend. It seemed wrong to put him in a Greek school and expect him to cope. We investigated the International School option, but at that time there wasn't one for secondary aged children. We decided between us it would be better for him to stay at the school he was attending and board, travelling home to us in the holidays. However, travel to Crete from the UK was difficult as there were no direct flights in the winter. The problems were stacking up and so we decided that we would have to look at moving to a country which would be easier to travel to and from the UK.

That's when we started to think about France as a possible alternative. It was easy to get to and the weather was warmer in the south. Gary trawled the internet searching for possible new homes and found that the south-west of France was the most suitable for our budget. Over the next eighteen months, we spent every spare moment we had visiting and exploring various areas.

It took over a year to find the right property and there were lots of disappointments and cliffhanger moments in the process. At one point, it looked like our dream was becoming more of a nightmare. But we came through it all and have lived to tell the tale.

We have gone through so many experiences since realising our dream to move abroad and I have so many stories to share of the ups and downs of life for us in France. We have seen many other expats come and go over the years. Some decide after a short time that their dream didn't live up to the reality. Some stay for a few years and then either move on to another country or go back to their roots. Others stay for many years, only to return after missing grandchildren or perhaps because their parents need care. Then, there are those, like us, who are in it for the long haul.

✧🙰✧ℛ✧

To give you a flavour of what life is like here, here's a snapshot of one morning back in 2011 when I first started writing about our experiences here in France:

May 2011. The dream versus reality.

I was sitting alone on the terrace on a Sunday morning in one of those quiet moments, so rare for a mother with young children. I was trying to recall all our reasons for choosing to move to France. It had been over seven years since we signed for our watermill in the peaceful countryside just an hour south-west of Toulouse. We moved in six months later with our three children and three dogs, and I reflect on all that has happened in that time. Renovating, having two more babies, starting businesses—we had certainly packed a lot into those first seven years.

The distant hum of Gary cutting the grass on the other side of the lake and the sound of the water cascading into the canal just beneath me filled me with a sense of contentment. The birds were singing, and I could hear the tapping of a woodpecker echoing through the trees. I singled out the distinctive song of a golden oriole calling near and sometimes further away in the trees on the other side of the canal. We would often hear, but rarely see them as they were in the very tops of the poplar trees. I wondered what happened to the nightingale that used to serenade us every night outside our bedroom window the previous summer.

My thoughts were broken as my two youngest children ran past giggling, sporting sandals, shorts and T-shirts, clutching a plastic box filled with leaves. No doubt they were hunting for some creature to befriend. I smiled to myself as I watched the back of their golden heads disappear behind the rose hedge. We had planted the roses over six years earlier and they were now a tangled mass of single pink flowers—they looked like they had always been there, but I knew better.

The sun was beating down—it was forecast to be at least 30°C later. It had been an unusually hot, dry spring and there had already been hosepipe bans in some of the surrounding departments. A lizard was basking in the morning sunshine just a few feet away. A black kite was gliding and circling high above me, its graceful lines cleanly silhouetted against the deep blue sky. There was not a cloud in sight and the air was still, with just the occasional breeze stirring the leaves in the tops of the trees.

I looked across the garden at the neat row of vegetables lined up outside our kitchen window—they were growing well, and I looked forward to eating the fresh tomatoes, courgettes, aubergines and peppers in just a few months. A couple of swallows swooped in through the broken window in the old barn next to our kitchen. They had already raised one clutch and were now on their second. I decided to take a peep inside the old wooden letterbox on the barn door to see if the baby great tits were still there, but they had already flown the nest.

I wandered out to the front of the house and admired the Trachycarpus (Windmill Palm), standing proud. It had more than doubled in size since we planted it. I sat on the wall of the little bridge crossing the canal and gazed into the water at a large carp that seemed, like me, to be enjoying the warmth of the sun. I noticed in the lake beyond that some of the lilies were already in bud. I looked forward to August when the lake was at its most beautiful and covered in pink lotus flowers. Only a few weeks earlier the water and the verges were covered with the white fluffy seeds that had floated down from the poplar trees—it had looked like it was snowing. I sighed contentedly; how I loved the spring…

"Aaaaaagggggghhhhh!" Suddenly an ear-piercing screech brought me back to earth with a bump! Three-year-old Marilene came running around the corner screaming.

"Mummy, Mummy, Robbie pushed me on the trampoline!"

"I didn't. She fell," retorted six-year-old Robbie, his cheeky smile replaced by a guilty pout.

And there we were—back to reality and the usual routine of screams and fights until bedtime. I took off my rose-coloured glasses and noticed that the roof of the barn opposite the house had fallen in and wondered if Gary would get the time to take it down before the guests arrived in the summer. The terrace I was sitting on earlier was surrounded by rubble—waiting for Gary to have the time to finish it. Our dream house was so enormous that it was unlikely we would ever be able to fully renovate and maintain it, not alone, and whilst trying to earn enough money to look after our larger than normal family.

It's fair to say that living in France hasn't given us a perfect family and home life where everything's roses and the children all love and respect each other. Children are children wherever they are, and sibling rivalry is alive and kicking in the McArthur household, wherever we are. However, we do live in a beautiful setting and our children have more freedom to explore and learn from their environment than we could ever hope to have offered them in the UK. I am confident that this will enrich their lives and give them lots of fond memories of growing up in the countryside. It already has. Of course, once they hit the teenage years—well, that's another story...

○෨◌ை○

We have had some spectacular highs such as welcoming some wonderful families to stay in our newly renovated holiday apartments, the birth of our two youngest children, opening the gates of our garden centre for the first time, and taking the first swim in our beautiful natural swimming pool. But, we have also had some devastating lows—financial hardships, battles with the famous French bureaucracy, challenges of extreme weather, even electrical fires to name just some. We've also had more than our fair share of health emergencies. However, despite all the dramas and difficulties, given the chance would we swap our lives here for our life back in the UK? No, we wouldn't.

I find writing the best way to express myself and sometimes my thoughts and feelings are more succinct when put in a poem. Here's one I have written about some thoughts on living in France:

Chasing the dream

I sit by the poolside, musing has life enhanced,
Since we packed up a van and moved to France?
What do we love here? What do we hate?
Has moving abroad improved our fate?

Let's start with the bad things, like the paperwork and cost,
If you have your own business, you will surely get lost.
Social and bank charges are shockingly high,
Bureaucracy and technology will make you sigh if not cry.

The educational system will not get my vote,
Unless kids are happy learning by rote.
With methods archaic and regimental,
Think carefully if your child has needs that are special.

Right up your bumper, French drivers will send
The calmest of drivers, straight round the bend.
If their dangerous driving doesn't cause you to gasp,
Inconsiderate parking will leave you aghast.

Some public toilets may make you frown,
When you find that it's simply a hole in the ground.
And your eyes don't deceive, you can clearly see,
That man on the roadside is having a pee.

France is known for its cheese it's true,
But I do miss our cheddar and stilton too.
I find French coffee is good generally,
But whatever you do, don't order a tea!

Now that the moaning is out of the way,
I'll move on to the good things I have to say.
Social charges and taxes are high indeed,
But so are benefits for people in need.

The health system here is second to none,
We owe them our lives more occasions than one.
From childbirth to strokes and organ transplants,
The service and care are much better in France.

Let's mention the weather lest we forget,
A reason we left England was that it is wet.
Summer is hotter, winter's not long,
The springtime is beautiful and full of birdsong.

The countryside is tranquil with so much to like,
The sunflowers, rivers and a long mountain hike.
The sunset is special as is the sunrise,
Our surroundings are truly a feast for the eyes.

Although the schools are a cause for concern,
Our children are freer to explore and to learn.
Being bilingual is a huge consolation,
There is more to life than just education.

The pace is much slower, we have more free time,
Life here is carefree, there is so much less crime.
No wasting our time in traffic jams here,
Just watch out for badgers and quick running deer.

Our home is enormous and a bit of a beast,
For the price of a small semi in the UK's south-east
Our grounds are large, we have plenty of room,
To be self-sufficient and grow our own.

Our French neighbours are all thoughtful and kind,
Sharing produce and giving us peace of mind.
Life is so different, perhaps you can tell,
Community spirit is alive and well.

Our lives are more wholesome and it's true to say,
Whilst we miss it, we're more healthy with no takeaway.
The markets, the olives, the bread is divine
Last but not least, there is always the wine!

So, on balance weighing bad against good
I hope that you won't have misunderstood,
Though we moan and it may not always seem,
We are blissfully happy chasing the dream.

○ ∞ ○ ∞ ○

Our life may not be perfect, but we are where we want to be right here and now. We live in a beautiful and tranquil setting and that is good for the soul. Life is full of challenges, wherever you are, but for us our surroundings are important. At this point in our lives, we are happy with where we live and that helps us through the difficult times. Will we stay here forever? I doubt it. We will move on when the time is right and chase another dream, but I don't see us returning to the UK anytime soon.

Life is too short to have regrets, what have you got to lose?

Find your dream and chase it, you never know where it may lead.

A Mother in France Series
by Nikki McArthur

This series of books follows a family who swapped their run-of-the-mill life in England for a life-in-a-watermill in south-west France. Nikki McArthur, aka 'A Mother in France', opens a window to her world and invites you to journey with her through the process of moving, settling, making a living and raising a family abroad. The first in the series published in 2020, *What have we got Toulouse?*, reveals why and how they moved and what it was like in the early years.

Follow the family's progress in subsequent books publishing soon, *No Time Toulouse* and *Refusing Toulouse*, with fascinating details on education, health, cultural differences, raising bilingual children and earning a living in France. An intriguing mixture of facts backed by true-life experiences and comparisons. A compelling read for anyone interested in or considering moving to another country.

Please visit her website for further details and sign up for her newsletter:
www.amotherinfrance.com

12

A Fridge too Far
ROB JOHNSON

Hello. I'm Rob, and I'm a smoker.

There. I've said it. Confessed to being one of the dwindling number of nicotine-addicted social outcasts. This might seem an odd way of starting a chapter about chasing the dream of moving to another country, but there's a reason for it, and I'll explain. Seventeen years ago when my partner (now wife) Penny and I set off from the UK in our elderly camper van to begin our new life in Greece, I distinctly remember saying, "I'll give up smoking when we get there because there'll be a lot less stress."

A lot less stress? Seriously? That was undoubtedly one of the most naive statements I've ever made in my life. I mean, moving house is supposed to be the second most stressful life event after bereavement, isn't it? But that's when you're doing it within the same country—possibly even in the same town—so how on earth I believed that moving abroad was going to be quite such a breeze is utterly beyond me.

For a start, we didn't actually have a house we could move into once we'd set foot on Greek soil. Okay, we had the camper van and a place we could rent for a very reasonable rate, but we were keen to find somewhere we could call 'home' as quickly as possible, and so began the nightmare process of house-hunting.

From the moment Penny and I had first decided to move to Greece, we were determined that we'd be as well prepared as we could be for such a life-changing event. This included reading just about everything that had ever been written on the subject of moving abroad and particularly if it was about Greece, of course. Once we were here, however, we soon realised how much of this stuff was inaccurate, out of date or just plain wrong. Here's a quote from the blurb on the back of one of the books, *Buying a Home in Greece and Cyprus* by Joanna Styles (2001): This book 'is designed to guide you through the jungle and make it' ... i.e. buying a property in Greece ... 'a pleasant and enjoyable experience'.

A pleasant and enjoyable experience? Buying any house is never going to be pleasant and enjoyable even in your own country where you're fluent in the language and have at least a reasonable knowledge of the process involved. I find choosing between different brands of frozen peas in the supermarket brings me to the verge of a nervous breakdown, and that's in the UK where I can understand what it says on the labels.

But pleasant and enjoyable or not, we had at least decided on a specific area we wanted to focus on, which was near a small town called Kyparissia on the west coast of the Peloponnese. The reason for this somewhat uncharacteristic decisiveness (on my part anyway) was that Penny had spotted a five-acre smallholding on an estate agent's website long before we came out here, and the views alone looked—and I hesitate to use the word—awesome. There was a small house at the top of the land, which was set in a natural amphitheatre of mountains and rolling hills, and from its height of about three hundred metres above sea level, the panorama of a perfectly curved bay with typically Greek blue waters was straight out of a picture postcard.

So, 'Xerika', as it's called, was the first place we went to visit, having first checked to see if it was still for sale. Amazingly after all that time, it was, although there were plenty of reasons why nobody else had been mad enough to snap it up in the meantime, but more on that later.

Even after we'd been to see the place and realised it was every bit as 'awesome' as we'd been led to believe, we thought we should at least have a look around to see what else was available before we rushed into a decision we might later regret. So that's what we did—traipsed round a whole load of other properties that were on the market and then meandered carefully into a decision we might later regret.

Eventually, however, it came to the point during the quest for our 'dream home' where neither of us could bear the thought of visiting yet another 'desirable property' which the estate agents decided to throw at us. More importantly, the stress involved in the whole house-hunting business was starting to get to both of us and resulted in several—sometimes completely irrational—arguments.

One such recurring argument was—and I hesitate to say this—mostly my fault and was usually along the following lines:

ME: Well, I never wanted to move to Greece in the first place.

PENNY: So you keep saying.

ME: Spain. That's where I wanted to go. I mean, it made perfect financial sense for a start. We already had the *Rough Guide to Spain*, a Spanish road atlas *and* the Spanish Linguaphone course. What did we have for Greece?

PENNY: Nothing until you bought me the *Rough Guide to Greece* and the BBC Greek language course for my birthday.

ME: Yes, but that was only after you'd said you'd rather move to Cleethorpes than Spain because you'd once been to Torremolinos or wherever on holiday and a waiter was rude to you.

Penny has always insisted that this wasn't the reason why she didn't want to move to Spain, but either way, it was arguments such as these which finally convinced us that it was time to gather together the reams of pros and cons lists we'd made for each property and make a decision.

This was when we came to the not at all surprising realisation that the clear winner of 'Finding a Place to Live in Greece 2004' was Xerika—the very place we'd seen on the internet even before we'd left England and well before we'd wasted vast amounts of time, energy, arguments and paper for pros and cons lists in our search for somewhere that might be ... 'just that little bit better'.

Not that we hadn't had a few niggling doubts about Xerika when we'd first spotted it on the estate agent's website, despite the photos of the stunning views and the typically gushing blurb: 'The estate dominates the region from a slope high above this picturesque village on the side of the mountains which surround Kyparissia'. Estate? Dominates? High above? What was it? Some kind of medieval castle? But then came the words which gave us our first niggling doubt: 'The single-storey house is functionally designed'. Uh-oh. I was beginning to sense the medieval dungeon part of the castle without the castle itself.

Our second niggling doubt arose from the website's description of the 'well-established vegetation'. Hmm. What now? A medieval dungeon surrounded by a jungle so dense you'd need a machete and chainsaw just to get to the place? Not to mention living in mortal fear of bumping into David Attenborough and a BBC film crew every time you ventured out of the house.

In reality, the description of the house as 'functionally designed' simply meant that it was very small. A bijou-sized fifty-five square metres, consisting of one bedroom, a minute bathroom, a combined living room/kitchen and a couple of small sheds. But so what? We'd be living outdoors for most of the time. Wasn't that one of the main reasons we'd moved to Greece in the first place? And in this case, outdoors meant two large terraces and five acres of land.

As for the 'well-established vegetation', we were relieved to see on our first visit that this was mostly grass—very long grass, it has to be said, but nothing a good scything with a quality, top-of-the-range Stihl strimmer couldn't handle. (People at Stihl-dot-com—manufacturers and purveyors of agricultural and horticultural machinery—please note blatant product placement there.)

In addition to the grass, the well-established vegetation may even have been intended to include the four hundred and twenty mature olive trees, sixty assorted fruit and nut trees and seventy grapevines. But whatever the intention, that's exactly what we'd be getting, and this leads me to another niggling doubt I had when we first went to see the place.

"Four hundred and twenty olive trees," said the agent, beaming with what—for an estate agent—seemed to be perfectly genuine enthusiasm. "Best olive oil in the world."

"But we don't know the first thing about growing olives," I said, wondering if the cultivation methods were anything like those for growing extremely large broccoli plants.

"It's not exactly rocket science," said the agent—or words to that effect. "You'll soon pick it up."

In hindsight, and with seventeen years' experience as an olive farmer, I have to grudgingly admit that she was telling the truth. There really isn't anything complicated about growing olives. However—and this is a big 'however'—it does involve periods of sheer bloody hard work and mind-numbing tedium. As for the olive harvest itself, this is an activity which should be registered with the Dangerous Sports Association and causes me night sweats for several months in advance. But that's a story for another time.

✧⁂✧⋈✧

It was, of course, a huge relief to be finally settled in our own place, and the only real downside was getting there from the nearest main road. As I mentioned earlier, Xerika is about three hundred metres above sea level, and as one of our early visitors remarked, "Well, at least you won't be bothered by Jehovah's Witnesses up here." Five uphill kilometres of potholes the size of small meteor craters, loose stones and dirt, which turns to a river of mud after a few millimetres of rain is not the kind of carefree motoring environment the VW camper van was designed for.

Many a low-slung vehicle has parted company with its sump on its way up to our place, and this is why we chickened out of bringing the van up the last particularly horrendous stretch of track below the house. Instead, we parked it in a small clearing and trudged the last kilometre or so, lugging whatever we'd happened to hunter-gather in town, regardless of sweltering heat or torrential rain. This could have presented us with a serious problem when we first moved in to a fridgeless and cookerless Xerika and realised we'd have to rectify this situation pretty damn quick if we didn't want to starve to death.

As it turned out, though, getting the fridge up to the house wasn't an issue. Nektarios, the guy in the shop where we bought it, just came straight out with the music-to-my-ears question: "When do you want it delivered?"

"As soon as possible?" I said it more like a question than a statement, expecting the usual Comet-stroke-Dixons-stroke-Argostype response of a shrug and a sigh and a "Hmm. Looks like we won't have a van in your area till a week next Friday."

But instead, Nektarios floored me with a "Would now be okay?"

"What, as in … now?" I had to grab the edge of the counter to stop myself from falling. He didn't even try and sell me some useless extended warranty like they always do in the UK. What was more, there wouldn't be any extra charge for delivery.

As we've discovered since then, getting stuff delivered comes under the heading of 'Things Which Are Better in Greece Than They Are in Britain'. Whether it's fridges, timber or bags of cement, there's never any of the week-next-Friday nonsense. There was even one time when the builders' merchant's truck got here before we did.

Having sorted out the problem of getting the fridge up to the house, we still had the issue of the two-ring cooker hob we'd just bought in a different shop and, more importantly, the ten-kilo gas bottle that went with it. I decided to try it on, knowing full well that if I'd dared to suggest such a thing in Britain, I'd get a response involving several sharp intakes of breath, a lot of tutting and a five-minute lecture about company policy on health and safety.

Not with Nektarios I didn't. "Of course," he said. "I'll bring it up with the fridge."

And so it was that Penny went in the pickup with Nektarios and his mate to show them the way, and I followed on in the van with Penny's seventy-odd-year-old mum, who was staying with us at the time. She and I had left the van in its usual parking space and had just set off up the hill with half a dozen carrier bags of groceries when we met Nektarios coming back down the track in his now empty pickup.

He pulled over. "What are you doing with all those bags?"

"Er, taking them up to the house?"

"But I could have taken all those in the pickup too," he said, giving himself a full-blooded slap of the palm to his forehead. "I am such an idiot. I should have asked if you had anything else to bring up."

It was all I could do to persuade him that it really wasn't his fault and that it was totally unnecessary for him to drive a couple of kilometres further down the track to find a spot where he could turn round and then ferry us and our bags up to the house.

There's a well-known saying here—even amongst the Greeks themselves—that nothing is impossible in Greece, but everything is difficult. Nektarios clearly demonstrated that this isn't always the case and that some things are much easier than you could possibly have hoped.

❀ℬℭ❀

Perhaps not surprisingly, something that we *have* found difficult—which is entirely our own fault—is the language issue. Even before moving to Greece, Penny and I spent a small fortune on CDs and books and diligently applied ourselves to the task of learning Greek. Seventeen years later, we still haven't reached anywhere near the level of understanding we'd aspired to and continue to fall into some of the numerous pitfalls that await the linguistically unwary.

In particular, there are many examples in Greek where two words that are spelt exactly the same have completely different meanings, depending on which syllable is stressed. This can lead to some highly embarrassing—and sometimes downright dangerous—situations if you happen to put the stress in the wrong place.

Take the time, for instance, when local father and son farmer duo, Thanassis and Yiorgos, came to help us set up an irrigation system for some of our olive trees. We were halfway through the job of laying a network of plastic pipes which led from a pump at the well, when Penny and I remembered that we had an appointment in town on some official business or other. It wasn't something we could get out of, so we apologised to Thanassis and Yiorgos for leaving them in the lurch and asked if we could get anything for them while we were out.

Their only request was for two soft, white loaves, which should have been perfectly easy except for one thing. The Greek word for 'soft' is *maláka* (pronounced mala-KA), which happens to be remarkably similar to the word *maláka* (ma-LA-ka), and that means something entirely different and not at all polite. The closest equivalent in English is probably 'tosser', and it's a word that you'll hear frequently in Greece, either as a kind of playful endearment or as a gross insult, depending on how it's delivered. Consequently, we rehearsed the appropriate pronunciation over and over again until we were absolutely certain that we weren't going to walk into the bakery and say, "Two white loaves, please, you tosser" and end up with our arses kicked—or worse.

In the rural and rather remote area of Greece where we live, there aren't too many people who speak English. And why should they? It's their country, after all, so it's up to us to do our best to fit in with *them* and not the other way round. Having said that, I must admit to a certain amount of relief when we come across someone that does speak English and—more importantly—is perfectly happy to demonstrate their knowledge.

However, out of respect for the fact that they may not be particularly fluent, we have to be wary of using slang or idioms which they very probably wouldn't understand. Since I'd previously taught English as a foreign language, this was something that wasn't at all new to me. Penny, on the other hand, had no such background, and I often found myself having to 'translate' some of her more obscure words and phrases such as 'We got ourselves into a right pickle', 'Bob's your uncle', 'That's a different kettle of fish altogether' and 'It all went a bit pear-shaped'. She wasn't entirely happy about my frequently correcting her, but she did get her revenge one day when I inadvertently used an expression that plenty of native English speakers probably wouldn't even know.

The gaffe happened when we were talking to a guy called Dionysis, who runs our local olive press. We'd been telling him that we were just about to go back to the UK for a week or two and we were desperately trying to get everything sorted out on the land before we left.

"One of the biggest jobs is getting all the grass cut," I said.

"Yes," said Dionysis, "and at this time of year, it keeps growing back again as soon as you've cut it."

"Exactly," I said. "So with twenty *strémma* (20,000 square

metres/5 acres), you have to start all over again as soon as you've finished. It's like painting the Forth Road Bridge."

I knew it was a mistake the moment the words were out of my mouth, and Penny shot me a look which could only be interpreted as 'Oh yes, Mr English Teacher, and I thought we weren't supposed to use that sort of language'.

But it was too late. The simile was already out of the bag, and Dionysis pounced on it before I had a chance to explain.

"So you have your own bridge in England, do you?" he said, clearly but erroneously impressed.

"No, not at all. It's just an expression which means that—"

"And that is why you're going back to England? To paint this bridge of yours?"

To Penny's obvious amusement, I floundered to come up with an explanation of what the phrase means, and eventually Dionysis seemed to understand. Or so I thought.

After we'd come back from the UK, Dionysis and his family invited us to their traditional Easter Sunday celebrations, which was really quite an honour. However, after lunch, I was sitting having a drink with Dionysis and some of his brothers-in-law (he has several) when he suddenly announced, "Robert has his own bridge in England, you know."

Five pairs of eyes popped in surprise.

"No, no," I began, but Dionysis was warming to his theme.

"Yes," he said, "and he had to go back to England recently to paint it."

I tried to interject and disabuse Dionysis and his brothers-in-law of the idea that Penny and I must be incredibly wealthy if we could afford to own an entire bridge, but by now, the floodgates were open, and I was bombarded with questions.

"So how big *is* this bridge?" asked one brother-in-law.

"Well, it's about two and a half kilometres long, I think, but we don't actually—"

"Wow," said another brother-in-law. "That's nearly as big as the Rio Bridge."

"Yes, but—"

"How many litres of paint do you need?"

"The thing is, you see, we—"

"What colour do you paint it?"

"No, you don't underst—"

"Do you do all the work yourselves or do you have help?"

As if my awkward embarrassment couldn't have got any more acute, Dionysis then threw in that this was our 'fourth' road bridge.

Eyes popped even wider.

"You have three other bridges?"

"But painting just one of them must be a never-ending job."

I attempted to explain that this was pretty much the point of what I'd been trying to convey in the first place, but I was interrupted by one of the brothers-in-law insisting that everyone drink a toast to "Robert and Penny's road bridges!"

Penny, of course, has never let me forget the Forth Road Bridge fiasco, and since then, I've never once dared to pick her up on her use of even the most obscure of English idioms. With what I consider to be one of the cruellest of ironies, though, I've since discovered that a far more durable paint has been developed which means that, in future, the Forth Road Bridge will only need to be repainted once in every twenty-five years. So, there's another stitch lost from the rich tapestry of the English language, albeit a potentially rather confusing one. (As a slight aside, I've been reprimanded by several Scots since I first told this story in one of my podcast episodes that it is in fact the Forth *Rail* Bridge and not the Forth Road Bridge. Sorry about that.)

✧෨✧ᘓ✧

While I'm on the subject of Dionysis, there's an incident that happened during our very early years in Greece that perfectly illustrates something about the character of the vast majority of Greeks. Their generosity of spirit.

It was towards the end of one of our first olive harvests when we discovered that Dionysis had overpaid us by two hundred euros for the oil he'd pressed from our olives, but when we told him about it, he simply said, "No I haven't."

"You have," I said and showed him the paper with his own calculations on it and the two-hundred-euro error.

Even then, he wasn't convinced, and it took several more minutes to persuade him that we needed to pay him back the money. Unfortunately, I'd forgotten to bring the cash with me, so I went back to the press two days later to hand it over.

"But you already gave me the two hundred euros," said Dionysis.

There then followed another debate about whether I'd repaid the money or not, but eventually he accepted it with an air of scepticism that said, 'Okay then, I'll take it if it'll make you happy, but I'm still not sure you're right'.

Never before in my life had I had to argue quite so hard with somebody—twice—that I actually owed *them* money.

The Greek people have a thoroughly deserved reputation for generosity, and even during Greece's financial crisis and ten long years of austerity, those who were no longer able to be as generous as they used to be in terms of buying drinks, giving gifts and so on are certainly generous with their time when it comes to helping someone out in an emergency. In fact, this is something that is deeply entrenched in the Greek personality and there's even a word for it—*philótimo*. Curiously, it's a word that's almost impossible to translate accurately into any other language, and even the Greeks themselves will struggle to explain its true meaning. Most would agree, however, that it represents a philosophy of 'doing the right thing' or 'stepping out from your comfort zone to help someone in need'.

During all the years we've lived in Greece, I've lost count of the number of times we've personally benefited from this *philótimo*, and what follows is just one example. (Coincidentally, this was when we first became acquainted with the Greek version of Harry Enfield's 'You don't wanna do it like that', which has frequently accompanied most pieces of advice we've been given since.)

It was our first winter at Xerika and soon after some seriously heavy rain when we got our camper van stuck in the mud. We'd been about to head into town for essential supplies (e.g. beer and tobacco) when I inadvertently backed the van off the concrete parking area and into nearly a foot of mud. Since the van is rear-wheel drive, this was definitely not a good thing to happen. However, because it was right in the middle of the olive harvesting season, there was no shortage of nearby farmers to come and offer their advice—and even practical assistance.

The first arrived within seconds of hearing the first slithery spin of the wheels and recommended the use of an olive net to give the tyres something to grip on. This succeeded only in wrapping a now very muddy olive net round the back axle.

"Netting's no good," said the next farmer to arrive on the scene. "You want to use wood."

I duly obliged with a couple of offcuts, which ended up being rocketed out from under the wheels at such a rate that they could easily have taken someone's head off if they'd been foolish enough to be standing within range.

"Any idiot knows that you need stones for this sort of job," said Farmer Number Three.

But all the stones did was to sink deeper into the mud as soon as I began to turn the wheels.

By this time, there were six farmers assembled around the van, and whenever two or more Greeks are met together for the express purpose of solving a particular *próbluma*, the arguments inevitably become heated to the point of deafening. To be fair, though, there's often as much shouting and arm waving when they're agreeing with each other, so it's sometimes hard to tell whether they're just about to slap each other on the back and adjourn to the nearest taverna or rip each other's throats out.

Every new suggestion for how to get the van out of the mud resulted not only in complete failure and more arguing but also in most of us being coated in yet another layer of reddish-brown gloop. This was especially the case when we all resorted to the brute force method of pushing and shoving at the back of the van, which in turn led to an extended period of head scratching and arguing.

It was eventually agreed that the only solution would be to use a tractor to tow the van out, but amazingly enough, not one of the six farmers had happened to bring theirs with them that day. After another lengthy debate about whose tractor would be best for the job, Andreas gave Kostas Moustaki a lift on his clapped-out old moped to fetch his from the village, which was—and still is—about four kilometres away. (Incidentally, Moustaki isn't his real name. It's just that there are so many men called Kostas in Greece that they often have nicknames to distinguish one from the other, and perhaps not surprisingly, this particular Kostas was so nicknamed because of his impressively large Viva Zapata moustache. Rather less charitably, some also referred to him as K-K-K-Kostas because of his occasional stammer.)

Once Kostas had returned with his monster of a tractor, complete with motorised winch, the job of towing the van out of the mud was completed in a matter of minutes. We were so grateful that I didn't even mind when all six farmers formed an orderly queue (unusual in Greece) so they could take their turn to inform me that "You don't wanna back the van onto the mud when it's been raining. You wanna keep it on the concrete." One of them actually accompanied this excellent piece of advice by tapping his forefinger against his temple, which is an internationally recognised gesture for 'use your head next time, you imbecile'.

So, I began this chapter by talking about the stress of moving to a foreign country. This definitely reduced over time, although a certain amount of stress is unfortunately inevitable in this day and age, wherever you happen to live. One of the great things about living in Greece, though, is the all-pervading approach to life that's embodied in the phrase *sigá sigá* (pronounced 'cigar cigar'), which translates literally as 'slowly slowly'. More loosely, it means 'why do today what you can put off till tomorrow—or the next day—or even the day after that?'. It can be frustrating at times, but the generally slow pace of day-to-day living has become one of the many things we love about Greece and its people. *Sigá sigá* doesn't by any means guarantee a stress-free existence, of course, which is possibly why I still smoke. Or maybe it's just because I'm incredibly stupid.

A Kilo of String
by Rob Johnson

Thank you for reading *A Fridge Too Far*, and if you've enjoyed it, you might be interested to know that there's a full-length book with a lot more about Rob and Penny's often bizarre experiences of living in Greece for thirteen years.

It's called *A Kilo of String* and is very loosely based on Rob's podcast series of the same name. There's also an audiobook version, narrated by Rob himself.

"Fabulously funny – a real must for lovers of all things Greek" is how one reviewer described the book, although many others have said that you don't need to be interested in Greece itself to find it "packed with fun and feel-good factors".

As well as *A Kilo of String*, Rob has written five novels, ranging from comedy thrillers to a comedy time-travel adventure, some of which are also set in Greece.

For more information, visit Rob's website:
www.rob-johnson.org.uk

13

A Long Way to the Castanets
JEAN ROBERTS

"Small innit?" said John as we stood outside in the sunshine in the dusty, narrow street, looking at the house we had just purchased. John was one of my husband Adrian's off-road buddies and we had jointly bought this house with him and his wife, Shirley. We had just come from the notary's office where the sale was completed and we hadn't seen the house since first viewing it three months earlier. In our collective memory it had been much bigger. There was a tiny window upstairs, a small window downstairs, and the front door, and there was a forest growing on the roof.

"Best go inside then," said John as he took the few steps towards the big metal front door.

As we stepped inside the light flooded in. It was light, airy, and much bigger than it looked from outside. It was wedge shaped, the narrowest part being at the front. I stood inside this wreck with its unevenly painted and broken cement floor, looked at the bareness, the blown plaster on all of the walls, the broken light fittings, and thought, this is beautiful.

There was no kitchen, no bathroom, but what it did have was a feeling of home. It was peaceful, warm, and welcoming.

"It's going to take a lot of work," I said, "but it will be worth it. It has such a lot of potential."

○෨♡૨○

To this day I have no idea why I was so consumed with having a house in Spain. I had never visited, knew little of the country, but was determined from a very young age that one day I was going to live in Spain.

I grew up in a post-war council prefab in a London overspill estate. I have lots of bad memories from my childhood but I also remember sunny days, laughing with friends, freedom to play outside, and loving the countryside that bordered our estate. The rows and rows of little white houses that made up the prefab estate were very neat and orderly, each was detached with its own garden, and there was a camaraderie amongst prefab dwellers. The all-in-it-together attitude that carried them through the blitz in London was still present. They were mostly young families that had come together after the war and lots of children were my age. Baby boomers. It was an okay place to live. I wasn't trying to escape from there, some aspects of home life maybe, but not the Harold Hill estate.

My father had been a Far East Prisoner of War and had been stationed in Malaya and Singapore before the Japanese invaded. He was captured at the fall of Singapore. His time in captivity was a taboo subject but he spun magical tales about the Far East, of rubber plantations, of palaces, friendships, and Dhobi rash. Yes, even an allergic reaction to the laundry sounded exotic. I blame him for my itchy feet. He was the first person to open my eyes to a world outside our asbestos walls. There was excitement and adventure to be had and it was going to be in my future. I listened to his stories and I promised myself that. Always an avid reader, I began devouring anything I could lay my hands on about the mysterious 'abroad'. I read the print off of Arthur Mee's *Children's Encyclopaedia* and somewhere along the line Spain became the focus of where I wanted to be.

In the 1960s the package holiday arrived. Suddenly foreign travel was available to everyone. I took on an extra job, worked hard and saved hard, and eventually booked my first holiday abroad. Desperate to get to Spain, where did I go? To Holland. I like tulips. Afraid to break away completely, I went with my mum.

Before the decade was out I took a step closer to my dream and booked a two-week package holiday to the beautiful island of Majorca. It was everything I had hoped it would be. The developers hadn't yet arrived; there were no high-rise hotels, no all-day breakfasts, no fish and chips and Sunday roasts, just calm, tranquillity, and small pensions. We stayed in a small village on the east coast, swam in waters teeming with neon fishes that surrounded us and danced in and out between our fingers when we tried to touch them. We walked along dusty streets, tasted wine in a bodega, and visited the breathtakingly beautiful Caves of Drach, gliding on a small boat soaking up the enchantment of the strains of Chopin drifting across the water. I was hooked. One magical day we were taken on a donkey and cart ride into the countryside where we caught our first ever sight of an olive grove. On the way back we stopped to watch hummingbirds hovering around a mud bank. It couldn't have been more perfect. This, added to the warmth and friendliness of the Majorcan people, cemented in my mind that I was right. Spain was where I was meant to be.

It would be almost twenty years before I returned to Spain. The intervening years were spent coping with a failed marriage, bringing up a family alone, working, studying, and building a career. Travel of any kind was virtually out of reach, but then in 1982 I met the person who turned my life completely upside down, brought with him adventure and fun, and somewhat awkwardly fitted into our little family. With Adrian, life, and love, expanded exponentially. And we started to travel again. Morocco, Egypt, Israel, Germany, USA, and even Hawaii, lots of far-flung and exciting places, but the few trips we made to Spain were the places where I felt most at home. On one trip to America I visited an exhibition of the works of Salvador Dali. I already had copies of paintings by Velazquez hanging on my wall at home but Dali was something else. Genius, glorious, fascinating, thought-provoking, moving, passionate, and completely bonkers! What kind of country could inspire this? What kind of country could inflame the strength of passion that these two artists conveyed, or the colourful, fiery artistry of the flamenco, or the vivid, evocative fervour of the Spanish guitar? I wanted to find out. I wanted to see, touch, and feel, Spain. I wanted to absorb it all. I wanted Spain in me.

○෨○෬○

The events that brought about buying a house in Spain had in no way gone the way I had planned. I had a career I loved, a family I loved more, and a beautiful home. All that was missing was the house in Spain. That was in plans for the future. I just had to convince Adrian that it was a good idea. In the end convincing Adrian became the least of my worries.

I worked for twenty years as a childcare social worker, for the last eight years managing a team of social workers in child protection. The work was hard, but worthwhile, and I prided myself on the standard of service we were providing despite lack of management support, funding or resources. My escape from the stresses of work was to go to property exhibitions, immerse myself in property magazines, and plan for the future. In the end that wasn't enough to relieve the pressure. As time went on budgets were restricted further, workloads increased, and I found myself managing three teams, the child protection team being the most intensive and stressful. Completely unsupported and with chaotic line management I found myself working anything up to sixteen hours a day just to keep pace. The situation was untenable. In the end, it broke me and I crashed out in spectacular fashion with a complete breakdown. It was four years before I was fit enough to work again.

One day Adrian came home from an off-roading event and said, "This will please you. John has suggested that we buy a little place somewhere in the sun."

We laughed as he told me how John was convinced that "all over Spain" there were 4x4 tracks and "a nice little base there" was of prime importance.

"What d'yer fink, Ade?" he'd asked Adrian.

Well, "Ade" thought he wasn't all that sure but he knew how badly I wanted, and at that point needed something, so he was happy to go along with it. John and Adrian weren't close friends; in fact they could not have been further apart in character, but Adrian found John entertaining and John always sought Adrian out at events. This suggestion, however, was a surprising turn.

"Ask yer missus. She'll love it," said John.

She would. There was a condition though. Whatever we found had to be less than €30,000; otherwise, financially, it was out of reach.

So that's how we found ourselves here, standing in a house that looked about to fall down about our ears.

With a lot of time on my hands and Adrian not interested, John and Shirley were happy for me to do the research needed to find the house. The following weeks were spent scouring the internet for houses and contacting agents. The limited finance took us inland to where property prices were a lot less and more could be had for our money. John had said that condition wasn't too important as he had a range of skills in DIY.

"Yer, look for a fixer-upper. I can sort it. Nah, Ade wouldn't 'ave to do nuffink. I can come for long weekends. Be done in no time."

Eventually, I found a young and enthusiastic agent who found us a raft of properties within our price range. All of them needed a considerable amount of work to make them habitable but with time to spare and a very limited budget we were convinced it was do-able. Our requirements weren't great. We needed a roof, walls, water, and electricity. We bypassed the ones with woodworm infestation, the one with the passed-out drunk squatter, and the one where the ceiling landed at our feet as we entered the door, and settled on a sound and cosy renovation project high up in the lovely hillside town of El Nacarino.

The cracks began to appear on our very first visit to look at properties. John and Shirley bickered continually, and John belched his way through meetings with estate agents, through viewings, through dinner. Wherever we were and whenever he fancied, which was frequently, he would throw his head back, open his mouth, and let the roaring volcano that was rumbling around in his belly come rattling out in a loud, rolling crescendo. There was never an opportunity missed to bring the percussion section into play. This was one circus that I definitely didn't want a ringside seat for.

"Adrian," I hyperventilated down the telephone, "are you sure the agreement is that we do not ever have to come over at the same time?"

"Absolutely sure," he laughed. "I take it you are getting the full John then."

"Not just John. You could have warned me."

"Where's the fun in that?" Still laughing he continued, "you wanted the house in Spain."

Pleased that my discomfiture was causing someone some amusement, and with the promise that we would not be sharing the accommodation at the same time, I ignored my own nagging doubts about the arrangement and signed the contract. The deed was done. Three months later we were standing outside, keys in hand, proud new owners of a ruin.

※※※※※

We walked around the house seeing it with fresh eyes and made note of what needed to be done. We were pleased to find that all of the upstairs was sound. It was clean and tiled, and completely liveable, in stark contrast to the lower floor. In typical old Spanish style, electric cables ran on the outside of the walls and we decided that when the re-wiring was done they would be buried and invisible. The front bedroom with the tiny window would be mine. I would replace the window with double doors and a balcony. It was the smaller of the rooms but by far the prettiest. There was no other work needed.

Downstairs was a completely different matter. There were two large rooms with uneven concrete floors and a wide passageway leading to an outside toilet, a miniscule patio, and a good-sized room where animal feed had been stored that was perfect for a kitchen. By sacrificing part of the patio there was room for the outside toilet to be extended to make a reasonable sized bathroom; a covered porch and a door would bring it inside the house. After that, some new windows, re-plastering, re-wiring, and tiling was all that would be needed. We were happy to see that this 'huge' renovation project actually wasn't so large after all. I had already fallen in love with the house; however, after John's reassurances of his DIY prowess, what I hadn't accounted for was the expectation that I would undertake making it liveable by myself. And I hadn't expected for it to take two years before it was complete, nor that the cost of the renovations would be more than we had paid for the house.

John's 'knock it off wiv an 'ammer' approach to repairs and his suggestion that we cut a kitchen worktop to fit around a bulging, plaster-blown wall quickly made it clear that we needed professional help. On the day we completed the purchase we met a young English couple, Tony and Sharon, in the notary's office who were doing the same as us. He claimed to be a builder having a portfolio of work that he had done in the UK and having just arrived in Spain he was looking for work. That same afternoon he turned up at the house.

"We just thought we'd pop in to say hello and have a look at your house, see if there is anything you would like help with." Having just arrived his work diary was empty. As it became apparent that John's attitude to work was 1) haphazard, and 2) he didn't really want to do it, this seemed an ideal solution. We didn't know anyone in the area, we had the opportunity of a builder who could start straight away, there would be no language barrier, and this nice young couple would have some work to start them off with. It seemed ideal. It would be a decision we would have time to regret. Taking his expertise on face value was to go on to cause us heartache, frustration, a ton of money, and embarrassment at our own stupidity.

Robbing bastard builders should come with a warning.

○✽✲◌✳

The renovations were underway in El Nacarino, and continued to be 'underway' for almost two years. Every time we questioned Tony on the slowness we were met with the explanation that it was a major job, it was going to take time, and it was 'a work in progress'.

Why did we allow this to continue for so long? Well, we were new in Spain and knew no-one. If we sacked him we would have no clue where to go to find another builder. Because we had nowhere comfortable to stay, our time in El Nacarino had been limited to short bursts and we'd had no chance to meet anyone else or explore other options. It was also difficult to get anyone else in to complete someone else's work. We did find another builder who came, looked around, threw his hands up in despair and left, muttering something about 'English houses' on his way out. We were in a hole.

My daughter Suzanne and I would come over for a week at a time and set to knocking off plaster, scraping walls, and wondering what Tony had been doing while we had been away. Each time we came there was another disaster or setback to deal with: badly fitting worktops in the kitchen, bare electricity cables sticking out of walls, uneven steps, building rubble and cement mixers left in the living room and, on occasion, unexpected Spanish workmen turning up asking for money. Finding our new gas bottles replaced with used and empty ones or items on purchase orders that were not for our house was commonplace. Despite giving deadlines for work to be done, almost two years later we were still living in a building site.

How on earth could it take so long to reform just the lower half of this tiny house? It just didn't make sense.

Finally it was done. The walls were plastered, the floors were tiled, the new patio was laid, and we had a usable bathroom, albeit with a leaky roof. We replaced the damaged kitchen worktop with granite and brought in a Spanish builder to correct all of the faults left behind. We asked him to level up the uneven stairs, to re-site the new air brick on the patio floor that allowed water to gush into the kitchen when it rained, and to re-set the new steps at the front and back doors that had been slanted inwards to funnel rainwater into the house. We brought in the Spanish national electricity board to sort out the dodgy electrics and breathed a sigh of relief at the safety and security we felt when it was done. Despite all of the problems and battles we had faced, the end result was beautiful. It was a lovely home; however, from time to time, we would still sometimes have reminders of Tony's time there.

One day I had washed the floors and the outside patio and was happily humming to myself as I tipped the dirty water down the drain. Suddenly there was an anguished cry of *"AGUA!!!"* from down below followed by a lot of indecipherable angry Spanish, followed shortly afterwards by a frantic tapping at my front door and a small, agitated, but smiling, Spanish lady frantically trying to tell me something. It didn't take a lot to guess that I was the cause of a problem. I struggled to keep up but the anxious *"Venga!"* ("Come with me") was unmistakable. I followed her to her house.

The houses in El Nacarino are built into the side of a hill and so the neighbour's house was below ours. My neighbour took me through her immaculate house and into her very wet, but otherwise pristine vestibule and pointed to a drainage pipe about halfway up the wall that adjoined our house, over which she had hung a small metal basket. When she took it off out tumbled a few very dead, very wet birds that had either scuttled in or been washed down the open drainpipe from our patio. In a stroke of genius Tony had simply knocked a hole in the wall and inserted this drainage outlet directly into their patio. Unaware that I wasn't connected to the mains drainage, every time I threw a bucket of dirty water down the drain I was pouring it into my neighbour's house!

While I was talking with the neighbour their small, yappy, very excitable dog was bouncing around. To return the favour, in his excitement he peed on my foot!

※❦☙❧☙❦※

While the renovations were underway I did make a few more trips over with John and Shirley. I had long since stopped eating with them. Finding it a stomach-churning experience I much preferred to eat and sleep at the house, however primitive it was. They stayed in the local hotel. We got together to go and buy things needed for the house.

One day we were returning from a shopping trip and I spotted a bed shop. I stopped the car outside and stressed the need to go in. John was very amenable but Shirley was sulking and refused to get out of the car. They had been bickering all day and she was being stubborn. With a "daft cow" thrown over his shoulder, John got out of the car and walked off into the shop.

We wandered around the shop and I chose a simple base and mattress, cheap but comfortable. John was looking at super-duper luxury range divans.

"They will be very expensive John."

"Nah, leave it wiv me. I'll sort it."

Okay, I thought, this is going to be interesting.

We sat in chairs across the desk from the sales assistant as she gave us the prices for both beds. Mine came to a very modest €149. John's was over €600.

"Ow much?!!! I ain't payin' that!" John's negotiating skills were falling a little short.

"I warned you it would be expensive."

"Yeah, but yours ain't nowhere near that."

Then the assistant chimed in with something that I hadn't, until then, considered.

"Perhaps you would like time to talk to your husband."

My husband! Oh Lord help me! No way! Gasping for breath, horror-struck, and engulfed by panic I blurted out, "He's not my husband! We're not married. My husband isn't here!"

Oh help! My mind was racing and out of control. She thinks I'm married to this oaf, thinks that I crawl into bed and cosy down with something this awful, thinks that I lack any kind of standards whatsoever. She thinks I can't do better, and I have just as good as told her we were having an affair!

You know the saying 'when you are in a hole, stop digging', well, that's what I should have done but panic had taken over. The awfulness of the last few days washed over me and I gabbled and babbled.

"He is not my husband. I'm not married to him. My husband is in England. He is working. His wife isn't here. We have just bought a house together."

The hole was getting deeper and deeper the more I spoke, but I couldn't shut up. I believe I even told her at one point that my husband was handsome. Here I was buying a double bed with a man who I wasn't married to and telling the assistant that both our partners were away.

I have never been so relieved to see anyone as I was to see Shirley walk into the shop. Concerned that she had let this treasure out of her sight for too long, she had decided to join us. I moved over and she sat beside him and grabbed his hand. In response John belched loudly. Ownership established.

Negotiations over, we all decided on buying two beds the same. The cheaper ones. Then it was time to pay.

"John won't pay until they are delivered, he never does."
What!
"Shirley, we have to pay now or we won't get them."
"But how do we know they will be alright? What if we don't like them?"
"That's not how it works. We've chosen them and now we have to pay or we leave without buying. It's that simple."
"Well, can you ask? Tell them we'll pay when we get them."
"No."
"Oh, but ... oh."

There was no way I was going to continue sleeping on a cement floor just so they could haggle over payment and having made it clear that I was not sharing a bed with John, illicitly or otherwise, I made to pay. They very meekly did the same.

On that same trip we had bought some garden furniture and some fold-up chairs. We had no garden but it came with a table, two armchairs, and a sofa and was ideal as a makeshift arrangement until we could get better organised. It was wooden framed with comfy squishy seats and it was self-assembly. While I put the table together John built an armchair. Just the one. For himself. His work in El Nacarino was done. Shirley and I perched on two hard folding chairs and John didn't lift another finger in the entire time we owned the house.

٠৪٠٠৪٠

With the renovations complete the house was beautiful and finished to a high standard by the excellent Spanish builder. I loved El Nacarino with its fascinating history, winding streets, and friendly neighbours and I wanted to spend as much time there as I could but Adrian was reluctant. With no outside space it meant a drive out to get any fresh air. Life in Spain is meant to be lived outdoors; we didn't have any and he missed it. A day in the sun meant a trip to the local pool or a drive to the lakes an hour away. Plus, being built into the side of a hill, whichever way we walked as we stepped outside the door it felt like we were climbing the north face of the Eiger. I had health problems and it was clear that, long term, this was going to become an issue.

As much as I loved that little house, Adrian hated it.

One day he said to me, "I live in countryside at home. Why would I want to give that up for a terraced house in a dusty town? If I wanted to live in a town I would do it at home. Look, I know you love this but it was only ever going to be a stepping stone on the way to getting what you really want. Why don't we sell this and look for something that we would both be happy with? Somewhere with a garden and, maybe, a pool."

John and Shirley had long since lost interest and hadn't been to visit the house in over a year. They continued to pay their share of the bills and the renovation work but their original enthusiasm had gone. They much preferred to spend their time with Shirley's sister on the Costa Blanca where, apparently, the beer was better.

"I'll speak to John," said Adrian. "All this is doing is costing him money so he may be amenable to either selling or to us buying their half."

He was right, of course. El Nacarino was beautiful and I loved the very bones of it but it wasn't where we were meant to be long term. We had warm and welcoming neighbours and we were in a place where our grandchildren were safe. The Spanish love of children is legendary and ours were fussed and fêted wherever we went. A ten-minute walk into town with a pram could easily take over half an hour as people stopped us to coo over the baby. Arriving late at night was guaranteed to have a neighbour coming to see if we had everything we needed.

"You have milk for the baby? Come and see me, I have milk."

They had welcomed these strangers into their midst and I couldn't have felt more at home. As an introduction to life in Spain El Nacarino could not have been more perfect. The Spanish love of life, the vitality, the vibrancy of the town and its people had drawn us in and I couldn't get enough of it. I was more comfortable here than anywhere I had been in my life. Could I really sell up and leave? Did I really want to stay in a tiny townhouse forever? I would miss my quirky little house with all its nooks and crannies. Built over several different levels it exuded charm at every turn. I would miss the whoosh of the church bells that vibrated through the house from the attached Ermita, and I would miss my warm and wonderful neighbours. I knew that if and when I left El Nacarino I would be leaving a big part of my heart right there. It was a big decision to make but I knew that whatever friendships we had made we would take with us so we took some time out and looked around, visiting other places in Seville that we thought we could call home.

A year later we had bought John and Shirley's share of the house, put on a roof terrace, put it on the market, sold it, and found our perfect new home in Acerico, just forty minutes away from El Nacarino. We were starting a new chapter of our life in Spain and moving on to new beginnings, to new friendships, to fun, and to a whole world of enrichment.

ೞೲೲಞ

I'm not good at giving advice so I don't generally give it; however, there are some things that are worth passing on. Based purely on my own experience:

- If a builder says he can start immediately RUN. There is usually a very good reason why he has no work. In our case we believed it was because he was newly arrived. We discovered later that they had lived in Spain for a long time ripping people off right, left, and centre, skipping back to the UK when it got too hot for him in the town.
- Go it alone. Don't buy with anyone else unless you are 100% sure of what you are doing and are confident that you can work together and co-exist. It works for some. It didn't work for us.
- Be careful who you use as a keyholder. Know them well or get references. Unknown to us ours was renting out our house when we weren't there—and we were footing the bills.

That's it. Just common sense really, something we were clearly very short of in the early days.

We are here, we are in Spain, and I love it. It is everything I ever hoped it would be, and more. Are there things I would do differently? Yes, of course there are. I have learned a lot from the experience, laughed a lot, cried a fair bit too at some of the disasters but nothing has taken away from the absolute joy of discovering this new country, these new people, this new life. I regret nothing. I finished my first book by saying how much I love Spain, how I love the spectacular scenery, the way the light seems brighter and clearer, making colours more vivid. I love that the smells are different, that the people are warm and welcoming, the liveliness, the sociability, and the overall happiness, and I love the way I feel when I am here. Yes, love is the right word for all of this. I love Spain. I love it all. Fifteen years on from arriving in Spain I still feel the same. Nothing has changed.

And you know what? It feels as if it has loved me right back.

The Castanets Series
by Jean Roberts

Jean Roberts fell in love with Spain as a child and dreamed that, one day, she would live there. In 2005 she and her husband Adrian bought a renovation project in the hills of Andalucia. With one foot firmly rooted in the UK and their hearts planted in Spain they began their lives as part-time expats.

Follow them as they battle rogue tradesmen, vicious local wildlife, the vagaries of the Spanish weather and discover that life in Spain is not all cocktails and flamenco. Laugh with them as they discover trees with testicles, struggle with the language, and stalk a neighbour. Above all, share with them their love of Spain, the warmth of the Spanish people, the friends that they make, and the happiness and joy that life in Spain has given them.

These books are a light-hearted, honest, and fun read of the author's passionate love affair with Spain.

Find out more via Jean's website:
www.jeanroberts.me.uk

Born to be an Expat
ANN PATRAS

"Pip, don't you think it's time you came back to England now?"

I received her airmailed reply a week later.

"I've got a better idea. Why don't you come and live in Canada?"

Pip had been my best friend and work colleague until she and her twin brother Andy went to live in Canada. I was a bit miffed about it, as she was my frequent alternative company to my boyfriend. Apparently they had an aunt and uncle over there so I had thought this would be just a temporary thing, but months down the line they were still in Canada, and having a whale of a time. It would seem no amount of pleading and whining on my part could persuade her to come home to England.

But her eight words made me think a bit. One day I mentioned Pip's comment to my boyfriend of two years, Ziggy, and his response was, "I think that's a great idea."

I was pretty demolished by this reaction, and thought (I'm going to swear here so close your eyes if you can't handle it) *well bugger you, Ziggy!* As his comment had intimated that my company wasn't paramount to his survival, I promptly put in an application to emigrate to Canada.

I never considered myself as adventurous, but can only assume that my lack of qualms at doing something so outrageous back in 1971 stemmed from the fact that I was an only child. Whilst my parents would let me have any friends of my choice round to play, or to accompany us on our outings, I did spend a lot of time by myself. Especially once I got my first pony.

I would go for rides on my own around fields alongside the River Trent, or trek off to nearby villages that held gymkhanas during the summer school holidays. In the winter I would occasionally go and join a hunt, usually bringing up the rear as we hurtled around the countryside over ditches and hedges. I never saw a fox and personally think they were all just running around to give the dogs a bit of exercise. When I look back, I guess I was never afraid to try something new, as long as it was legal.

Honesty was an integral part of my upbringing. I was brought up chiefly by my Nannan (grandmother), mainly because my parents were busy working for her corner grocery store. On several days of the week my mum and dad also operated a mobile shop which served a council estate on the other side of town, so I didn't see a lot of them. Despite this I enjoyed my childhood; life always seemed very full, with plenty of music and laughter.

When they heard my plans, and after my application was accepted, my parents were pretty devastated, but they never tried to dissuade me from my course of action. One bright morning in May 1971 saw me flying out of Heathrow Airport on an Air Canada 747. These planes were pretty new on the scene and having flown around a fair bit already in my life, I was almost as excited about my flight on a jumbo jet as at the thought of going to live in Canada.

I received a very warm welcome from Pip and Andy, as well as their respective flatmates, and my new life began. I must confess that on the first night in my Canadian bed, I lay awake wondering what on earth I had done. But my apprehension, apart from being too late, soon disappeared.

To get my emigration papers I had to have a job to go to, so Pip's uncle had offered me a secretarial position with the company he worked for. When I pitched up at his office two days after my arrival in Toronto he announced, to my absolute horror, that he had only given me the letter to help with the formalities. There was no job! But he was sure I would have no trouble finding one. Holy moly, what now?

When she returned home from work that evening, I told Pip of my dilemma. She was somewhat surprised, but shared the same feelings as her uncle on the matter.

"I'll ask around the offices I work at. Someone might have a job there."

Within the week I was working for an industrial real estate agent in the same office block Pip worked in, though the boredom of that soon saw me moving on, into the more familiar field as a legal secretary.

We had a great life. While never overly flush with money, we kept our heads above water and maintained a pretty decent lifestyle in a little townhouse we shared with Jan, a Canadian girl Pip had befriended before my arrival.

We lived in an area of Toronto called Downsview. The development we lived on was a large grassed area surrounded by two or three low-rise blocks of apartments and some rows of townhouses. Pip and Jan had originally lived in a two-bedroomed apartment, but when management found out there were now three unrelated girls living there, they advised it was against the rules. They offered us a two-bedroomed townhouse instead! We couldn't quite figure that out, as Pip and I still had to put our beds in the same room, but we weren't going to argue about this incongruity as the townhouses were even nicer than the apartments.

Unlike the terraced accommodation in Burton which I had been used to, our townhouse was equipped with central heating—a wonderful hot-air version. And apart from a lovely modern kitchen there was a basement, equipped with a washing machine and even a tumble dryer. Such luxury!

I think the thing which had surprised and impressed me the most initially, was how new and gloriously spacious everything was compared to my home town.

The weather was certainly different. For a start, it hardly ever rained. There was sun in the summer and plenty of snow in the winter. We enjoyed trips to various places, even managed a weekend excursion over the border into the United States. And of course, we took in the magnificent Niagara Falls, which were just a couple of hours' drive down the road.

I wrote loads of letters home, telling them all about my new life (well the bits a 21-year-old could tell her parents) and at their insistence I phoned my folks once a week—reverse charge calls— which they were still paying for long after I returned home. I also kept in touch with Ziggy who apparently was now wishing he hadn't encouraged my move, but he arranged to visit me for Christmas.

We had a smashing two weeks together, deepening our relationship. Ziggy said he also wanted to move to Canada but his qualifications at that time made it very difficult to get a job. I was also concerned about any prospect of raising a family in Toronto, as it had come to my attention how easy it was to obtain drugs. I was big-time anti-drugs and didn't relish the idea of bringing up children in a country where they were so readily available from across the border. It shows the level of my naivety that I hadn't considered this would become a problem throughout the world in years to come.

So it was that at the end of March the following year I returned to England to eventually marry the love of my life, much to the delight of my parents and Nannan, as well as my husband-to-be.

I had thoroughly enjoyed my time in Canada and have no doubt that this experience opened my heart to further travel, even if it was going to turn out to be a vastly different experience.

○ຂ◇෬○

Ziggy and I got married in 1974. As years progressed he became a mechanical construction engineer, latterly in the petrol chemical industry, and the very nature of his job meant he worked mostly on the coast. Our home town was smack dab in the centre of the English Midlands, so most projects saw him working away from home from Monday to Friday. I was kept busy at home, raising our three children. As these little blighters were born very close together, the twins (Victoria and Leon) arriving when Brad was only seventeen months old, I had my hands full.

Then in 1980 the specialist division of the company Ziggy worked for was dissolved, and he was made redundant. He took advantage of the small redundancy payment to take more time in looking for the right job, one which would involve less time spent away from home.

He found one which sounded perfect for us, one where he would even be home for lunch every day. It was a two-year contract, in Zambia!

And I barely batted an eyelid at the prospect of moving there. The job sounded like it would be a great challenge for Ziggy—Site Manager on the building of a new cobalt processing plant. And I loved the idea of all that African sunshine and warmth. The whole project became even more interesting when we found that the company paid for all accommodation and services, a company car, medical facilities, and for private schooling once our kids were old enough to attend.

Of course, all of our friends thought we were completely off our heads.

"Are you mad? Upping sticks with three young kids under the age of four, to go and live in the middle of Africa?"

I guess we must have been, especially when you consider that we knew absolutely nothing about what life would be like. There was no internet to search for information on Zambia, or what it might be like to live in Africa. And in those days the only programmes shown on TV about that continent involved lions and elephants which, frankly, wasn't terribly helpful.

When Ziggy's application for a work permit went through, we did receive a brochure by the Zambia Tourism authority, which told us next to nothing of any use. However Ziggy's new boss answered a few questions Ziggy put to him, but suggested that when it came down to the finer details and requirements of life in Zambia, it would be far better if *I* spoke to his wife. He said I should phone her, reversing the charges, at any time.

Remembering how long it had taken for my folks to pay off my many reverse-charge calls from Canada, I waited until I had a full list of things to ask before giving the boss's wife a call. She was very sweet and gave me what I thought at the time was a lot of information, finishing with the words, "… but if you'll miss it if you don't have it, bring it with you!"

Something I failed to mention earlier is that when I went to Canada I also sent a trunk via sea freight containing my prized possession—my sewing machine—which I knew I couldn't do without. It also contained essential things like bed linen etc., which I knew I would need, as well as a painting I'd been given on my 21st birthday and a few other nick-nacks. That turned out to be a very good move, as they made me feel much more at home in my new surroundings. I lived in Canada for less than a year, though it seemed much longer, so when I knew we were moving to Africa for two years, it made sense to be even more thorough.

Within a week of arriving in Zambia I realised that her intimation of there being a lack of certain commodities was the understatement of a lifetime. But never fear. Following behind us on a paddle-steamer were thirteen crates of our possessions.

I had packed the entire contents of our kitchen cupboards, wardrobes (except for very cold-weather stuff), hi-fi and records, kids' toys, pictures and framed photographs and my huge Imperial typewriter, of course, for my letter writing. You name it, I packed it; everything apart from furniture, television, lead crystal glasses and the contents of our tool-shed.

The company had promised to pay for freighting five large crates of stuff, so the rest we had to pay for ourselves. But oh boy, was I glad we did!

The first couple of months in Zambia we lived in temporary accommodation while we awaited the arrival of our freight, then we moved into what one of the kids named The Big House with all our possessions. When the boss's wife came to visit us there for the first time she was astounded by all the stuff I had brought over. She was also delighted.

"You know Ann," she said, "we have offered every couple who have come to work here the same opportunity to ask questions, but you are the first one who has actually phoned me. Others have just bitched and moaned about what's missing from their lives after they've arrived, causing some wives to even return to the UK before their contract was finished. Seeing your setup here, I know you will be happy in Zambia now."

I was.

Because of that initial good impression, she was always there for me if I needed to know or find anything, and boy did I ever have loads of questions. There was so much you couldn't get in Zambia in the way of groceries, it was mind-blowing. There was no such thing as convenience food, apart from baked beans and corned beef. No pasta, no frozen food, no sauces, no cake-making extras (I had three kids to spoil for goodness' sake!). Often basic essentials weren't even around, like flour, salt, sugar, oil, soap and toilet rolls. Oh I could tell you some tales here. Anyway, I'm veering off track. Where was I?

Back in the early 80s there was a large expat community in Kitwe, the town where we were living. There would be different batches of folk who hung around together depending on work-place and preferred sporting interest or social scene. Talking of social scenes ...

After my return from Canada my parents moved out from the corner shop and, following a dream they'd had for years, took on a pub. Pubs were big where I came from. I don't mean big in size; I mean in importance to the social scene. I came from Burton upon Trent, the most internationally famous beer-producing town in England. Back then there was at least one pub at every street junction, and one to be found every 200 yards or so if the streets were long. Pubs were where everyone met. Nearly all of them had regular darts, dominoes and/or cribbage teams who played in the various leagues. Pubs were part of our lives.

So can you imagine my horror when we arrived in Kitwe to find that there was no such thing as pubs? It was an issue we had given no thought to (what?) but we were told that socialising centred around sports clubs. That's all very well and good, but the only sports we ever played were darts, dominoes and crib!

Of course, we soon adapted to this new way of life and joined three clubs. We had wondered why Ziggy's contract had mentioned including club fees in his package, now we knew. The expat community in Kitwe was great, and I made some very good lifelong friends there.

Our third two-year contract was with a different company, based in Lusaka, Zambia's capital city. When we moved there it was a different kettle of fish initially. The expats were more diverse, so there wasn't the community spirit we had experienced when we first arrived in Kitwe, where work had centred around the government copper mines and ancillary private companies.

But again, once we got ourselves established in one of the sports clubs, this time the Lusaka Gymkhana Club, we soon found that amazing camaraderie again, and here too made many wonderful forever friends.

To my absolute horror the end of that two-year contract saw us returning to England. I was devastated.

Of course, it came as no surprise to find that the typically daft things that seemed to fill our lives in Africa didn't stop just because were back in Burton. But to my great relief we eventually returned to Zambia, where we then continued to enjoy more crazy experiences in the sun. As a nation the Zambians were very friendly people, but security was quite an issue and measures had to be taken to guard against intruders. Due to the basic lack of mod cons (including washing machines), the employment of domestic staff was essential for just about all expats, and theft from that quarter was not unknown either, as I related in my first book. Bearing in mind that this was back in the 1980s, we had never experienced security problems in the UK, but in Zambia it was one of those things one had to learn to deal with.

When my husband announced our second departure from Zambia I refused point blank to return to England again. It was only when I had been back on holiday that I realised living abroad had changed me, though it is difficult to describe exactly how.

In the majority of situations when living overseas, expatriates tend to gravitate towards each other. I don't think it is purely as simple as speaking the same language in a foreign country, although this would be a draw. It could also be because of the familiarity of like-minded souls sharing new and unusual experiences. The peer support and camaraderie generated by living in new surroundings can be very strong, and quite different to any friendships still remaining from one's previous life.

I think there is rarely a middle road to expat life; people either love it or hate it. You need to be open to change, and to challenges. I could no longer enjoy the predictable lifestyle of the England I knew (and its lousy weather!). I reckoned I was born to be an expat, and I loved it.

So it was that in 1989 we moved to South Africa, though this took us into a completely different scenario.

In some respects, moving to South Africa was the more traumatic of the moves I had made so far in my life. We did know a bit about the place, having spent a couple of weeks on holiday there one year, so that was an advantage I hadn't had on the previous two migrations. But our holiday had been spent on the coast in Durban, and we were going to live in Johannesburg, where most of the engineering work was to be found. Ziggy had flown down from Zambia for a couple of weeks job hunting, and had found a suitable position. But that was all.

We had nowhere to live, and knew not a soul there. But hey, I was an old hand at this game now. I was sure we'd get sorted, except this time we weren't going accompanied by thirteen crates of possessions. In fact, we weren't going south with much at all.

We stayed in a hotel for a short time while I found out what areas I should, or should not be looking at to live, and searched for a suitable rental property. Key to this was schooling for the kids. By now they were in their final years of primary school, so we needed to make sure there was also a good senior school in the area too.

We eventually settled in a suburb about as far north of Johannesburg as you could get without falling off the edge, insofar as Joburg (as it's known locally) ended just a couple of kilometres up the road from our house in Fourways. Fortunately it also lay just beyond the main highway, which gave easy access to many areas for work and shopping. And what a pleasure that was. Shopping! We could buy anything we wanted, as and when we had the money. This was such a luxury after the incredible non-availability of stuff in Zambia.

On the downside, there was no expat community like we had known in Zambia. The area we lived in was primarily English-speaking and, like Zambia, most houses were surrounded by high brick walls or fences, so I only saw people when I went shopping or to school. There didn't seem to be any social gathering places where we could meet people. There were definitely no pubs. Again!

Then there was another shock to my system. While Ziggy's post was reasonably well paid, it soon became obvious that we needed an additional income, to buy basic things like furniture, school uniforms, a car for me, the list went on and on. It was clear that for the first time in thirteen years I had to get a job.

The upside was that we both gradually got to know people through work, and as our neighbourhood rapidly began to expand, a few pubs did spring up, where we got to know people more local to us. But it wasn't as easy as it had been in Zambia, even though many folk were imports like us. A lot of white people were second or third generation South Africans who had no need to expand their social network to include foreigners.

I guess my use of the 'white' word sparks a question here. Apartheid. When we had visited SA from Zambia we had been appalled at seeing 'whites only' bars and beaches in Durban. But we knew, when we decided to move to SA a few years down the line, that things would be changing. They did, and on that memorable day we watched TV with friends as Mandela was released from prison.

So our life progressed and as we realised that we were happy to settle now, we sold up our house in England and bought one in South Africa.

People who know us, either personally or through reading my books, won't be surprised to hear that in SA we continued with our habit of doing stupefyingly ridiculous things. They may be quite surprised to hear that we also had a lot of wonderfully normal experiences too. I will be writing about both varieties in my next book(s).

In 1995 all three kids completed their schooling (yes, all three going through matric and taking their final exams at the same time, but I won't go into *that* experience right now). They got jobs, ultimately all going their own ways. First Vicki, and then Brad, went to England where they could earn *proper money* to be able to travel a bit, while Leon stayed to take in the many wonders of South Africa.

In 2009 I retired from my last job, as an admin manager for a national art society and gallery, so that I could get stuck into writing my first book. "None too soon," a lot of people said, given that I bought my first computer in 1987 for the purpose of doing that very thing. As it turned out I reckon I got through more computers than my husband had cars, before one was finally used for the intended purpose.

After quitting his first employed job in SA, Ziggy chose to work as a contractor, being a Project Manager in the petrol chemical or mine processing fields. But as we neared the end of the new millennium's first decade, projects were beginning to dry up. He'd been a bugger for taking time out between projects; then we would have to live off our savings until he started another contract. Now that I had stopped work I could see our funds would diminish pretty rapidly.

Essential private medical insurance was a big drain on our resources, so I decided it was time we did something sensible. Well, we had already done one thing sensible and that was to pay into the British state pension scheme so that we could draw a British pension on retirement. It would also cover medical treatment for us if we were living in the EU. So I decided perhaps we should go and live in Spain.

"I don't want to move to Spain. I'm quite happy where I am, thank you very much. I love this house."

What? Ziggy had mentioned early in our married years that he would love to retire to Spain, so I figured he'd be delighted with this suggestion.

"Well you'll have to be happy living somewhere else," I told him, "because I'm going to Spain, and if we split up, this house will be sold anyway to share the proceeds!"

That told him! All our previous moving decisions had been based on his working life. Now it was my turn to call the shots. He mutteringly agreed. (Sorry, I have a tendency to make up words, as you may have noticed earlier.)

This time I was able to make all sorts of wonderful investigations on the internet. And what's more David and Heather, our two best friends from Lusaka days, had moved to Spain, and I was able to go and stay for a month with them, checking everything out and making sure that this was where we would be happy.

I decided it was and returned to South Africa to sell our house.

Another trip over to Andalusia to house/dog-sit for our pals while they visited their son and his family in the Far East, gave me the chance to learn even more and to look around for a property to buy. Just before returning to SA I found the perfect place for us—a finca.

It is a small, unassuming house on about an acre of land, on the edge of town. In fact, from the main road it is only a five-hundred-yard drive down a dirt track which leads to a few properties and a dead end.

Our finca has a wonderful outlook over a few lightly inhabited hills with a backdrop of mountains. It is very peaceful, with only the sound of birds, the occasional barking of dogs and, in the height of summer the one-hundred-and-fifty decibel cacophony of cicadas buzzing in our pine trees. This is more accurately and musically described by those in the know as, "a clarion of blunt saws on sun-hardened almond trees" or "like an army of battle-hardened insects announcing the impending heat by scrapping their swords against old, out of tune, metal violins." But you get used to it.

Oh, sorry, I got a bit carried away there ...

So 2011 saw me packing once more. Again, nothing big apart from a washing machine and a couple of coffee tables with sentimental value, though I still managed to fill seventy-two cardboard boxes with 'stuff'!

And while I said a **very** sad farewell to Africa, it will remain in my heart forever.

○〜○☆○☜○

You have no idea how many crazy exploits I have to tell you about our twenty-two years spent in South Africa, but here we are now, almost ten years down the line, living and loving life in sunny Spain—my husband fell in love with the place very quickly once we settled in. And I am not sorry to tell you that the silly stuff *still* happens to us.

Before saying goodbye, perhaps I should mention that if, after reading about all our to-ing and fro-ing, you're inclined to think what a terrible mother I was, dragging my kids all over the place so that I could be happy, I can hold my head up high. Not only will my 'kids' tell you of their own volition that they loved their unusual upbringing, they are proving it. Because they too have all now moved to live here in Spain.

I guess they were also born to be expats.

Books by Ann Patras

Ann and her young family left England in 1980 to live in Zambia on a two-year contract. They finally left in 1989.

She wrote scores of letters to family and friends telling them about their pretty unbelievable lifestyle—stupendous shortages, incredible insects, wonderful wildlife, and hair-raising happenings. This resulted in pleas to 'write a book about it'. She did—three of them!

Writing like she speaks, Ann recounts the miscellany of hilarious experiences in Zambia as they went *Into Africa with 3 kids, 14 crates and a husband*; *More Into Africa with 3 kids, some dogs and a husband*; and finally, *Much More Into Africa with kids, dogs, horses and a husband*.

From Zambia they moved down to South Africa where they lived in the northern suburbs of Johannesburg for twenty-two years, before finally settling down in Andalusia, Spain, in 2011, with no intention of moving again!

You can find out more about her books on her Facebook Page: www.facebook.com/AnnPatrasAfricaSeries

15

Winter Fruit
VERNON LACEY

"Can I board?" I gasped.
The guard shook her head.
"I'll miss my flight."
The guard peered down the platform. The engine rumbled.
I dreaded a return home across sub-zero London.
"Quick," the guard said, flinging open the door.
I pushed my bike through the entrance and leapt aboard.
"Lucky," the guard said. "We should have left by now."
The train creaked and soon we were gliding out of the station, passing through Victoria, heading for Gatwick.

I stored my luggage and took a window seat. House lights glowed and the frosted rooftops glistened in the lamplight. An hour ago, in the dead of night, I'd closed my flat door on piles of unmarked schoolbooks and exams and hurried to the Underground on icy streets. It was February half-term, and for the first time I was setting off for Spain.

Three hours later, I was looking through a plane window at snow-capped mountains, somewhere in the middle of the Iberian Peninsula. There was not a cloud in sight. The gloom of London. The cold. The Underground train clattering through a black tunnel. All suddenly gone. It seemed I'd woken from a dream. The plane wing rose, flashed in the sunlight, and the arc of the horizon expanded.

It was just after nine when we landed in Alicante. My rucksack trundled out on the carousel, but when my bike appeared in the special luggage area I froze. I'd forgotten my cycle tool kit. I could see it in my mind's eye, a thousand miles away on my dining room table. Now I had no way of assembling my bike, and I cursed my forgetfulness.

"*Hay un autobus para Alicante?*" I asked a fur-coated woman, trying my phrase-book Spanish. She swivelled her head, owl-like, and nodded towards a row of buses.

On my way, a white-haired taxi driver called from his cab. "You speak English? I take you ... where you goin'?"

"South. La Marina."

It was 1997. Pre-Euro Spain. "Fifteen thousand pesetas," he said, winking. "Everything go in the boot. Bike. Rucksack. Twenty minutes we there."

I did the maths. £60, I reckoned. He was trying it on. "Not me. I'm a teacher. I don't earn that much."

"A teacher? English?" the driver said, getting out of the cab. "I know teachers at the Academy in Alicante. I take them to the airport. They have a nice life. Nice holidays. Easy work."

"Easy?"

"Yes. Easy. Four months of holidays!"

He pointed at my trolley. "Specialised. Good bike. Good." He bent down and prodded the tyres. "Not good. Empty of air. Not good."

"I forgot my tools. *Que tonto!*" I said, cobbling together a phrase.

The taxi driver laughed. "You know a little Spanish."

"What's your name?"

"Paco."

"Vernon."

"Bairnon?"

"Vernon."

"I tell you what I do. I help you." He dashed to his vehicle, opened the boot, and lifted up a flap. "Here," he said, rolling out a greasy canvas tool pouch. "You can make your bike."

"Free?" I joked.

"Of course."

He watched hawkishly as I installed the pedals, tightened the wheel bolts, and fixed the seat in place.

"But the tyres?" The taxi driver said. "Where you go with tyres so low? You have no ... *bomba?*" He made a rapid pumping motion with his hands.

"No pump. I forgot everything."

"You go nowhere. Nowhere. Come. Come with me." He led the way to the car and opened the boot.

"Look. I don't want a lift. I can't give you fifteen thousand pesetas."

"No. No. No," the taxi driver said. "We go to *gasolinera*. There we find air."

I watched impotently as he put the bike in the boot, and grabbed my rucksack with his quick hands. From the back seat, I memorised his dashboard licence number. The driver wound down his window and lit a cigarette. He lifted the packet and looked in the rearview mirror. "No. No thanks," I said.

As we set off, I looked for road signs. Any clue to our direction. Was he driving to La Marina where he'd demand payment?"

After about five minutes the driver indicated. "Here. Here," he said, wagging a finger.

I looked ahead, relieved to see a petrol station.

He sucked on his cigarette, twisted the stub in the ashtray, and flung it out of the window. "Smell badly," he said. "Not good for taxi. Not good."

Paco parked and sprang out of the vehicle. I watched through squinting eyes as he took my bike out of the boot. A tight-jeaned youth with his motorcycle helmet cocked back on his head strutted towards the petrol station entrance. A pot-bellied truck driver stood with his arms crossed as diesel pumped. I was still in a post-flight daze. Still doubtful about Paco's intentions, I was glad for signs of everyday life.

The air hose hissed a last time. "Here. Strong tyres," Paco said, prodding the rubber walls. Now you ride the bike to La Marina."

"La Marina? Yes."

He pointed the way. "Two kilometres down. Then turn the right and follow the coast … over Las Salinas. Past Santa Pola."

I put my hand in my pocket.

"No! No!" Paco said, wagging his forefinger.

I recalled his winking eye and felt a pang of guilt for doubting his motives.

"You saved the day, Paco."

He got into his car, raised an arm above the roof and waved as he set off on the highway in the morning sun.

The salt flats of the Las Salinas wetlands, south of Alicante, were a silver sheet, and I cycled the road around them with the sun on my back and a balmy breeze blowing from the south. Hours of sunshine lay ahead. The Mediterranean glowed. The freedom was exhilarating.

❁❧☼☙

I'd taught for three years by now. Things will get easier, older teachers had said. You'll get into a routine. Don't take too much on. But the routine had not got easier. It had got harder. Sixty-hour weeks. I taught two hundred and forty pupils a week. I spent most evenings and weekends marking, preparing, calling parents. My voluntary group for struggling pupils was full. But I could no longer give my best. When the holidays came, I'd collapse on the sofa and mindlessly gorge on TV.

This time, I said to myself, it would be different. A proper holiday. A real break in Spain. Somewhere warm and quiet. I'd return feeling better. Easter didn't seem so far away. Six weeks. It would be spring. The cherry blossoms around Hilly Fields where I worked would be in full bloom. I loved the cherry blossoms. A resounding sign that winter was over.

I found the key to the villa where the owner said it would be and plucked it out of the bougainvillea pot half-astonished by how visible it was.

The interior was cool and dark and smelled of flowers. I went from room to room, opening the windows, pulling up the roller shutters. Sunlight flooded in, and soon the interior was a scene of pinewood furniture, white linen, terracotta floors, walls decked with hanging tiles depicting the Alhambra and the Mosque of Cordoba, a Picasso print of Don Quixote, and a table on which stood a bottle of wine, a packet of muffins, and a bunch of green-skinned bananas. I held up the bottle. Marqués de Cáceres. Reserva. A tag hung around the neck of the bottle. *Welcome to Villa La Paloma*, it read.

A warm breeze blew through the windows, and I threw myself onto the bed in exultation. I had no plans. No commitments. Time had stopped. I was the kid on the beach patting sand. The youth cycling through countryside on a summer's day. The carefree student in a late-night bar. I closed my eyes and fell asleep in the midday silence.

The evening of my first day I went down to the beach where a wide, beige strand stretched as far as I could see. An onshore wind scattered sand across miniature dunes and shook the surface of an inky sea. There was not another person to be seen, and I pulled off my sneakers, rolled up my trousers and paddled in the spume. A far-off liner emerged from the haze, and the sinking sun turned the sky blood red.

In the dusk, I sat in the villa courtyard with a blanket around my shoulders. Screeching starlings whirled above the rooftops and dots of starlight pin-pricked the sky. All around me I could hear the flow of torrential Spanish cascading from interiors where raucous families and clinking crockery marked the mealtime.

The jasmine gave off a sweet scent, and for the first time in months, I opened a book and read for pleasure. It was my desert island book choice, my *Mornings in Mexico* by DH Lawrence with its curled edges and cracked cover. His exotic world suddenly came close. Landscapes of sun in winter. The green parrots and the smell of carnations, ocote wood, and coffee. Don't imagine the grandiose and the distant, Lawrence says, in the opening passage. Don't imagine the person who writes a book is so distant and remote from you. Imagine a real person. Fat. Thin. Small. Tall. On a chair. On a bed. Writing. Composing the very thing in your hands. You are the person. The traveller. The morning in Mexico is your morning as much as mine. They are not so far away as you imagine. *"It is morning, and it is Mexico. The sun shines. But then, during the winter, it always shines. It is pleasant to sit out of doors and write, just fresh enough and just warm enough."* It was evening now in Spain, south of Alicante, and I lost myself in Lawrence's peculiar sketches of another south.

The following morning I set off for Elche. My goal was to see La Palmera, the famous date grove. I have always loved dates. My dad would have a store of them at Christmas. I loved their sticky skin. Dark, wrinkled beads. Sweet like liquorice. "If we planted the pit, would it grow into a date palm?" I once asked my mum. "Not in Cheshire," she said. "Not in England."

The excursion did not disappoint. Shafts of sunlight pierced the palm fronds, and I walked under the towering trees with my neck bent backwards. La Palmera was first started by the Romans whose aqueducts brought down water from the mountains to the north, along the Vinalopó river bed. Christian and Islamic civilisations expanded the site. Every year tens of thousands of white palms are gathered for the Palm Sunday Procession of the town. They are exported also to the USA for the Feast of the Tabernacles. The place breathes history, spans civilisations and religions, and it was strange to walk under the canopies, thinking how a single species could mean so much.

Outside, I entered a shop. Oval boxes with dates imprisoned under tight, see-through wrapping lined a shelf. A basket of loose dates lay on another. There were rows of date loaves, *pan de dátil*, bread made with pitted dates and almonds and woven with white palm leaves. Bags of flaked almonds. Baskets of oranges. Lemons. Figs. And red pomegranate bulbs stacked like cannon balls. I wanted something of everything.

A hazel-eyed assistant approached.

"Two kilos of dates," I said. She weighed them silently on white enamel scales and poured them into a brown paper bag.

"*¿Algo más?*"

"Yes." I held up four fingers and pointed at the pomegranates. "*Cuatro granadas. Y dos.*" I pointed at the figs … "*Higos.*"

In a plaza nearby I stuffed a couple of dates into my mouth when the waiter went off to make *cortado* (short coffee). "*Gracias,*" I mumbled when he came back. The dates were exquisite. Oozing sweetness and stored up memories.

I packed my pannier bag and set off for my villa in the mid-afternoon. Cars whirred by and pounding trucks left whirlwinds that forced me to grip the handlebars and squint through dust clouds. Whenever it was free from washed-down hill debris, I cycled the rain gulley. I'd read about truck wing mirrors. They stuck out far enough and were at the right height for a cyclist's head. At the first sign of a diesel engine chug, I made sure I was well out of the way.

Tired of the danger, I took a minor road. It was off my map, but I knew the general direction to the coast. I was in no hurry. I had no appointments. And there were hours of daylight left. I'd easily make it to my villa before nightfall.

Half an hour into my ride I heard the heavy panting of an animal from behind. I cast around, and immediately a black, wolf-sized dog let out a gut-wrenching bark. It was soon abreast, and my only relief was a meshed fence that separated us. I scanned the field perimeter ahead, dreading a break in the defences, and picked up my pace, pressing as hard as I could, only to be outpaced by the wild-eyed dog. Any breach in the fence and I would be easy prey.

The road rose steeply and my pace slowed. I gripped the handlebars and forced down the pedals with all the ferocity I could muster. I moved into the middle of the road. There were no vehicles. If the animal found a gap in the fence, I thought, I'd have a chance to turn around and take advantage of the descent.

Still I pressed ahead. Still it pursued me.

A pickup truck shot up from behind the brow of the hill and went slicing past with its horn blaring. The dog let out a frenzy of barking. Finally, I caught my first glimpse of the sea. And as the ascent turned to descent my speed picked up and I raced down the hill with tyres whining. Hundreds of metres away, I turned to see the dog standing defiantly at the hilltop.

A few kilometres further on, I stopped at the edge of a fruit grove. Dozens of oranges had fallen and spilled over the border fence and lay in the rain gulley. End of harvest surplus. A few days in the sun, and they'd be spoiled. I collected a few, put them in my pannier bag, and continued my journey.

In the evening I set out a patio table with dates, coffee, oranges, figs, and date bread. It was my second day in Spain. I had a whole day left before I flew back to London. As the shadows thickened and the rooftops gave up the last of the sun's glow, I sat in my hermitage patio under the light of the kitchen, and listened to the starlings as they swirled maniacally around the rooftops. And to the cascading Spanish blabbing from TVs, and the cluttered conversation of the evening meals.

What if I could come and live here? I asked myself. In Spain where the light and the sun had awoken buried longings. To teach freely, without the pointless bureaucracy. To have time to socialise, play my guitar, and go cycling.

Stay. Stay. I heard. *You'll get promoted. Head of Department. Deputy. Inner London Allowance. Educational Services. The potential is enormous. London is growing. Demand is high.*

Go. Go. I heard. Brian, my colleague, who taught drama. *Look at me. Dingy flat in Lee. Tiddly pension for London. Fifty-five and still living in a one-bedder.*

I thought of his words. His entreaties. The London property market in that year, 1997, had rocketed. I did the maths constantly. If I saved all my disposable income for the next four years …

Secretly I knew it was too late. In four years the property prices would be too far up the mountain. A teacher's salary could never keep up.

Go. Go. Go while you're young. It's a chance that might never come back. Brian knew my desire to live overseas.

I lay down with a troubled mind. Only to wake in the early hours to discover a strange guest. I rubbed my eyes and watched the shadow it cast on the ceiling. The window was closed. The shutters were locked. How did it get in? Its beady eyes glared. It moved its silicone fingers with miniscule movements.

It was a grey-skinned gecko, stalking a daddy-long-legs. I dreaded a sudden attack. The gecko might fall and land on me. With my eyes trained on the reptile, I pushed my sheet slowly to one side and got up. I switched on the light and the gecko turned from grey to pink. It did not move and was simultaneously deadly and aloof in its regal indifference to interruption. It had one evolutionary purpose. A meal.

Silently, I crept backwards out of the room, and took up position on the sofa opposite where I could observe the lizard from a distance.

The arrival of the gecko was something new. It would not be rushed. It was not frightened. It had come in the quiet of the night, unbothered by my presence. Now I was the second comer. The guest. I had never seen anything like it so close up. So freely using my home as a hunting ground. I'd held up twitching crabs on the

Llŷn Peninsula in Wales. Peered into hedgerow nests to discover fledgling blackbirds with gaping mouths and quivering pink flesh. But here was a proud and consummate thing, claiming its place on my bedroom ceiling.

It twitched. I jumped up from my vantage point. And from the doorway I scanned the ceiling but found no trace of the daddy-long-legs.

I slept that night on the sofa. And by morning there was no sign of my late-night visitor. Gingerly, I lifted clothes with a wooden spatula. Opened drawers. I pushed a mirror under the bed, wondering if it had glued itself to a mattress slat where it would stay until night came. I stood back as I opened the wardrobe. I scoured every centimetre of the room, but it was nowhere to be found. I concluded it had either slithered through the louvred blind in the night and escaped into the backyard, or was hiding somewhere in the villa. Determined not to be interrupted a second time, I closed my bedroom window, rolled up a towel and placed it at the door bottom. This way I'd be able to sleep without fear of intrusion.

On my last day, I cycled the coastal road to Alicante. I wanted to ascend Mount Benacantil, to see Santa Bárbara Castle, and look out to sea. I love vantage points, and none can be so alluring than those that look out over both land and sea. Like the Great Orme in Llandudno, where one view is of the Orme. The town. The promenade. Places you can visit. Get familiar with. And the other of the dark inconstant sea. As if, simultaneously, you're standing between the predictable and the mysterious. Safety and adventure.

On the Avenida de Jaime II, a car horn blared from behind. I was in a taxi bay, map-reading and the horn blared again. I raised an arm apologetically, stuffed the map into my pocket and set off. Again the horn blared. I looked around and saw a hand raised above the roof, waving. Beep. Beep. It was Paco. The taxi driver from the airport. I waved and again his horn blasted out in the morning air.

Minutes later he pulled up next to me as I cycled up the hill. "Induráin. Induráin," he shouted through the open window, saluting homage to the great Navarran cyclist. An elderly couple in the rear looked worriedly across. "*¡Arriba! ¡Arriba!*" Shouted Paco. With a final toot and rev of the engine he pulled away never to be seen again.

An onshore wind blew over the Santa Bárbara Mount. Alicante shimmered in haze. I could trace the route I'd taken. From the coastal road, past the harbour, the palm-lined promenade, through the dense streets of the town with houses and their shuttered windows and flowerpots resting on sills, and up the winding hill road. Inland the knuckly mountains thrust upwards, and out to sea the sun carved a silver path across the calm water.

That evening I sat for the last time on the patio. A murmuration of starlings swirled and screeched above the villas. The TVs blabbed from neighbouring homes. And the raucous voices of families at mealtime added to the hubbub and the sense of routine.

I worked on my finances. I'd saved £10,000. I could get by for a year, I calculated. While I learned Spanish. Got to know the country. Found a flat and looked for a teaching job.

Teaching.

The singular word awoke a calling. A love. A joy of being with young people. Maybe I could find a post in an international school. At least give private lessons.

It had to work out. *Go. Go. You have one life. What can go wrong? Go.* Go. I would.

I'd resign straight after I got home. I'd write the letter. Resist the pull of promotion. The voices in my mind saying stay. Here was a chance. Here was my next landing stage.

At midnight the wind whispered the sound of the sea and the moon lit the rooftops.

I went inside and pinched a corner of the rolled-up towel at the bottom of my bedroom door, lifted it and shook it. No sign of the reptile. I eased open the door and a light shaft fell on the beady-eyed gecko. Perfectly at home in the middle of the ceiling with his little hands spread fan-like.

Books by Vernon Lacey

Vernon Lacey's *South to Barcelona* portrays the writer's experiences of moving to Spain. Faced with prohibitive property prices and a punishing workload at a London comprehensive, the writer sets off for Barcelona in search of a better life.

The memoir covers the first two years of the writer's stay. It deals with themes of finding a home, discovering a new city, the trials of learning a new language, and making friends. It is a story of personal development and belonging.

Kidding Around (Bradt Travel Guides)

In *Kidding Around*, an anthology of unusual stories about parents travelling with children, Vernon Lacey reveals his command of short travel accounts. His contribution, *The Best Medicine*, recounts the temporary disappearance of his child in Cornwall, and was one of the winning entries of the Bradt Travel Guides award for new writing.

**For more information visit his website:
www.vernonlacey.com**

16

Travel is in my DNA
RACHEL CALDECOTT

I learned the hard way that truthfully answering the teacher's question, "What did you do over the summer?" wasn't a good idea. It didn't make me popular at school. While tales of my mother taking our dirty laundry to the launderette and leaving it on the bus did.

I have a sneaky suspicion that emigrating is in my DNA. Since the 18th century (possibly even earlier) every generation of my family has moved country. Whether to avoid war, political persecution, or for love, the grass has always been greener on the far side of a national border. The result is that I am a genetic mongrel with a predisposition to relocate, but devoid of any real sense of belonging anywhere.

My personal love affair with travel started young. My parents firmly believed that it was an essential part of education and therefore 'good' for us. Instead of having a house with central heating, a washing machine or other mod-cons, they gave us one foreign holiday a year.

As soon as I could travel on my own, I went on as many extended holidays as I could manage. But my first attempt at truly living abroad started in 1982, immediately after college, when I moved to Italy.

A friend of a friend wanted to exchange a flat in Rome for private English lessons. What could go wrong with that? Of course, there were downsides. Firstly, she did not *want* to learn English, but neither would she let me teach anyone else—so I had no income—yet I still had to cover the bills. Secondly, she used her flat for assignations with her various lovers, all the while living with her parents, and conducting a very staid relationship with her official fiancé. Luckily for me, one of her 'friends' was the head of the restoration of the Sistine Chapel and he allowed me to mount his scaffolding, right up to the ceiling. I even touched it! For a former art student, that was a big deal.

I stuck it out for over a year before moving into a shared flat with friends in an isolated building just next to the high-security prison. We had the joys of being stuck in the middle of nowhere, being disturbed by sirens at odd hours, and blinded occasionally by searchlights. There were few other buildings around at that time, and as I didn't drive, getting to and from anything interesting or even a shop involved several very long bus rides. It couldn't have been less like Three Coins in the Fountain if it tried. Friends back in England may have been envious, but I certainly wasn't living, or even chasing the dream, at that point.

My return to the UK turned out to be serendipitous as I landed a series of really great jobs which kept my mind busy for the next couple of years. But I never got Rome out of my system. I loved it. It had entered my soul and wedged itself there. During this period my father became gravely ill with cancer and died. His last words to me were, "Go back to Italy. It suited you." However, I couldn't. I'd just landed a dream job working for the organisers of the 1990 concert at Wembley Stadium for Free South Africa. As Mandela had always been one of Dad's heroes, it broke my heart that he died three months before the great man's release. It was a bitter-sweet time.

As soon as the Wembley thing finished, I did a TEFL qualification at International House, London, then headed 'home' to Rome. I was much better organised this time around. I had a real job at a language school, and I taught in banks, oil companies, and government offices. I also had a brilliant shared apartment around the corner from the Colosseum. Carrying on a fine tradition since ancient times, my road was known for prostitutes and my downstairs neighbour was a bona fide lady of the night. Carla decided she liked me and became fiercely protective. (She also enjoyed showing me her knitting, but given her constant stream of callers, I'm not sure when she had the time for it. Probably best not to ask.) Situated in the heart of Rome, I could walk everywhere. Of course, it was noisy and crumbling, but I'd have happily lived there forever, had the landlady not decided to sell.

My next apartment was an Art Deco affair in a rather right-wing area, where locals, on discovering my name, would say warmly, and in my opinion quite worryingly, *"Che bello, come la moglie di Mussolini!"* ("How beautiful, like Mussolini's wife!"). I was still living in that flat four years later—teaching English and running art classes—when my life took an unexpected turn.

✧∞✧⚘✧

I'd gone back to Bath on holiday to visit my mother, and in my honour, she had organised a dinner party. One of the guests was a man my mum had already described to me as "a charming glassblower". We met, fell in love, and I returned to Rome to pack up my life. We married just over three months later in December 1994.

At the time we met, Chris had just gone back to glass after a short break and had set up a new studio in Bath, where he quickly became known as the most eligible bachelor in town. I had to deal with quite a few disgruntled women who deeply resented me snatching him away.

Later, once our daughter was born, we took her with us to deliver Chris's glass to galleries around Europe, and she slept under the counter when we did large craft fairs. Then, while I was pregnant with our son Stan, Chris was asked to make the glass for the film Gladiator. It was great fun and well paid. In fact, it was probably the best-paid job Chris had ever done.

We had a few good years before things started to go awry. Our rented studio was sold off from under our feet to developers, and although we tried to cling on, it wasn't possible. So, at fifty years old, Chris retrained as an HGV lorry driver.

He did a removal job that took him to the Languedoc region of southern France. It turned out to be the job that changed our lives. He awoke one morning, crept out of his tent to admire the sunrise, and something about the light, the hills, and the nearby river captivated him. He returned home, desperate for me to see it too. I have a clear image of how it must have been for him, partly because he talked about it *a lot*, and partly because I have now experienced the special magic of an early summer morning in the Hérault; looking across the vineyards to the hills while the pastel sky gradually lightens and nature sings.

When we first found the Stinky House, in May 2002, we saw only its potential. The sun was blazing down, blinding us and bleaching the sand-coloured buildings white. Light bounced off the nearby rivers while swifts chased insects overhead. The house offered a welcoming cool retreat from the southern French heat. Yes, it was shabby; yes, it had no plumbing; and yes, it had no electricity. But it possessed oodles of charm as well as the pathetically small skeleton of a kitten and a rather ugly stencilled frieze of beige flowers around the top of each room.

By mid-June, we'd borrowed enough money to buy it. By mid-July, we were back in the UK, shell-shocked and excited. However, as we proudly showed photos to family and friends, we were puzzled by the looks of horror that crossed their faces. My mum even burst into tears. We spent the next few months trying to reassure her.

"It'll be all right, don't worry. The roof is fine, the walls are solid. There's not that much work to do. What do you expect for that sort of price? It's a *fixer-upper*. That's what *fixer-uppers* look like! You're supposed to buy a ruin and fix it up!"

I took to writing excited round-robins to all our friends. The first gushing email went like this:

Driving through the rain in northern France with the kids moaning, demanding, and arguing, we nearly gave up the whole trip. Suddenly, the heavens cleared, the views became more beautiful and the flowers more abundant. I particularly liked the mix of red poppies and wild blue lupines. As we headed south, our spirits lifted and we were unfazed by sticking brakes—which pulled us unexpectedly off-road—or the unnerving and unpleasant bubbling radiator incident.

Just for fun, we'd made an appointment with an estate agent in Clermont l'Hérault and therefore we spent much of the journey trying to make up a convincing line to give him to disguise the fact that we hadn't a penny in the world: "We won a bit on the lottery." "An elderly relative just died."

We arrived perfectly on time (anyone with kids will know that this was impressive) and were shown a couple of nice, but not spectacular properties in the £20-30,000 range. Suddenly, the agent pulled out a photo of a house which cost a mere €11,000. Although it was still out of our price range, we were enjoying the whole fantasy thing and wanted a peek at it anyway, and its leafy balcony was intriguing. We ended up falling in love with it.

And that's when things got weird. Chris's new friends suddenly offered to lend us enough money to buy it. Wonderful, exciting things just keep happening every day and we both feel that we have found where we are meant to be.

WISH US LUCK!!!! COME AND VISIT!!!!

PS The best bit is that our house is built on the site of Emperor Nero's coin mint, so guess who's going to be investing in a metal detector? I thought we could manufacture coin-shaped, embossed peppermints and flog them to tourists as 'Nero's Mints', alongside the wine produced in our vat called 'Emperor's Tipple'.

Needless to say, we did neither, but we did lurch into our new lives with more enthusiasm than sense.

After completing the purchase, we spent a few months deciding what to do with it. As we pondered, Chris started the monumental task of making it habitable while I stayed with the kids in England. In the spring of 2003, he was invited by the Lodève Trader's Association to give an open-air glassblowing demonstration at the town fête. My second round-robin went like this:

For the demonstration, Chris built a furnace on the back of a borrowed trailer. This had the advantage of being fully portable and raising the door of the furnace to a perfect working height. Unfortunately, the fête coincided with a huge funfair in the local park (i.e. on the other side of the road), so most locals were over there. It also rained. The few people not at the funfair wandered quickly past, heads bowed against the downpour, ignoring us. The glass also refused to cooperate. It took much longer than expected to melt, so there was a lot of hanging around, and when Chris eventually did get it out of the furnace, it was almost unworkable. The raindrops caused interesting, but unwanted, patterns on the surface of the molten glass, and Chris started to get frustrated.

We'd asked a local, Maurice 'La Bouche', to act as translator and presenter. He proved to live up to his nickname, 'The Mouth', by being simultaneously extroverted, egotistical, nutty, childish, and unbelievably loud! Chris battled on grimly through the rain without knowing whether our reputations would ever recover.

We did survive the demonstration, but packing up on Sunday night was another matter. Cheech, an Italian tattoo artist, was passing by and offered a hand to hold the trailer while Chris removed the supporting blocks. One of them must have let go at the crucial point. The trailer tipped over and the car park was soon covered in molten glass and red-hot bricks. Luckily, by that point, nobody was around to see. Except for Cheech and he wasn't going to tell anyone.

We returned to England, where discussions continued about whether or not to move over permanently. Signals at the time indicated it was a good idea, and the number of people we met with a connection to Lodève was becoming spooky. Clearly, the universe was telling us to move there! Back on planet Earth, our reasoning was that my mother was fit enough to leave behind and our children were young enough to adapt. Unfortunately for the kids, we'd just moved into a lovely house in a hamlet outside Bradford-on-Avon, a short walk from Florence's wonderful primary school. Both lost no time in declaring it the best house in the world and refusing to have anything to do with the idea of moving to the horrid, stinky French house.

We weren't completely heartless in ignoring the wishes of our children. We genuinely believed this move would be good for everyone. Lodève town council had already promised us a start-up grant of €1,000. This offer confirmed our belief that France would and could provide a more fertile ground for a small arts-based business. After all, France had always been known for its famous artists, hadn't it? Surely there was a good reason for that? Anyway, we had nothing to lose. We were not, and probably never would be, homeowners in the UK and the glass equipment was already in storage. So why not take the plunge?

Once the decision was made, we had the logistics to deal with. We bought an old Securicor delivery van for £500. It was a seventeen-ton Mercedes truck and Chris was totally in love with it. That was fine by me; it meant I didn't have to put up with him shouting every time he saw a lorry, "See that! I could drive that!" Now he had his own and we could shove everything in it and move to France by ourselves.

There were a few issues getting it through the MOT. After being parked on a farm, its undercarriage was so encrusted with dung that the MOT testing guys refused to touch it. It took two sessions with a professional steam cleaning firm before they'd have a look at it. I'll save tales of its lethal cargo of bomb-making ingredients for another time. I'm just happy Chris survived.

But we finally made it to France. We arrived with all our precious glassblowing equipment and household paraphernalia intact, and a total of €500 in our pockets. We had nothing in our bank accounts and no real knowledge of French.

Our children named it the 'Stinky House' with just cause. It squats, as it's always done, like a toad in the shade of the surrounding buildings in the poorest part of an impoverished town where unemployment is high and morale low. Before we came along, it had sat there, sad and empty, for nearly forty years; abandoned by all except for spiders, scorpions, and rodents, patiently waiting for someone to love it. While it may not have been the obvious choice for most Brits looking for a place in the sun, we really did love it. It may not have a pool, a garden with views, or even a decent courtyard, but it has played host to some great parties, meals, singsongs, ghostly encounters, water fights, and chestnut-roasting sessions. It hasn't yet lived up to its full potential and it is over-full, messy, and chaotic, but it is also open, warm, and welcoming.

The town itself is shabby, and there are many empty buildings on the brink of collapse, but if you wander through it you can still find little hidden gems: the communal washhouses, the town hall with its colourful roof tiles and elegant proportions. In autumn, my favourite tree, a ginkgo, glows as bright as the sun itself, scattering pure gold onto the pavement with each gust of wind. Then, of course, there is the Cathedral of St Fulcran, one of the finest bits of Gothic architecture in southern France, and nearby is the other major tourist attraction, the Museum Fleury. This is one of the best regional museums in the country. A new public library has also just opened and is architecturally interesting, as are the museum annex, council meeting room, and shiny new sports complex.

By the time we'd uprooted the children, broken my mother's heart, and moved over full time, the numerous friends who'd previously waxed so lyrical about Lodève only months before suddenly changed their tune. A horrid sinking feeling nestled into the pit of our stomachs when we realised we might have made a whopping boo-boo. As if sent to confirm this, an old English resident accosted us one day.

"Why did you come here? Why bring your children? Lodève is dead. There is nothing. This is where people come to die." Our kids looked worried, but they looked more than worried the following week when several of our immediate neighbours died. They turned to us accusingly.

"What have you done? Why did you bring us here? We're all going to die!"

Although on paper there are plenty of affordable activities for children to do, my kids didn't necessarily want to do them. At first, there was the problem of language, and then later we discovered the problem was they didn't particularly like the other kids. Luckily, Florence suddenly discovered a riding school and took riding lessons for about a year. Then, sometime later, Stan took up the trumpet and joined the town's marching band.

For all its shabbiness, the town is perfectly located, with one of the best climates in France. When they were little, the children learned to swim in natural rivers and pools, and once old enough, spent long summer nights camping under the stars at Lake Salagou, or learning to drive on virtually empty motorways and country roads. There is an easy forty-minute drive south to child-friendly beaches, and about the same distance north to skiable mountains. The immediate surroundings are geologically and therefore botanically varied, and picnic spots abound. This beautiful landscape helped shape our children into the environmentally aware, artistic adults they have become.

✧৯০✧ৎ০✧

Of course, shit happens everywhere; in our case, it wasn't long in coming. But, being in France, we had to deal with it in bad French.

We moved to France in July 2003. By September, we had to get the kids into school.

Although I'd been trying to introduce them to the language for the last year, they still knew very little by the time term started.

Our town has three catchment areas, just as strict as any of the English ones. We were not in the right area for the school with the best reputation, which sat virtually opposite our front door. Instead, Florence had to go to another one a little further away, and which everyone in town hated. There she was subjected to such a traumatic and horrible start to school life that we quickly took her out. Not only could she not keep up with the work on the first day, and was subsequently shouted at, but she was chastised for daring to cry. It was worse on the second day. On the third day, I went with her and asked to sit in at the back of the class. The teacher would have none of it and even shouted at me. To cut a long story short, at one point another teacher, who spoke English, joined in. He thrust his finger into her face and shouted, "Do you love your mother? If you love your mother, you'll stop this nonsense right now!" He and the headmaster then physically ejected me from the school. I took her out the next day. Then, until the following April, when she could start at the fee-paying Catholic primary, we encouraged her to play in the streets with all the assorted local kids, and both of ours happily learned French without even thinking about it.

After seventeen years here, I have finally identified some of the main problems with French schools. Certainly, this is how it was for us, and I know I'm not alone in finding this, although I concede other families may have had better experiences.

Schools here are harsh environments, where teachers pit children against each other. They regularly humiliate students and stand by, arms folded, when obvious bullying is happening in front of them. Often the bullying is done by the teachers themselves. Both my children witnessed their friends being hit or kicked by teachers or belted to chairs for several hours. In the nursery section where Stan was, a little girl was forced to pee her pants because the teacher wouldn't give her a bathroom break and then punished her for pissing her pants, making her stay in wet clothes until home time.

Despite the French education system, our kids turned out fine. But it wasn't an easy ride; a lot of damage was done to them along the way. Stomach ulcers and other stress-related conditions are very common amongst school children in France, and both of ours used to suffer from persistent tummy aches. Florence ended up dropping out at fourteen—which was illegal—although no one bothered to find out why she had left. My son, Stan, dropped out temporarily but returned to attend the three years of Lycée and graduated with excellent grades in his Baccalaureate in science.

While all this school drama was going on, in February 2004 Chris was unexpectedly hospitalised, and diagnosed with kidney stones. Chris thought it was his appendix, but without French, we couldn't convince the local doctors. It wasn't until he was transferred to Montpellier did anyone think to check him for that, and even then it was by accident. It was a horrible couple of days. All of us believed he was going to die. He was grey, feverish and convulsing. To add to the stress, while I was trying to register his arrival at Montpellier's ER, I was presented with a bill for €168. I didn't understand what for or why. All I knew was they had wheeled Chris off somewhere and I was stuck at a desk with a woman who may as well have been talking Martian. I'm ashamed to say that in frustration I burst into tears. To my surprise, nobody asked me for any money after that. I caught up with Chris in a darkened corridor where he was lying forlorn and forgotten on a gurney. A passing surgeon prodded his belly and instantly diagnosed appendicitis and sent him off to surgery.

He spent the next two weeks in Montpellier before being sent home for another two weeks of daily nurses' visits. During his stay in hospital, our new friends rallied around, providing child-minding services, and daily lifts to visit him.

In February 2005, it was Florence's turn. She woke in agony and begged us to take her to hospital. I didn't need language to understand the doctor. He came out from the examination room, sat me down, and patted my knee. "We've called an ambulance," he said.

"Kidney infection." If my French had been better, I would have asked if this was the only diagnosis he could make. I then spent the next five days living at a Montpellier hospital with her, while Chris and Stan made do at home.

✧୨୧✧

France, like any other country, is not perfect; however, they have a really excellent healthcare system. We used it so frequently that we almost qualified for our own parking spot. As it turned out, although we didn't know at the time, we were to get very familiar with the law courts in Montpellier too. I certainly know where the toilets and coffee machines are.

In October 2005, our lives fell apart, when Florence, still only nine years old, was sexually molested by a seventy-two-year-old neighbour. With the help of some extremely kind *gendarmes*, we managed to get the old bastard into court. It was a confusing and terrifying experience. The trial was postponed at least once and when the case was finally heard, we couldn't find our lawyer. Chris waited outside for her, while I sat inside waiting. Suddenly, I heard Florence's name and realised that we were up. There was still no sign of our lawyer.

So, red with embarrassment, shaking, and with a sudden urge to find a toilet, I made my way to the bench. Everybody stared at me, and it was all I could do not to cry. The panel of magistrates stared at me as if I was mad, as I blurted out in English, "I am Florence's mother, but I can't find my lawyer." Suddenly, a complete stranger introduced herself and the case proceeded.

Legalese is bad enough in English; after all, lawyers have designed it that way to exclude normal folk. But in French! I vaguely followed the proceedings and it seemed to be going well until our lawyer suddenly asked for €10,000 in compensation. I was not aware that we had asked her to do that, or agreed to it in any way. But I have been tormented ever since with the thought that, somehow, because of our terrible French, we'd sanctioned it and so lost the case.

The old bastard was let off with a warning. But it wasn't over. We were forced to move house for about six months. This was partly because Florence would freak out every time she saw him, and partly because he and his wife took to spitting at us in the street. Our problem with him only resolved itself when he was found shot dead some months later.

○ℰ✧ଓ○

While life went on, Chris also needed to work, and his search for the perfect studio resembled Goldilocks' quest for the perfect porridge. While he physically searched for a suitable building, I tackled the paperwork. Anyone moving to France must be aware that life revolves around paperwork. It is horrible, confusing and often illogical, designed in the inner circle of hell and sent to Earth to torment us.

We had several workshops over the years and all were variations on a theme. The theme being disgusting hovels with no passing trade! Fundamentally, these were empty buildings with no window panes, electricity, gas, or water. In each, we had to install mains water and electricity, but the gas was delivered in large bottles from a town fifty kilometres away. For some reason, it was cheaper to do that, than having it delivered from Lodève itself.

Only our second studio was glorious, and we could see a bright future ahead. Chris had fun doing glassblowing demonstrations for school children, and for months, he couldn't leave the house without a small child pointing him out to their parents, *"Voila, c'est Monsieur Crease, le souffleur de verre!"*

However, to get it to a useable state, Chris and a friend had to create windows and remove a huge diesel tank from the premises. Meanwhile, the services—mains gas, three-phase electricity, and water—were the responsibility of the landlord. And that's where all the problems lay. The landlord was an evil psycho and we spent many years in legal battles with him. He put in a temporary electricity supply rigged up to a fuse box tied to a drainpipe fifty metres down the road. In bad weather the box sometimes fell off onto the pavement. He also rented out space to several other businesses, all getting their electricity from the same box. It would frequently overload. At which point, we'd be plunged into darkness unable to work. He also neglected to finish the roof, and for weeks at a time we'd be flooded out, and our blowing irons would rust.

On one level, the move to France worked well. The children became bilingual, and at ease with all sorts of people and situations. Of course, we had the usual problems that can beset anyone anywhere, but in general, Lodève provided a lot of the simple pleasures which so enrich life. We certainly had ups and downs; probably because we'd wilfully broken the laws of the universe, which in hindsight, I would never do again.

We'd bought the first house we'd seen (bad move).

In an area we knew nothing about (also a big mistake).

It needed major building work (we knew nothing of restoration).

Other adventures have befallen us, including Chris's kidnapping at gunpoint by a local drug dealer, and a spooky invasion of the house by angry spirits. But I simply don't have the space to tell you about them here.

Certainly, on more than one occasion, we've wanted to give up. But generally, at every low point, our friends here have come through for us. Of course, there has been a near-constant struggle with money. But we manage just about to make ends meet (or rather we did pre-Covid), selling Chris's glass and my jewellery on street markets, and I'm now known locally as that Smiley Earring Lady. I quite like that title, although Sexy Jewellery Goddess suits me better (honest). Chris, meanwhile, is known as either Bill or Mr President, because of his similarity in looks to a certain American statesman.

I don't know whether we'd have all been better off staying in the UK. Overall, our kids thank us for the chance to live in such a beautiful place, although both have chosen British universities. I do know we would have missed out on some wonderful experiences and people if we hadn't made the move. I can't advise anyone else to leave everything and settle abroad, and I don't know if we'll stay here much longer. But I can say that life is for living and sometimes you've just got to take risks to really live it.

Books by Rachel Caldecott

Blown out of Proportion – Misadventures of a Glassblower in France
"You must be mad! Why set up a glassblowing business in one of France's poorest regions?"
The Thornton family moved to southern France with a lorry full of glassmaking equipment, two young children, and only €500 in their pockets.
Alongside the anticipated problems of moving abroad on a budget, they encountered Dickensian teachers, perverts, corrupt politicians and gun-toting kidnappers.
The tales of their misadventures are all told with compassion, humour and a smattering of historical and cultural facts.

The Panopticon Experiment (Young/New Adult speculative fiction)
At a time when humans and animals are considered equal and interspecies telepathy is the norm, two young human telepaths battle to save their utopian society from a handful of rebels determined to bring back the old ways—when mankind ruthlessly dominated the planet.

For more information, visit her website:
www.rachelcaldecott.com

In Sight of Aconcagua
RONALD MACKAY

"Look!" Giorgio gestured towards the jagged Andes that separate Chile from Argentina. Viviana and I watched Aconcagua's snowy peak flush pink in the setting sun.

"We call that the *'Aconcagua smile'*." There was awe in Emma's voice.

The highest Andean peak in South America deepened into fiery red against a mauve sky. We were sipping wine on the patio of Giorgio and Emma's house set in a quiet fifty hectares on the south side of the Aconcagua River. Water gurgled. An owl hooted. Jasmine scented the air.

Viviana's contentment confirmed that we shared the same feeling. *This is where we would like to spend our retirement—here in Chile's timeless Aconcagua Valley. The Pacific to the west, the Andes to the east.*

In Canada, only one month earlier, the organisation Viviana had been employed by for twenty years had closed down.

"Is this my fiftieth birthday present? A challenge to reinvent myself?" Oddly, she appeared empowered.

I was approaching sixty. We had planned five more years of work before retiring to our plot of land in Ontario where we had begun to plant ornamental curly willow and holly trees that bore bright red berries. In time, they would yield a crop of decorative cuttings much prized by flower wholesalers. We planned to build a small house, expand our floral business, and enjoy retirement.

Now? Sudden derailment! On the balcony of our Montreal apartment that summer evening, we discussed our options.

"I could retire immediately," I suggested. "We could camp on our property and do most of the house-building ourselves. Once the structure is enclosed, we'll sell this apartment, and move to Ontario."

But Viviana possessed that rare gift, inherited from her Italian and Peruvian grandmothers, of inventing novel solutions when plans floundered. She saw a bigger, better and brighter option.

"My cousin Giorgio in Chile. He's been inviting us to visit him, Emma and their children."

"Holiday in Chile? When we should be saving?"

"Not a holiday, a radical change. We both speak Spanish and

love Latin America. Let's visit Giorgio and explore setting up a small agricultural enterprise in Chile. Leave Ontario with its long winters behind forever."

Viviana's enthusiasm was infectious. Before darkness had fallen, we had a plan. We would investigate Chile as a potential new home.

Giorgio and Viviana shared the same great-grandmother. Their families had kept in touch across a century and more as members moved from Italy to Argentina. Some, like Viviana's grandfather, to Peru, others like Giorgio and Emma, to Chile. An Italian family afraid of nothing, whose abiding love of kinship guaranteed acceptance.

Now, having flown to Chile, we are installed in Giorgio and Emma's guest suite and getting to grips with what it might mean for us to resettle here. We pose no burden to our hosts. Their home boasts three self-contained wings—parents, children, guests. Dinner, served by the housekeeper at 10.30 at night, is the only weekday meal we take together. Their seven children, some working, some still at school, live independent lives and dine earlier in their own quarters. We see them all on Sundays when family tradition demands that they congregate for a loving family lunch together on the patio, in sight of graceful white egrets stalking the edge of the river. It's a joyous occasion where they all laugh, talk at once about school, work or their expeditions on horseback. They all grew up riding and refused to believe I never had. One day they persuaded me to join them. All went well until, on the way home, they raced to see who could arrive first. My horse insisted on joining in. Though I'd clung on to the bitter end, the experience so terrified me that I refused ever again to mount.

Giorgio lent us a yellow Jeep. "Look around. Make up your minds. No hurry."

We were free to explore on our own.

✿֍✿ଜ✿

We immediately felt at home in this part of rural Chile, a series of fertile valleys whose rivers flowed from the Andes. The floor of this, the Aconcagua Valley, was planted with vineyards and cash crops. Green lines of plantation trees were beginning to creep up the arid yellow mountainsides.

Inviting side-glens beckoned us. We would come upon idyllic villages of white adobe splashed scarlet with geraniums, a goat tethered by each cottage. Hens pecked. Piglets scrambled in the ditch. Often, there would be a ruined manor house guarding the village like the ghost of the aristocratic Spanish colonist who had built it.

After a week of lone exploring, Giorgio and Emma took us to view their flagship plantation. In its centre, under the shade of pepper trees, was a rustic, single-storey building clad in purple bougainvillea. Giorgio's administrative and finance staff ran the entire business from there. It had an executive boardroom and an elegant dining room overseen by a smiling local woman, Juanita, who both cooked and served. Giorgio needed an appropriate place where he could meet and negotiate with fruit buyers from overseas supermarket chains. Driving together on the well-maintained tracks that divided the plantation into huge sectors of table grapes, mandarins, and grapefruit, they gave us a better insight into what we had been seeing on our explorations.

When Spain conquered Chile, the land had been divided into vast estates granted to Spanish nobles. Social reform in the mid-20th century had seen estates divided up among landless peasants. Disinherited landowners had retreated to the capital, leaving their grand houses to fall into decay. Many peasants worked their lands cooperatively sharing labour and machinery; others rented their land to entrepreneurial farmers who needed vast tracts to make agribusiness viable.

Giorgio was one of these tough new entrepreneurs. He negotiated a rent on under-used land and turned each enormous parcel into a plantation. There, he grew fruit to supply North American and European markets. For some years, he had been pioneering the planting of avocado groves on the barren sides of the mountains.

Giorgio drove us up the steep zig-zag mountain track linking the avocado groves that grew in skirted layers on a thousand hectares. Using plants that followed the contours, he had created geometric patterns of great beauty where previously there had been only a chaos of cactus and thorns.

Over lunch in the executive dining room in his office complex, Giorgio explained, "Demand for avocados is growing annually." He gestured to the vast plantation we had just driven through, planted out ten years earlier. "Each tree yields twenty kilos. Here, I have two hundred thousand mature trees. From this plantation alone—and I have more—we export millions of kilos annually."

That evening, as we changed for dinner, Viviana and I speculated about settling in the valley. Our funds were limited. We were considering something modest along the lines of our twenty hectares in Canada. But Giorgio shattered our illusions.

"How much can you invest?" He invariably cut to the chase.

"Our entire savings."

"How much exactly?"

I told him.

"That's all?"

Embarrassed, I added the value of our apartment in Montreal, our land in Ontario.

A long silence.

"¡Poca plata!" Giorgio palmed away our wealth as he might dismiss an unpleasant odour. "That won't buy much."

Viviana shot me a look that said, *'We're not giving up that easily!'*

Another long silence.

"Stay and work for me." Giorgio looked at me and me alone.

Viviana shifted uncomfortably in her chair. Years ago, she had escaped the machismo and sexism of Peru. Had she returned to have it smother her now, here in Chile, when she was still in her prime?

"And Viviana?" I ventured.

"I will introduce Viviana to my friends. We meet in town for coffee most days." Emma smiled.

After two decades as a professional mentor who trained

biological scientists to manage agricultural research projects, Viviana was not the meek woman satisfied to retire and chatter in cafés.

"Start work tomorrow." Giorgio continued to address me. "Viviana can accompany you if she wants."

Viviana's encouraging glance to me said, *A foot in the door is better than nothing.*

"Fine," I agreed. "What do I do?"

"Nico is my eyes and ears in our plantations across the river on the north side of the valley."

We didn't know that Giorgio also farmed on the north side; didn't even know how to get there.

"You will be my eyes and ears in my smaller avocado groves on this south side. Nico will show you what to do."

Nico was Giorgio's 26-year-old son who rarely appeared for meals. Impressed, we had watched him on horseback twice at rodeos where he had shown great skill driving and roping calves in competition with other horsemen dressed as traditional *huasos*, Chilean cowboys.

Later, I asked Viviana what serving as Giorgio's eyes and ears might mean.

"In Latin America," she explained, "an employer places more trust in family members than in employees. Giorgio's inviting you to oversee the operations in his smaller plantations—not the flagship one where his offices are—to discourage abuse of any kind by his workers. It's not a job delegated to a woman."

We looked glumly at each other. We had envisaged more for our retirement together.

✧ℰ✧ଔ✧

"Ready?" I hid my impatience to get started. Nico finally appeared in the yard, mid-morning. His Toyota Hilux pickup was parked in the shade of a jacaranda tree, purple-blue in the sun.

"Don't fasten your seatbelts!" He had inherited his father's habit of speaking in the imperative.

"Why … ?" Viviana began. But he drove directly to the riverbank and plunged into the raging water.

Alarmed, we heard the tyres scrape for purchase on the gravel. Water seeped through the door seals. The current tugged us. Now we understood. If we overturned, we might escape more easily.

"Is there no bridge?" Viviana ventured.

"Thirty kilometres to Chagres and thirty back."

Viviana's look said, *Sixty minutes is a cheap price for safety.*

We lurched up the north bank and came upon an even simpler world. No road, just a rutted track. Smallholders' cottages bright with bougainvillea. Goats grazing on thornbushes raised their heads in curiosity.

Nico stopped at a once-grand colonial manor, now demoted to serve as a barn. It snuggled so serenely in a green basin-like valley. "Shangri-La!" I murmured, gazing at it in wonder.

"Throw a dozen bales into the truck bed." I obeyed. The beauty of the spot meant nothing to Nico. We lurched off towards a lone avocado grove etched into the barren mountainside.

Nico braked as a middle-aged man approached.

"*¿Como va todo?*" ("How's it going?") Nico asked.

"*Todo bien, Señor,*" ("All good, Sir,") came the response. And off we lurched again.

Nico repeated the same brusque routine at three more plantations. He then drove several kilometres to a modern metal-roofed barn surrounded by green, irrigated paddocks. Nico greeted a worker with a smile and strode into the barn where a dozen mares nuzzled their foals. He spoke gently to each one and fondled their ears.

In the final stall, a mare had foaled overnight. Nico examined the foal gently while the mare nibbled his hair. Nico was a horseman. Avocado groves bored him.

Mid-afternoon, we drove back across the perilous river.

"You get the idea?" Nico looked at me.

"You mean, I ask '*¿Cómo va todo?*'"

"Right! And make sure that the answer is 'All good'." Nico drove off to his beloved horses.

On the patio under a blue sky overlooking the sparkling river where the great white egret stalked, with the peaks of the Andes in the distance, the housekeeper served us tea. Alone, Viviana and I analysed the day.

"It looks like being Giorgio's 'eyes and ears' demands little more than asking a single question for which the only acceptable answer is, 'All is well'."

Viviana understood the culture better than I. "Here, this is an acceptable role for the son of a landowner." When I looked sceptical, she sighed. "I know. You want a more meaningful challenge."

She was right. For decades, I had been involved in agricultural projects in the developing world funded by Western governments to help increase crop yields to reduce hunger. My role had been to determine if the project was accomplishing its goals. If it was not, I had to discover why it was failing and how it might be put right.

Viviana, too, had worked in development projects. Her work ensured that project personnel learned the practical management skills they needed to operate effectively from day to day.

"I see a challenge for us here," Viviana said. I noted with satisfaction she was including herself. "We need to understand what an avocado grove is, how it operates and what each worker needs to do to make it a success." She looked optimistic. "In time, we may find a niche for us both. I want to show my cousin that even a woman can be of real use to him."

I nodded, pleased at Viviana's enterprise.

"Nico has shown you the ropes," Giorgio announced at dinner. "You start on this side of the river tomorrow. The yellow Jeep is yours." Giorgio poured a finger of wine into our glasses.

"Giorgio," I needed reassurance, "of the foremen in those groves in which I will be your eyes and ears, who is the one you value most?"

"Conrado at Lo Campo," Giorgio answered. "He's been with me since I started work on that plantation. Why?"

"Viviana and I," I let both names sink in, "need to spend the first week, all day every day, exclusively with him. We need to learn all that's involved in running an avocado grove. Only then will we be in a position to watch and listen for anything that might pose a risk to your interests."

Emma looked surprised that Viviana would not be joining her for daily coffee in town. "As soon as a woman leaves Latin America she turns into a man!" We all laughed, and the tension was broken. Viviana's relief at having escaped from the traditional passive role of the Latin woman was obvious.

Giorgio nodded. "That makes sense. Do it!"

There and then at 11 p.m., he called Conrado to give him instructions. An employee in Chile is at his employer's beck and call, day and night.

Before sunrise, at 7.30 a.m., Conrado, a stalky man in his forties, greeted us formally when we arrived. The deference he showed to Viviana because of her family relationship with his employer was extended even to me.

As the sun rose over the Andes flooding the valley with light, I explained to Conrado that we needed to get an overall picture of all the elements that made up a plantation, who did what, when and why. He understood.

"I've worked for Don Giorgio from the clearing of cactus off the mountainsides to the excavation of the roads. I've supervised the installation of the water cisterns and the irrigation system that delivers water to every individual tree. In a week, you will learn all I know." He smiled. "But now the buses have arrived with the workers! We must split them into work groups, each under a crew boss who understands the work I want done today."

Five buses belching black diesel fumes disgorged more than a hundred men and women of all ages, brought from surrounding hamlets. Plantation work was labour intensive.

Conrado exceeded his promise. We learned how and why avocado groves were being carved out of mountainsides. That semi-tropical trees cannot be planted on the cooler valley floor, so Giorgio had negotiated rents on frost-free mountainside. First, he hired gangs to clear the cactus and burn it. Then he had operators use hydraulic excavators to etch narrow, parallel tracks along the mountainside eighty metres apart to allow access. Once hydraulic pumps and irrigation pipes were installed, the tiny avocado trees in soil pots were planted in vertical rows at right angles to the access roads. In a short time, barren mountainsides were converted into neatly tiered sets of shiny green avocado groves containing hundreds of thousands of trees.

While I sought to uncover and understand the technology and agricultural practices, Viviana accompanied one or other of the work crews to every part of the plantation to discover what they needed to know and do, and how good they were at it.

Each evening, sitting on the patio watching the jagged peak of Aconcagua turn red in the setting sun, Viviana and I would compare notes and share what we had learned. Later, over dinner, we would quiz Giorgio on any matter we didn't fully grasp. Giorgio seemed satisfied at how seriously we were taking on the role of becoming his eyes and ears. Emma listened, mystified at why any woman would choose to spend the day in boots and work-clothes on a mountainside in the burning sun.

Viviana's questions to Giorgio were mainly about the workers, bussed in daily to his avocado groves from the nearby hamlets and villages.

"Dayworkers are my biggest challenge." Giorgio shook his head in frustration. "We need more at some periods, fewer at others. We spend time showing them what to do but the same workers don't always return, so the crews never become really skilled. As a result, they break equipment, trample plants; they waste herbicide and fungicide; they take risks. I don't want an accident."

Viviana understood.

My questions were about the technical infrastructure the plantations depended on and the cultivation practices employed to ensure healthy growth.

"I've got the technology down to a fine art," Giorgio assured me. "Now my biggest concern is trees that shed the avocado fruit before it matures. Instead of yielding twenty kilos, a tree will abort fruit and so yield little. I've planted varieties other than the Hass avocado to promote cross-pollination, but we still have a problem."

Over the next six weeks, Viviana and I observed, asked questions and read, honing our skills as Giorgio's eyes and ears south of the river. As we did so, we were planning roles for ourselves that promised to be far more useful than the simple task Nico had initially shown us or that Giorgio expected.

Our pride and interest in gainful employment urged us to think outside the box. We invested all our spare time searching for potential projects. If Giorgio gave us the green light, we might create valuable niches for ourselves by benefiting his operations in ways he had not thought of.

✧෨✧ෆ✧

"We've found a house you can rent." Emma was delighted. "It's fully furnished."

"Almost," Giorgio corrected her. "It belongs to Miguel, a friend of Nico who trains horses. He's been living alone for several years, so it may need tidying up."

"I told Miguel you'd view the house today." Emma handed us a sketch map.

"You can reach any of my avocado groves in minutes from that house." Giorgio saw it as a done deal.

We'd been their welcome guests for almost four months.

Leaving the main road, we entered a narrow glen that led into a serene, rounded valley circled by mountains. A place both timeless and beautiful. Wildflowers grew from dry-stone walls. Tidy fields of tomatoes and artichokes crept across the valley floor. Horse-drawn carts laden with freshly harvested vegetables lumbered towards a village.

"This must be the house." Viviana pointed to a Spanish-style bungalow in the middle of a vineyard. Its white walls and roof of curved orange tiles were partly hidden by an Ombú tree with pendant white blooms, more beautiful than any sculpture.

"But how do we get there?" The track was flooded by irrigation water.

"Here's how!" Viviana took off her shoes and socks. Laughing, we began wading. Two horses ambled to greet us from a decrepit stable that appeared to be under renovation.

"Apparently, Miguel has left the door unlocked so we can go inside."

"This is furnished?" Viviana's voice betrayed disappointment as we stepped inside.

In the sitting-dining room a rickety table, two upright chairs and a wood-burning stove. In the bedroom, a bare bedframe with a crucifix guarding it. In the kitchen, bare electric wires dangling from walls.

Discouraged, we stood in silence. Then a clip-clop of hooves and Miguel arrived.

"Welcome to your home!" He dismounted, a tall, tanned, handsome man, thirtyish. His smile disarmed us. We shook hands. "Everything is in order." He nodded vigorously as if to give credibility to this fiction.

"Emma said the house was furnished."

"Yes, all furnished." Again, he gave an encouraging nod.

"But there's no mattress, no cooking stove, nowhere to sit."

Miguel looked offended. Then his face broke into a smile. "I know you prefer to buy personal items for yourself." He nodded earnestly.

"Come, I show." He led us to the stable under renovation. "I make a place for me here." In the open loft lay a mattress, an armchair, and an electric stove. He smiled. "Here am I. You will buy the extras you want in San Felipe."

"Extras?" Viviana's mouth hung open.

"Please, when you connect new electric stove ask electrician to connect mine also." His angelic smile and affirmative nodding left Viviana no margin to object. His nod acknowledged that we had accepted the house as it was, at the rent he had set.

Ever practical, Viviana began to make a list of all we would need to turn the bungalow into our home.

And so, each afternoon, after we'd exercised our eyes and ears for Giorgio, Viviana and I drove to San Felipe to make our purchases. We transported them home in a trailer behind the Jeep. Ever courteous, Miguel assisted with the heavier items, nodding his approval at each.

When Giorgio had his electrician make our wiring secure and install the new appliances, Miguel had the electrician run a cable from the house to his stable.

"You've connected your stable to our electric meter," Viviana pointed out.

Miguel adopted his offended look. "I set the rent low, so already you enjoy compensation."

We said nothing, knowing that we could never outsmart Miguel's peculiar reasoning. Nor did we want to risk his reversing his promise to fence off the stable to keep his horses out of our garden. Meekly, we returned Miguel's smile.

But very soon, Miguel won our hearts. One Sunday some weeks later, bathed and dressed, we were driving the Jeep to Giorgio's to enjoy lunch with the whole family. We'd come to delight in these noisy and intimate gatherings. Suddenly, one of the Jeep's front tyres hit a loose rock on the track and exploded. We stopped. Resigning myself to getting dirty, I searched for the wheel-jack. It wasn't in the Jeep. Then I remembered seeing Nico removing it a day or two earlier for reasons of his own.

At that moment, Miguel came along on his horse. "May I help?"

We pointed to the problem. "Wait here! I come!" He smiled and galloped off. Minutes later he was back with his truck and a jack. He changed our wheel while we, unsullied, watched. Filthy, Miguel threw the offending tyre into the bed of his truck.

"I take it to garage for fix."

As clean as when we had started out, Viviana and I drove off happily in the opposite direction.

We agreed that we were going to get on well with Miguel.

Acting as Giorgio's eyes and ears was taking up half of our day. Viviana and I were able to dedicate afternoons to thinking deeply about the two most valuable and viable ideas that we planned to discuss with Giorgio.

Viviana, with her background in training, was developing an idea to train close-knit teams in the essential skills that would fit them to execute effectively the multiple manual tasks demanded by an avocado plantation. I was working on ways to boost successful cross-pollination of Giorgio's Hass avocados and so guarantee a heavier crop of mature fruit. We'd discovered that as the natural growth was cleared off the mountainsides, the insects who were the natural pollinators also disappeared. We were looking at introducing hives with honeybees. We would need thousands of them.

Finally, the day came. We felt ready to approach Giorgio with our novel ideas for the first time.

"Tell me your ideas!" Giorgio was all ears.

Briefly, we outlined these, our two most promising ideas, while Giorgio sat expressionless. We finished and held our breath.

Finally, he nodded. "Submit detailed proposals for both projects to my financial director. You know where Don Arturo's office is in our offices within our flagship plantation. Your proposals must be complete. Leave nothing out."

Giorgio's curt directives allowed us to breathe freely once more.

Viviana took the lead on the training project; I on pollination. Together, we spent a month, talking to plantation foremen, dayworkers, commercial beekeepers, officials in local government. Painstakingly, we gathered all the information we needed to come up with well-founded proposals.

Finally, we were ready. We delivered two slim binders to Don Arturo.

"*¡Gracias!* I will study these. Please prepare a summary of each for Giorgio. He will read no more than a single page. Make sure he gets them tonight and that everything is precise and accurate."

Two days later, we drove to Giorgio and Emma's home. We left the two single-sheet summaries with him after we finished dinner.

"Finally!" was all Giorgio said, and took the pages from us as if they were of no importance whatsoever.

An entire nail-biting week passed before Arturo telephoned.

"Giorgio wants you both to give a brief presentation of each project this morning at 11 a.m. in the boardroom."

"At least he wants to hear what we have to say." Viviana had almost reached the point of despair. "This will determine whether we stay or not!" Unless Viviana and I had solid remunerated roles to play, our only real option was to return to Canada.

In Giorgio's office, sunshine streaming in the window, we made our presentations. Viviana began with the training project; I followed with pollination. Each lasted just eight minutes. Each made detailed projections as to the many ways that not only Giorgio's business would benefit, but the economy of the entire valley, including those who lived in its villages, would thrive.

Neither Giorgio nor Don Arturo interrupted or smiled as we explained. When we finished, Don Arturo looked at Giorgio.

"Lunch is ready!" was all he said.

We filed into the executive dining room and sat at the table. A smiling Juanita usually served us wine with lunch but today she looked serious and there was only water. Viviana and I exchanged glances.

Does this signal the inglorious end to our efforts, to our dream of a new life in Chile?

Juanita served Giorgio first. We ate in silence. I was convinced all was lost.

Giorgio addressed Juanita as she cleared the table. "Bring me the bottle from the fridge in my office."

Juanita returned with a bottle of sparkling wine in her right hand and four flutes between the fingers of her left. Giorgio uncorked the champagne, filled the flutes and handed them round. He raised his glass and nodded to Don Arturo.

"Giorgio approves both projects with two modifications." Our hearts sank. If Viviana were to be excluded from either project just because she was a woman, we could not accept. Don Arturo paused. "One, you must purchase personally the two extended cab long box pickup trucks you have included in your costs. And two, your personal monthly salaries need to be reduced below your projected figures."

I paused to gather my thoughts. We had given long and deep thought to the entire budget and specifically to these items. Viviana had learned from Nico the salary his father paid him, and we had entered exactly that figure for each of us despite his being less than half our age and that we would be undertaking work of far greater value than his hollow ritual.

Viviana, thinking faster and smarter than me, jumped in. She addressed both men evenly and directly.

"You understand the importance of efficiency, Giorgio, and so do I. If these two projects are to operate with maximum efficiency, each of us needs a vehicle fit for the job. We must be capable of transporting a dozen beehives at a time to exact spots in the plantations where the bees can pollinate most effectively." She let her point sink in. "We must also be able to carry several workers at any time to locations on the plantations that would otherwise take them up to an hour to walk."

Viviana crossed her arms.

Giorgio sat stock still, stony-faced. I thought I detected a smile flit across Don Arturo's face as Viviana continued.

"The bottom line, Giorgio, is that these trucks are essential to success. They are not merely toys for us." She paused to let this sink in. "Reduce our salaries? No! We investigated the pay scales for agriculture-based operations in this region. The figure we suggest is the average, neither above nor below."

Viviana waved the back of her hand with the same eloquent Latin gesture of dismissal that Giorgio had made when he had banished our life savings as unworthy of consideration.

Giorgio's eyes bored into Viviana's; a muscle ticked in his cheek. Suddenly he threw back his head and roared with laughter.

"You know what, cousin? Emma is right. When a woman leaves Latin America and gains experience in the North, she turns into a man!"

He laughed again. Viviana laughed with him. Don Arturo joined in. I sat there wondering if I would ever truly understand Latin American culture.

Giorgio raised his glass. "Cousin, you are exactly the kind of woman I need in my organisation! I have my doubts about your Scotsman though! Nevertheless, I welcome you both!"

We drank.

So began our life-changing adventure in Chile.

Memoirs from foreign places
written by Ronald Mackay

Ronald's dreams and travels, like those of many émigré Scots, were driven in equal measure by adventure and necessity. Both impulses have been amply satisfied. He has undertaken assignments in the Canadian Arctic and behind the Iron Curtain, worked under risky regimes from Morocco to Mexico and engaged in agricultural development from the Andes to the Amazon and from Bolivia to Bangladesh.

In *Fortunate Isle* (2017) Ronald writes sensitively about his youthful exploits in the banana plantations of Tenerife in the early 1960s long before the Canary Islands became a tourist destination.

With candour and humour, he offers a first-hand account of life in Romania under the communist dictator Nicola Ceaușescu, in *The Kilt Behind the Curtain* (2020).

For more information, please visit
www.amazon.com/Ronald-Mackay/e/B001JXCBL8
Or type B001JXCBL8 in the search box on Amazon.

Tuscan Dreams
TONIA PARRONCHI

What am I doing here? I thought, as baby James screamed for me to read Postman Pat, again. He then petulantly flung his toy rabbit so it rebounded at the end of its elastic and hit me on the nose. James was usually very sweet tempered, but being confined to the cramped cabin of the boat while Daddy was outside, on a choppy but very hot day in the Mediterranean, had made him grumpy.

He, like me, had the kind of skin that turns red at the first sight of the sun and then proceeds to peel and turn back to white again. What a shame he inherited my English complexion instead of his dad's bronzed Italian skin! So, while Guido blissfully sunbathed, for the two-hour sail from Ponza to Palmarola, my tetchy toddler and I were trying to have 'lots of fun!'

Lots of fun, magical, adventurous! This is how my husband, my Italian 'action-man', had described our new life on a forty-two-foot sailing boat, Whisper. He had decided to take early retirement from Alitalia at the age of forty-six, buy a boat and sail across the Med, from Rome to the Aeolian islands. He is a very convincing and persuasive man when he talks about his passions and I had been quickly sold on the idea, but the reality of setting off for my very first sailing jaunt with a small baby, was rather less romantic than he had made out. Where my legs weren't tender from sunburn, they were black and blue from climbing into the high bunks in our cabin. However, it wasn't all bad. We had some amazing times alongside more than our fair share of storms, slipped anchors and engine problems that summer.

James is now a strapping twenty-six-year-old, with a beard and the irritating habit of patting me on the head and calling me 'little mum'. Guido and I are still together after more than thirty years and we still have a sailing boat, although I remain a rather reluctant sailor.

So, let's backtrack a little. When I first met Guido, in Greece in 1990, I fell in love with his exciting tales of travel and adventure. He had been travelling the world since he was sixteen, and his adventures would need a whole book for themselves, but his two main passions were sailing and flying. Our first date was on a sailing boat, so I should have been prepared for what was to come. Guido invited me to stay with him in Rome, for a short holiday on my way back to the UK from Kefalonia. Needless to say I didn't make it all the way back to England.

They say opposites attract and we are certainly opposite. I love reading and writing; he loves any extreme sport and is good at just about every sport he tries. The only sporting activity that I have ever enjoyed is swimming. We both love travel, good food and better wine though, so our chance meeting was the beginning of my long love affair with Italian men and the country itself.

For the first few years of our life together we lived in Ostia, the beach-resort of Rome. Then, after he retired and James was born, we moved to Guido's family home in a small Tuscan village. Over the years that followed Guido built himself a small plane in the workshop below our apartment, to avoid getting bored during the winter months. He delighted in flying in it above the stunning countryside of our Tuscan valley, while planning our next summer's sailing itineraries. I grew to enjoy the boating life, although never as much as the rest of the family. It prompted me to write my first book, a kind of 'memoir-of-a-reluctant-sailor' and after that, writing became my passion. For the first time I understood how time slips by so beautifully for Guido when he gazes out across an endless seascape.

He quickly learnt what it is like to live with a writer obsessed with her work. Any suggestion of his would be met with a smile of happy agreement, but afterwards I often had no idea what he had said to me. When I write I get so involved in my characters and the story that I often forget to cook dinner and my poor men feel rather abandoned. I have fun adding a spiritual element to my books, such as a ghostly presence, and I can honestly tell you that these characters are often the most fun to write, and the most demanding. The old wise-woman/white witch, Fiammetta, in my first novel, took over completely. Her voice would wake me up during the night with some witty remark and a gleeful cackle. I could never finish the washing-up in peace, rushing to dry soapy hands quickly as she encouraged me to write down a twist in the plot, or some herbal recipe.

"Write about camomile, my girl; how to pick the flowers while the dew is still on them."

"Alright Fiammetta! But I'll do it once I've finished, okay?"

"You won't remember it, you know! Stop washing those dishes and brew yourself some camomile because you're getting tetchy again!"

Dialogues like these echo in my head all day and at times my characters become friends and seem more real than many people I meet.

I absolutely love living in Italy now, although the early years were quite difficult at times. Certain things took some getting used to: Italian bureaucracy, non-existent queuing skills and general excitability. Then there are over-loud voices that sound as if people are arguing when they are just having a friendly discussion about … everything, and different driving techniques—break every rule as long as you can get away with it and never drive slowly.

The food is undoubtedly fantastic, although there still isn't much choice if you fancy ethnic food and in the early years, if I wanted anything other than Italian food, I had to learn to make it myself. I went up two dress sizes the first year I was in Italy because I couldn't say no to the amazingly generous hosts at dinner parties, who would pinch my cheek and insist *"Mangia, Mangia!"* even when I had already eaten more pasta than I usually did in a month. Now I have learnt to restrain myself around pasta, pizza, *cornetti* (an Italian sweet breakfast croissant) and other carbohydrate-laden delicacies.

In one way I have become almost Italian now. I use my hands to gesticulate wildly while talking and find it really hard to keep them still when in the company of British friends!

I missed England a lot in the early years, not just my wonderful family and friends but also the countryside and the cool weather. Once we moved to Tuscany I began to really fall in love with the country. It was partly due to being able to communicate as my language skills improved, but mostly because of the beauty of this valley, with its gnarled olive trees and dark cypresses, glorious sunflowers and mist-wreathed hills. I take long walks every day with my adorable dogs. These walks allow me to observe the intimate details that slowly change as each season unfurls: frosted cobwebs in the undergrowth, soft moss in old dry-stone walls, poppies rioting in olive groves and the silvered olive leaves that dance like shoals of darting fish as the wind plays through their branches.

From this love of place and the people who live here—my lovely neighbours with their warm hearts, country ways and entertaining eccentricities—came my first novel. I will always be considered 'the English woman' but have been accepted as part of local life here and no longer feel the need for the things I once found essential as a young woman in London. I do sometimes crave the social life I enjoyed then, with the abundant choice of theatres, exhibitions and cultural pastimes but have found that this pace of life suits me very well and gives me an inner peace I have always craved.

✧✧✧✧✧

I hope I manage to capture the true essence of this part of Italy in my work, as well as the hint of magic which I find in every lichen-clad stone and dew-trembling leaf. I love the simple village life with its culinary traditions. Unsalted bread which enhances the strongly flavoured prosciutto, salami and cheese. Pungent olive oil. Strong, local, home-made red wine. Porcini mushrooms, smuggled home in baskets swinging from the arm of well-camouflaged old people. I always wonder about their choice of attire. Is it that if they blend well with the forest, the mushrooms will not be able to escape? Or is it that they are intent on keeping their particular mushroom spot in the forest a secret?

The villagers still screw up their faces in deep concentration when I speak. I am actually quite fluent now but my accent means they are convinced they won't understand a word. For some reason I am always exacerbating this problem with my choice of names. 'Stella', my first dog, was fine, meaning star and being a good Italian name. 'Drake' is totally impossible for them to pronounce, unless they roll the 'R' for several seconds. I had the same problem with James's name and the poor kid suffered years of being called JAM-EGGS at school.

Every summer there is a charming village fair. The majestic Chianina cows arrive, their white hides decorated with bells and tassels. They are probably better known as Florentine steaks—delicious as well as beautiful! Other farm animals are penned around the edge of the fair too and stall holders set up to sell honey, olive oil and an array of local produce. One year, and one year only, they organised a dog show, with three arenas on the sports field for dogs of different sizes. I think I know why they did not carry on with this idea. It was my Stella!

James wanted to enter her in the competition because, after all, there had never been such a beautiful German Shepherd. Although I agreed with him wholeheartedly I was also aware that what Stella had in the looks department was not matched by her obedience skills. However I agreed to James's plea. What could go wrong after all?

The rather pompous judges asked James to trot his dog around the ring then make her sit. Child and dog did a great job and I felt really proud of them both. Then the judges wanted to inspect Stella's teeth.

"Just open her mouth for me, son. She doesn't bite, does she?"

"Of course not! Stella, open your mouth, like when you let me rescue my toys that you steal. Well done, girl!"

So far, so good. Then disaster hit. No one has a clear memory of what happened next but I think that when James leant over to praise his darling dog, he inadvertently slipped the clasp on her lead. Stella had been quite enjoying the fuss but was in an arena with only two other German Shepherds, while a short distance away were two other rings full of noisy dogs of all shapes and sizes. She did what any dog would have done. She escaped. James stood there holding her lead in astonishment while I shrieked her name. Of course she paid not the slightest attention to me. As I ran across the ring and out into the crowd I had no doubts about the direction in which my dog had run. A cacophony of barks, shouts and scuffles from both the other arenas made me unsure of whether to follow her or try to encourage the ground to swallow me up. Stella quickly tired of the other tame dogs on their leads and took off across the field towards the tempting, distant woods. Halfway across the field James and I gave up our pursuit.

"Isn't she fast, mum?" said James in awe. I could think of several more satisfying adjectives but, to shield my son's delicate ears, restrained myself.

Of course Stella came back. She enjoyed a good long run and then missed us and bounded back. She allowed me to clip her lead on again then walked, in a dignified manner, back to the arena to finish the show. I do not think I have ever been so embarrassed, but now, whenever I tell the story, it makes me laugh. In a drawer somewhere I still have the certificate Stella won that day. Third prize! I don't have to tell anyone there were only three dogs in her category, do I?

Having pesky dogs and a dare-devil husband and sons has taken its toll and I now have rather a lot of grey in my hair. Age, you say? Absolutely nothing to do with age! It is the reaction to things such as Guido phoning me from a field in the middle of the Chianti hills, as I was preparing a Sunday lunch. He told me he was fine and then, once that reassurance had made my legs go wobbly, gave me sketchy details about an emergency landing he'd had with his friend's plane. While he was talking I could hear the sound of helicopters whirring above and men's voices shouting,

"Who needs the stretcher? Where are the pilots?" Since I could hear one of the pilots talking to me and his friend shouting back to the paramedics that no one was hurt, I told Guido I would turn off the oven and make lunch later. Then I calmly put the phone down and sat there for about an hour before my legs felt strong enough again.

Or, how about the time Andrea (Guido's adorable son from his first marriage) entertained us at dinner with stories of his underwater diving adventures. He does underwater caving and apparently one time got stuck in a tunnel when his oxygen tank wouldn't fit through a hole. He managed to dig his way through, since the bottom was quite sandy. Obviously the story had a happy ending because he was sitting there shovelling pasta into his mouth, oblivious of the effect his story had on me. I went into the kitchen for more water, stuck my head in the fridge to cool my cheeks and decided I'd better take in more wine too, if I was going to have to listen to more 'fun japes' such as this.

Fortunately James takes after me more than his father. When he came to prise me away from the fridge, I shook my head and asked him to please assure me that he would not EVER do anything so dangerous.

"Don't worry, Mum ... the worst I'm likely to do is burn myself while I'm cooking," he laughed. I am so grateful that he loves to cook!

✧ଚ✧ଔ✧

So, as I said, I'm going grey and here we find a big difference between Italy and the UK. A lot of friends in England embrace their grey. Italian women do not. As they age they try many improbable shades, from the brightest Barbie blonde to a rather odd shade of reddish-purple, but never a strand of grey is allowed to poke through. Even once they become truly ancient, white hair is given a blue or pink rinse. I started out being very pragmatic and going grey gracefully, but the pitying looks and sorrowful head-shaking got to me. I'm glad to say that I joined the Italians at that point and have been a 'natural' blonde for the last few years.

Italians are born with a style gene, which is often sadly lacking in the average UK high street. I started out working in fashion, in London's West End, before moving to Italy and, although nowadays I'm more often in old jeans and dog-walking shoes, I am still a sucker for a bit of girly sparkle and glamour, so I appreciate the fact that even a trip to the supermarket is an excuse to dress for the occasion. I haven't yet succumbed to wearing full make-up and jewellery on the beach though, and I tend to dress for the weather rather than the season, so I will never pass as a proper Italian woman. Fur coats or huge puffer jackets are *de rigueur* from November onwards, while I am comfortable sitting outside a bar at lunchtime on Guy Fawkes Day, wearing a T-shirt. Scarves get wound around every Italian neck throughout the winter regardless of the temperature and they have a garment which I believe only exists here: the *maglietta della salute*.

This mysterious item of clothing translates as 'the vest of health' and not wearing one, of course, marks me out as a foreigner again. It must be worn throughout winter, often in autumn and well into spring. Going without one can seriously damage your health.

There are other things that damage an Italian's health, which I grew up happily ignorant of. You should never go swimming after you have eaten. Italian mothers shriek at their offspring who have just scoffed an ice cream if they put even a toe in the sea. Certain foods are *calorosi* or inflammatory. Eating these will set your haemorrhoids off if you are unfortunate enough to have them. I had never heard of this, maybe because, luckily, I don't suffer from this nasty affliction, but you cannot live in Italy without being aware of the perils of such foods. I can never work out what to avoid as the list seems enormous: figs, chocolate, alcohol, spices, coffee, aubergines, bananas, tomatoes. I could go on, and on!

Quite honestly I have come to the conclusion that Italians are total hypochondriacs. The average Italian medicine cabinet is overflowing with thermometers, bandages, salves and over-the-counter medicines of every type. They were obsessed with measuring their temperature, just in case they had a touch of fever, way before this Covid-19 crisis. Growing up, our family medicine cabinet held one bottle of stinky embrocation oil for rubbing on muscles, an ancient packet of Aspirin, some plasters and a tin of Germolene. I liked Germolene because it was pink and it got smeared over any cuts or grazes we had. We also had a disgusting liquid to swallow for whenever we had tummy ache, called Milk of Magnesia. Just thinking about that makes me queasy.

When we bought our first sailing boat, our local doctor gave us a bag full of medicines that we might need. It was a kind gesture and summed up the Italian obsession with health. There was no room in the boat's head to stow even half of the stuff he gave us. I think I might still be working my way through the plasters and things without an expiry date.

We had a rather eccentric friend called Tony who owned one of the most beautiful sailing boats I've ever seen, a Sciarelli fifty-foot schooner called Elisir. Sometimes, when between boats, we went sailing with Tony on Elisir. It had a spectacular bathroom; all honey-coloured wood, with brass fittings and the most ridiculous mirror. This latter covered the inside of the door, so that you could admire yourself while performing. It was very off-putting to say the least, but he also kept a copy of Jerome K Jerome's *Three Men in a Boat* and Dante's *Divine Comedy* there, as a good means of distraction. I have no idea if he kept any medical supplies. Possibly not, because his cure for anything at all was a bottle of Rosso di Montalcino. He filled every corner of the boat with this delicious wine, so it was a veritable joy to go sailing with him.

My latest novel started in a very different way to my others, with the death of this wonderful friend. I found it very hard to accept the tragedy and I had been searching for the perfect love-interest for a great new character I wanted to write about; the frosty, sarcastic Miss Angelina Snow. I found myself thinking about Tony so much that I decided a cynical, pigeon-chested, wine-drinking hero would be the perfect foil and wrote him into the book. The events in the first chapter were very hard to write about with a sense of humour, because in real life there was no happy ending. We will never know exactly what happened to Tony but he had suffered two aneurysms shortly before he disappeared from his boat on the Tevere River. His body was discovered ten days later near the mouth of the river, floating out to the sea he had so loved. Of course the events and character in the book are mostly fictitious but I like to think I have given Tony the life he should have had, and that he would not have been too disapproving of my story.

☼☙☼☙☼

So, after many happy years of being a full-time mum, with a few sporadic teaching jobs alongside my writing to keep me busy, I found myself the mother of two adult sons who no longer lived at home. Guido had his latest sailing boat, Mistral, to play with all summer long but I decided that I needed a project of my own. I became involved in helping a good friend with his taxi business. Stefano retired early, bought a shiny seven-seater Mercedes van and got his

NCC license. He was all set to go but spoke no English at all. I gave him a few lessons and we discovered that we shared a passion for this stunning territory of ours. Being born here he knows all the best local places to visit in our valley which, so far, is off the usual tourist routes. We are within easy reach of the art-cities of Florence, Siena and Arezzo and, as far as we are concerned, our wild and dramatic countryside is even more beautiful than the Chianti hills. The wine and food are really amazing too. Doing airport runs was okay but what Stefano really wanted to do was share our local treasures. So we began to work on interesting itineraries together and were well on our way to developing a small tour-operator business. We were even contemplating getting an off-road vehicle and doing a kind of Tuscan safari tour. Seeing people's happy faces at the end of a day's excursion really thrilled and inspired us.

Then this coronavirus hit and Italy was at the forefront of what has become a world-wide pandemic. Lives and livelihoods have been destroyed and we are very grateful that we have been able to put our business plans on hold, rather than suffering as many other businesses and families have. As soon as people can travel again we will start back with our 'Tuscan Travel Tours' and in the meantime are trying to share any interesting events and offers on social media.

This pandemic has had a profound effect on Italy. It is hard to explain to people of other, less flamboyant, nationalities just how difficult it is for an Italian to say hello without cheek-kissing and a huge hug. Keeping distance from others is not as easy as it is for the average English person. Italians just do not have the same personal-space boundaries. I used to love to see teenagers of both sexes sitting on park benches, intertwined and happy; or a group of elderly men outside a bar gesticulating wildly, each shouting to be heard above the rest and merrily slapping one another on the backs. This habitual camaraderie has been suppressed and hidden behind masks, which everyone has been really good about wearing. In fact, the usual Italian way of cutting corners and taking cheeky short-cuts whenever possible, has been replaced by a stoic following of rules for the good of all. I have felt very proud of my adoptive country over these last difficult months. Our medical staff, teachers, supermarket workers and many others have made enormous sacrifices, as they have around the world, to keep us safe, healthy and fed, during the harsh lock-down periods. I truly hope we will be able to defeat the virus and that one day it will be a vague memory but I think that, sadly, it will be a slow process and too many small businesses will close and people will lose their jobs. It is quite a bleak scenario.

I feel even luckier than ever, here in my little bit of paradise. I have the woods close enough to walk with the dog and my little garden to potter around in, once the weather stops being gloomy and sulking its way through winter.

In the meantime I have another project which is keeping me sane and hopeful. I am renovating a little apartment here in my village to use as my writing retreat. The lockdowns have resulted in a lot of squabbling over who gets to use our computer first. Fortunately James, who is back living with us due to the Covid-19 situation, has his own computer, otherwise this chapter would never have been written. Guido is coping with the frustration of being cooped up in the house by searching the internet for the perfect future boat. When he gets bored with that he flies around the world on his flight simulator. So, a place of my own, to lose myself in my writing, will be bliss. I will probably use it as a B&B in the future too.

Of course, we are in Italy and so the renovation is not going quickly. Quite apart from council and lawyer's offices being closed due to Covid, even when we are not in lock-down it is quite hard to rally the team of builders, electricians and plumbers. My son told me today that, given I am not renowned for my patience, I have been surprisingly relaxed about the delays. Maybe I am actually becoming a bit more Italian.

If something is not finished today, it will get done soon. I have now had a toilet and radiator in the bathroom for two weeks, but my bidet and basin are still waiting patiently in the bedroom. It's true that I have no front door to my flat yet, but I have some spectacular lighting. I especially adore my rainbow-crystal chandelier and the way it sends sparks of light across the newly white-washed walls. I was a bit worried when my grizzled electrician, the chain-smoking, joke-cracking Enzo and his son Andrea tackled this light.

"What's this thing? Take it home and stick those bits on for me, there's a girl. It's enough to give me a heart attack!" Enzo muttered from around his cigarette.

Looking at their huge, grimy hands next to the crystal droplets, I agreed. I painstakingly attached the long strands at home, then an hour later carried my assembled, glittering beauty back down the street, ignoring the curious looks I got. The smell of smoke hit me as I entered the building. Enzo does not believe in no-smoking zones or ashtrays. I handed the light up to Andrea, who is luckily much taller than his father, as the pair balanced precariously on a builder's scaffolding block and a wonky ladder. In spite of a few tense moments the rough hands finally managed to affix the light to the ceiling. The worst that happened was when Enzo dropped his cigarette and I learnt a few new Italian swear words to enrich my vocabulary. Yes, you cannot rush builders, or bureaucracy, in Italy but things have a way of working out perfectly in the end.

The world as we know it no longer exists. This is not an exaggeration now, after so long living with the daily death toll on the evening news. Things get brought harshly close to home whenever there is a death here in the village. A van pulls up across the road from our house and a masked council worker pastes another death announcement to the billboard there. Losing members of our close-knit community is very hard. No matter what the age of the person, their families suffer greatly.

However, Italians are so resourceful and resilient. Their spirit is undauntable. We will return to our natural hugging, kissing, shouting and cheek-pinching ways, I am sure.

In the meantime there is always PASTA. Someone put the pan on please!

The Italian Connection Books
by Tonia Parronchi

Life is all a journey, don't you agree? Whether it is a trip to distant destinations, an inner journey of the soul or simply travelling in your mind within the pages of a book, we all need 'the dream'. Tonia's dream was to travel the world, having exciting holidays. She never imagined living abroad but Italy has now been her home for over thirty years. It inspires her every day and whatever she writes, no matter what genre, has a strong Italian connection.

Immerse yourselves in the mystical beauty of her cypress-studded Tuscan valley, sail the unpredictable Mediterranean Sea with her family or laugh with Leonardo Marconi as he wryly observes the British way of life.

Enjoy your journey and never stop dreaming!

For those of you who loved *The Song of the Cypress*, Tonia is currently writing the prequel.

For more information on Tonia's books,
visit her Amazon Author Page:
www.amazon.com/Tonia-Parronchi/e/B00GNTVLG4
Or type B00GNTVLG4 in the search box on Amazon.

Melbourne - the Wonder Down Under

SIMON MICHAEL PRIOR

February 2005, London, England.

Fiona's pregnancy bump resembled the pointy end of a submarine. She wiggled uncomfortably in her seat, as we finished our evening spaghetti Bolognese.

"Simon, now we're having twins, I want to move to a new house."

"But we've only just moved to this one. It's got three bedrooms; how many twins are we having?"

"I need to be nearer my family."

"Your family lives in New Zealand," I said.

"Yep."

I took a deep breath. Fiona looked as radiant as Simon Cowell's teeth. She loved being pregnant, and we were overjoyed at the thought of two babies in our home. But we didn't need the stress of emigrating again at this point in our lives. Unfortunately, once she had an idea, it was hard to derail it.

"This isn't like when we backpacked in 1996, Fiona. There'll be four mouths to feed on one salary when they're born, and I work for an international insurance company. I can't leave my job; I'm in line for promotion. New Zealand's South Island's too rural, there are no big businesses."

"I don't mean living in the same street as my family," said Fiona. "But I want to be nearer to them. I want the kids to grow up knowing their grandparents."

"My employer has an office in Singapore," I said. "Is that any good?"

"Not really."

"Fiona, I'll consider it; could we please put this on hold until the baby stage is out of the way?"

"I suppose we'll have enough to think about for a couple of years. Pass me the *Gina Ford* book, please. I need to read the breastfeeding chapter again."

Two years later
February 2007, London, England.

Subject: Mandatory all-hands department meeting.
Time: 11.00 – 11.30 a.m.
Location: Boardroom.

"Carl, what's this all-hands about?"

"Dunno, Simon. Keith's been with the director all morning. Must be something big. Let's go. It's almost eleven."

I entered the unfamiliar boardroom and sat in a luxurious green leather swivel chair. My shoes disappeared into the sheep-soft carpet. I worried about leaving fingerprints on the mahogany-brown table which was more polished than Tiger Woods' trophies. Latecomers stood around the edges of the room, murmuring amongst themselves like tennis spectators at an exciting breakpoint.

The director entered, followed by Keith, our boss. They sat at the head of the table. A projector displayed our company's logo behind them, next to an unfamiliar one.

The director spoke. He sounded brusque and efficient.

"Ladies and gentlemen, I'll be brief. The decision's been made to outsource this department to an American company. Once this happens, you'll become employees of OuterSys Incorporated. Your roles will be unchanged, but your employment contract will be with them. If anyone does not wish to transition to OuterSys, voluntary redundancies will be available. May I reassure you; nobody will be forced to leave. The process will take about six months, and we'll give you regular updates as we go forward. Any questions?"

Silence. No-one wanted to be the first to speak.

The director concluded.

"There'll be an intranet site to give you information as it's available. Keith will answer questions in the meantime. Thank you for coming today."

The director stood and strode out of the room.

Keith appeared abandoned and bewildered. We looked to him for some reassurance.

He put his head in his hands, then raised it.

"If it's any consolation," he said, "my job's affected too."

✧☙✧☙✧

"You're being made redundant again?" asked Fiona that evening, as she stirred a pot of our daughters' favourite tomato soup, tasting it to ensure it wouldn't burn their mouths.

"Not exactly. They're offering me the 'opportunity' to transfer to OuterSys. I've done some research, and OuterSys isn't a good company to work for. They drive you into the ground, never give pay rises or bonuses, and you're always at risk of your role being offshored to India."

"That doesn't sound good," said Fiona. "Did you say they mentioned voluntary redundancies? Why don't you ask for one of those? Then we can move nearer my folks."

"But New Zealand's no good for my role. I need somewhere with head offices, big corporations."

"What about Australia? There are bigger cities and companies in Australia. New Zealanders seem to be able to live there without any visa application process. Some of my old schoolfriends live in Australia."

"Australia?" I asked. "I don't know anything about Australia. I holidayed in Brisbane once, years ago. Remind me how long it takes to fly to New Zealand from there?"

"Slightly over three hours from most Australian cities. Close enough. We could still see my family a few times a year, and they'd be able to visit us easily."

I had an idea. "I work with an Australian girl. I'll ask her about it tomorrow."

✧☙✧☙✧

"Hi, Louise. Are you okay, after the big announcement?"

Louise looked up from her computer, her long blonde hair tied in a ponytail. She took off her spectacles and smiled at me.

"I'm going to ask for one of those voluntary redundancies,

Simon, and return to Brisbane. I've lived in London for four years; I miss the sunshine and the beaches. And my folks, of course. What about you?"

"Funny. I'm also thinking of moving to Australia. My wife and I have twin one-year-old girls, and she wants to be nearer her family."

"Is she an Aussie?"

"She's a Kiwi; I understand New Zealand citizens and their spouses can live in Australia easily. Would you mind if I asked you some questions about your country? I know nothing about it."

"Sure. Coffee? I can't be bothered to do any work."

✧෨✧ʚ✧

"A large latte, please. What will you have, Louise?"

"A flat white, thanks."

We sat near the café's gas fire, cosy from the February cold and grey, which was more depressing than a doctor's waiting room.

"I'm not going to miss this weather in Brisbane," said Louise. "Which part of Australia are you moving to?"

"I'm not sure. I need a corporate job, so I have to live in a big city."

"Okay, that narrows it down," she said. "The largest cities are Sydney and Melbourne. Brisbane, Adelaide and Perth are smaller and don't have many head offices. I don't want to do IT support any longer; I'll find a job working outdoors in Brisbane."

"Which is nicer, Sydney or Melbourne?"

"They're both great cities," said Louise, "with lots going on. I went to university in Melbourne; it's fantastic for restaurants, cafés, live music, art galleries. I didn't enjoy winter there, though. It's not as cold as London; it never snows or freezes, but you'll still need a coat."

"What about the summers?"

"The other three seasons are perfect," said Louise, "although the weather is changeable. They have this extraordinary phenomenon called 'the cool change'. On an unbearably hot day, forty degrees or more, the temperature might suddenly drop to twenty-five; people can't wait for the relief. At least in Melbourne you only suffer one scorching day at a time. But all you do is stay indoors and hide in the air conditioning."

I'd never considered hot weather to be a negative thing; this would be a novel experience.

"And Sydney?" I asked.

"I haven't lived in Sydney," she said, "but I believe it's got nicer beaches than Melbourne, and warmer winters. But it's very humid in summer, and I hate feeling sweaty."

We sipped our coffee. Outside, the 4 p.m. darkness fell.

"Are there lots of big companies in both cities?" I asked.

"Four big banks, Telstra, Qantas, they all employ thousands of people. You'll have no problem finding a job with your experience."

"Thanks, Louise, I appreciate your time."

"No problem, Simon. Ask me anything. Another coffee?"

✧෨✧ෆ✧

"Fiona, I chatted to the Australian girl at work today. She reckons it's easy to find a good job in Sydney or Melbourne. The other cities might be too small."

"Why don't we do some research on the computer after we put the girls to bed? Let's study suburbs in both places, see what houses we could afford."

We gave our daughters their evening bottle and incarcerated them in their timber-railed cots.

Fiona typed in *www.realestate.com.au* and browsed to the Sydney section.

"Does the website let you search within an easy commute of the city centre and walking distance to a beach?" I asked. "I've always wanted to live near a beach. This might be a good chance."

"Yep, we can browse by map. What's our budget?"

"Our house would sell for about £300,000. The exchange rate is $2.50 to the £, so that's $750,000."

Fiona clicked on the website. I sipped a glass of Australian shiraz.

She ran her finger down the laptop screen. "Hmmm. Nothing in Sydney's in that price range, unless you want to live miles out of the centre. We could only afford a small apartment near the beach, or an old wreck, which would need another £300,000 in repairs."

"How about Melbourne?" I asked.

Fiona clicked some more. I topped up my shiraz. Red full-bodied Barossa Valley wine in mid-winter assisted my emigration dreaming.

"Melbourne's more affordable," said Fiona. "We could buy a beautiful house, close to the train line, and in a beachside suburb. For instance, this one: four bedrooms, two bathrooms, two living rooms, two garages, all within our budget."

"Wow. Let me see."

I studied the photos. It looked enticing. The house even had a fitted barbecue, an outdoor dining area, and a shed which could have comfortably contained David Beckham's car collection.

"What time is it in Melbourne?" I asked. "Shall I ring the estate agent?"

"Hold your horses, Simon," said Fiona. "It'll be sold by the time we arrive. We're trying to get an idea, that's all."

"I'm keen on Melbourne," I said. "I don't want to live in an apartment or a wreck, so Sydney's out. What about jobs?"

Fiona typed *jobs in Melbourne* and browsed to a website called seek.com.au.

"What should I enter for your job description?" she asked.

"Try data networks, IT project management."

Fiona tapped the keyboard. I poured myself some more shiraz, and dreamt about eating barbecue food in my outdoor dining area on a warm evening, Fiona sitting next to me in a summer dress, the twins playing in the shade of a gum tree.

"I think you'll be okay, Simon. According to this site, there's 3,150 IT project management vacancies in Melbourne today."

ಲಿಸಿಲ

"Keith, I wanted to ask about one of those voluntary redundancies."

"You too, Simon? That's half the bloody department. Have you found another job?"

"No, my wife wants to move back down under; we're considering emigrating to Melbourne."

"It's like rats fleeing a sinking ship. If you can stay until May the 31st, they've offered a retention bonus, on top of the redundancy payment. They're trying to keep some staff here until the handover to OuterSys. The last one of us left better turn out the bloody lights."

"Excellent, Keith. I'll need all the money I can get. With flights, accommodation, and everything else, this is an expensive exercise."

"You definitely want the redundancy?"

I paused, and looked at him. I was going to be unemployed, with a wife and twin toddlers to feed.

"Yes."

Three months later
May 2007 - London, England.

The estate agent stepped out of his black BMW, his grey suit and icing-sugar-white shirt topped off with a bright purple breast-pocket hankie, which matched his tie. He held out his hand for me to shake as we met on the doorstep.

"Congratulations, Simon. They offered the full asking price. And they're cash buyers, they want to move quickly."

"Great, I suppose."

"You should be pleased, you did well."

"I guess I am. Thanks for your work."

I walked back inside. Fiona taped up an enormous cardboard box, filled with more toys than Hamley's bargain basement. My emotions bubbled up as I watched her stuff one of our daughter's favourite teddies in the top.

"Fiona, what the hell are we doing? I've two weeks left in the best job I've ever had, we've sold our lovely family home, a bloke's collecting the car tomorrow and we're moving to no job, no home, no friends, nothing."

"Do you want to change your mind?" she asked. "I'm sure you could keep your job; they like you."

"We can't back out now; we've invited forty people to our leaving party this weekend. We'll look stupid."

"Sure?"

"I'm having last minute nerves," I said. "The expat website said they're normal."

"That site's been a godsend, hasn't it? Although I can't believe we're staying the first few weeks in Melbourne with someone you met on the internet."

Our leaving party
May 2007, London, England.

White fluffy clouds scudded over a pale blue sky. The red 'sold' sticker on the sign outside our semi-detached suburban house glared at me accusingly, and I felt disloyal to the home my children had started their lives in. I looked down at the ground, shook my head, and sighed.

Fiona shouted from a window. "Simon, can you serve drinks please?"

I walked into the back garden and poured sparkling sauvignon blanc into a tray of glasses. The wine smelt fresh and crisp. I spilt some, and looked around for a cloth, while a toddler clamped herself to my leg.

A stranger held his hand out to me.

"Hello, Simon, I'm Darren. My wife, Tracy, worked with Fiona. Thanks for inviting us to your leaving do."

I tried to prise the toddler off, but she giggled and clung on tighter.

"Hi, Darren, pleased to meet you. Thanks for coming. Help yourself to a drink."

"So, you're moving to Melbourne?" asked Darren.

"Yes, Fiona's family's from New Zealand. She wanted to move nearer to them. My employer offered me a redundancy, and we took this opportunity."

"I've always wanted to move to Australia," said Darren. "My cousin lives in Queensland, and he loves it."

"Why don't you, Darren? You're young enough to apply for a skilled visa. What's your line of work?"

"I'm a plumber."

"They're desperate for plumbers in Australia," I said. "You'd have no problem."

"Is that right? Shame we can't go," said Darren.

"Why not?"

"Tracy's afraid of spiders."

"Really? They won't be crawling over you every night. I'm sure the Australians manage."

"I suppose," said Darren. "But what about the dog? He's five, might be too old to move him."

"Five's not old for a dog, is it?"

"And Tracy's mum. She's on her own; we can't leave her behind. She'd miss us terribly."

"Well, Darren, if you want to move to Australia, I'm sure you'll find a way. Please excuse me, I need to offer some drinks round. Candice! Get off my leg."

I clumped off carrying the tray of drinks, the toddler clinging on like a convict's leg-irons. I stopped in front of a colleague.

"Hi, David, thanks for coming. Have a drink."

"Thanks, Simon. This is my wife, Karen. So, you lucky things, moving to Australia, eh?"

"We're going to come and visit you next year," said Karen, as if she were doing us a massive favour by gracing our new home with her presence.

"You are? Err, wonderful."

"Yes," said David, "we're thinking about moving to Australia too, and wanted to do a bit of reconnaissance. We thought we'd stay three weeks with you. The two of us and the kids."

"Err, well, I don't know how large a house we'll have yet. I mean, it would be lovely to see you, but …"

"Oh, and can you lend us your car while we're there?" asked Karen. "During the days, while you're at work."

"Um, well, I suppose so ..."

"Excellent," said David. "And maybe you could drive us round at weekends, take us to the best restaurants, show us the sights?"

"Erm ..."

"Great, that's settled," he said. "I'll email you when we've booked the flights."

"Right, okay. Ah, hello, Auntie Susan. Thanks for coming. May I offer you a wine?"

"Thanks, Simon. You're really going to Australia?"

"We are, in two weeks."

"You shouldn't be leaving," she said.

"We shouldn't? Why not?"

"What about us? We're going to miss your gorgeous girls. You've no right to take them away, flitting off halfway round the world, chasing the dream. We'll never see you again. It'll be like you've died."

"I'm sorry you feel that way. You could always come and visit?"

"You can't make me fly on a plane for that long, Simon. It's too far. You're being bloody unreasonable, you are. You can't do this."

"I can't? Sorry, Auntie Susan, I need to give Fiona a hand with the food."

I strode into the kitchen, disposing of the juvenile leg-irons on the way.

"Fiona, this is horrible. I'm glad we're going. I can't wait to leave all these people behind."

Fiona hugged me.

"It'll only be us in Australia, and we can make friends with whoever we choose. A new start. I can't wait."

July 2007
Mornington Peninsula
Near Melbourne, Australia.

"Simon, why are you taking a picture of mid-air?"

"I can't believe how blue the sky is, Fiona. It's the middle of winter, and there's not one cloud. I want to photograph the blue."

"Why does everyone have jumpers on?" she asked. "It's eighteen degrees."

"I guess we'll acclimatise. Nice to be in a T-shirt in mid-winter. I'm so impressed by the play parks. Look at the smiles on the girls' faces. Everything's clean. I haven't seen any litter, or graffiti."

"And everyone's friendly," said Fiona. "The lady I spoke to with the young girl and the baby invited us to a barbecue tomorrow. I can't remember her name. Should we bring anything? Oh, Simon, your phone's ringing."

"Hello? Yes, this is Simon. They do? When do they want me to start? Do you think I could delay a couple of weeks? I need to find somewhere to live. Thanks, talk to you later."

"Fiona, that was the employment agent; the interview I had yesterday. They're offering me the job."

"Fantastic, when do you start?"

"They want me to start on Monday; I told them I need a couple of weeks to find a house."

"Where's their offices?" asked Fiona.

"Southbank, in the centre of Melbourne. We must find a house nearer the city. It's beautiful on the Mornington Peninsula, but I haven't moved across the world to spend four hours on public transport every day."

"Let's investigate *realestate.com.au* for rental properties this afternoon."

※⁂※⁂

We sat with the laptop while our daughters had an afternoon nap.

"Where do we begin?" I asked. "I don't know anywhere, apart from the city centre, and here, where we're staying."

"Well, you wanted a reasonably short commute," said Fiona. "Your new office is directly opposite Flinders Street Station. Let's see how far the train travels in half an hour."

Fiona looked at the Melbourne transport website *ptv.vic.gov.au*.

"After thirty minutes," she said, "you'd be in Mentone, and after forty-five, Edithvale. Let's investigate the suburbs in between those two."

She refined the search terms, and we ended up with a shortlist of houses.

I rang one of the agents. "Hello, is that Roy Black real estate? I want to view a couple of rental properties on your website. On Saturday? Not before? All right."

"Fiona, it works differently here. The agent opens each house for fifteen minutes per week, and everyone who's interested turns up all at the same time. This'll be like the first day of the Harrods' sale."

✿❀✿❁✿

The house stood in its overgrown garden, pale blue paint peeling from its weatherboards. Green water stains indicated where a downpipe should have been. A rusty bicycle wheel propped open its purposeless, perforated screen door.

"This is the right address, isn't it?" I asked. "It looks nothing like the photos on the website. Ah, here's the real estate agent."

A pair of stockinged legs and black shiny high heels appeared from a two-seater Mercedes, followed by a middle-aged blonde lady in a smart navy suit with a bright green cravat, the colour of the agency's logo. An uneven spray tan decorated her face. She was aged fifty, going on twenty-five.

"Hi guys, won't be long. I'll put the flags out."

She erected advertising sandwich boards, and a banner as big as a tablecloth, which proclaimed, 'Open Home'.

We stood outside, and waited politely.

At exactly 2.45 p.m., as if responding to a summons, several cars arrived from both ends of the street. Groups climbed out of them. They joined us on the pavement.

"Are they all for the open home, Fiona?" I whispered. "There must be fifteen families."

"Funny way of organising viewings, isn't it?" she asked, "I don't like the way they're looking at me; it's competitive."

The front door opened, and the blonde spray-tanned lady stood to one side of it with a clipboard. She asked for our names and mobile phone numbers.

We entered the house, along with the other families.

A smell of cleaning fluid and mothballs greeted us.

Under a chipped laminate worktop, pale green kitchen cupboards surrounded an enamel oven, benefiting from a greasy eye-level grill, controlled by black Bakelite knobs. Cracked linoleum curled up at the edges of the room, where it met nicotine flavoured skirting board. A lonely bare light fitting adorned the centre of the empty space.

In the living room, orange, heavily patterned carpet sat under another unattired lightbulb. Stains on the floor looked suspiciously like someone had tried to erase a police body outline.

Fiona and I looked at each other.

"I'm glad the girls stayed with the babysitter today," said Fiona. "I wouldn't have wanted them crawling on this."

We popped our heads into a pale pink bathroom, and navigated round a plump man exiting. A chipped bath with a brown stain leading to the plughole, and a pink sink on a pedestal, stood on more cracked linoleum.

"Fiona, where's the toilet?"

"No idea. Here's the back door. I'm going to investigate outside. Ah. I've found the toilet."

Accessed via the garden, a small room contained a pink toilet with a chain-operated flushing system. It housed an impressive cobweb collection. I started humming the theme tune to *The Amityville Horror*.

"I've seen enough, Simon. Let's go before we catch something."

The agent gave us a broad white smile as we left. "Thank you! What did you think?"

"Erm, it didn't really resemble the photos on the website."

"Those photographers are clever, aren't they?" she replied, without a trace of irony.

"I hope the next one's better," I said to Fiona, as we programmed the satnav to lead us to a street one suburb away.

"From the photos, it looks brand new."

"Yes, but so did the last one."

✧❦✧❧✧

We entered the door of property number two, a townhouse standing alongside three identical ones. I recognised the faces of most of our fellow applicants from the first viewing.

"This is an improvement," said Fiona, as we entered the kitchen, which still had plastic wrapping on the pristine appliances.

"It would be amazing to live in a home no-one's lived in before," I said. "But it's a bit small. It looks bigger because there's no furniture in it. Where will we put the dining room table?"

"Maybe in front of the window?" said Fiona.

"But then you couldn't open the door to the garden."

"Well, how about against that wall?"

"Sure, but where would the couch fit?"

"I don't know," she said. "Let's examine the outdoors."

We stepped out of a sliding glass door and stared at a fence directly in front of us.

"Too small," I said. "A tiny decking area and a gravel path. Nowhere for kids to play."

"This won't work," said Fiona. "We need something bigger. Let's have another look at the laptop this evening."

We jumped back in our car, and followed the satnav's directions towards our accommodation.

Fiona pointed. "Simon, turn in here. I saw a sign saying, 'Open Home'."

I swerved down a side street, and the satnav lady objected.

"Perform a U-turn where possible. Perform a U-turn where possible."

A group of children passed a ball around in the road. I slowed down to a crawl, and they scattered on to both pavements.

A red advertising banner flew outside a modern home, opposite a park, in a tree-lined avenue of family houses.

The agent stood at the open front door, her dark hair tied up in a bun. She looked about nineteen, and bored.

We walked up the path, and she immediately entered professional mode with a wide grin.

"Hello, I'm Leanne. Could I make a note of your names and mobile numbers please?"

"Certainly," I said. "This house is for rent?"

"Yep, three bedrooms, two bathrooms, two reception rooms, $400 per week."

"Sounds interesting. Are we the only people viewing it? We've always seen several other families at open homes."

"There's been a bit of a mix-up," said Leanne. "It hasn't been advertised online yet, so no-one knows about it. We were going to cancel the open home, but the landlord insisted we run it."

The wide front doorway framed a high-ceilinged hall with a contemporary black polished concrete floor. An integral garage led off the entrance, and in front of us, a tall door led into a modern open-plan kitchen, dining area and living room. Beyond, a small, fenced garden, with a lawn, flower beds and a patio invited further investigation.

We strolled through the downstairs and stepped outside.

In the far corner of the garden, a wooden children's playhouse stood on small stilts.

We looked at each other and smiled.

"Shall we go upstairs?" I asked.

"Lead on, Simon."

The open-tread stairs led up to three bedrooms and two bathrooms. A huge timber-floored playroom provided sufficient space for ballroom dancing, in the unlikely event we wished to enjoy this activity. A glass sliding door led out to a balcony overlooking the park.

"What do you reckon, Fiona?"

"It's perfect. Clean and modern. Exactly what I wanted."

We walked downstairs to see the agent.

"Are we close to the train line?" I asked her.

"About ten minutes' walk. Straight across the park and keep going."

"Fantastic. We'll take it."

"No problem," she said. "We'll do the paperwork back at my office."

"Great," said Fiona. "The playroom's perfect for the girls, the garden's safe, and when they're older, they can play in the park across the road. I love it."

We were home.

April 2021 - Melbourne, Australia.

"This steak's tasty, Simon, isn't it?"

"Yes, although I've learnt, if you want a steak medium-rare here, ask for rare-to-medium, otherwise they overcook it. Unless you go to a French restaurant."

"And this shiraz, it's smooth, bull's blood." Fiona sipped from her glass. "We're lucky to have such fantastic vineyards a short drive away."

"It's amazing to think it's almost fourteen years since we arrived."

"It's flown by. I can't believe the girls will be driving next month. It seems only a few years ago they started school."

"I'm glad they've been educated here," I said. "The class sizes are smaller; there's more individual attention."

I put down my cutlery and gazed at the view from the vineyard's terrace. Rows of grapevines marched up and down the slopes in the autumn sunshine. Three sulphur-crested cockatoos skrarked loudly, as they flew between gum trees.

I refilled our glasses.

"Would you do anything differently if we were emigrating all over again?" I asked.

"I don't know," said Fiona. "I loved living in London. I wish we'd seen more attractions before we moved. And I regret the girls aren't experiencing any of Britain's heritage; the castles, the historic homes."

"I don't miss not making eye contact with anyone on the train, or our next-door neighbour threatening me when I complained about his loud music, or spending thirty minutes trying to find a parking space in Sainsbury's. I didn't enjoy any of those parts of London life."

"I loved being able to go overseas easily to countries with different cultures, such as France or Italy," said Fiona, wistfully. "We can't do that here."

"But how often did we go? Once a year? We've been to New Caledonia. It's the same as going to France; Paris in the Pacific."

"I know," she said. "I do miss Europe though; the art galleries, the museums, the outdoor markets."

"There's plenty of culture in Melbourne. We loved Open House day, where we saw the Immigration Museum, the old churches, and inside the vaults of the Treasury."

"I suppose. Let's say you were back on that expat website, Simon. What advice would you give to someone moving to Melbourne now?"

I paused, sipped some wine, and chose my words.

"It's different, compared to when we came. I reckon it's harder. House prices have rocketed; nothing in our suburb sells for less than a million dollars. And the value of the pound's fallen; your money goes nowhere near as far. But wages are higher compared to England. I can't believe how much our teenagers earn in their part-time jobs."

"I don't mean financially," said Fiona, "I mean lifestyle. Most people emigrating are looking for a better life."

"Well, Melbourne's been the most liveable city in the world many years running. The weather's better. It's ten degrees warmer than London all year round. It's like London with a beach. And we own a boat. The girls would never have learned to wakeboard in England. Here we can launch at the end of our street. Ellie loves paddle boarding with her friends. She couldn't do that in London; we were sixty miles from the sea. In how many other cities could our daughters snow ski on Saturday, and water ski on Sunday?"

"Yep, can't argue the beach lifestyle's amazing," said Fiona. "I love my morning run along the cliffs, looking at the clear turquoise water. I saw the dolphins again today."

"And what about the city of Melbourne itself?" I asked. "The restaurants, the little coffee shops, the trams, it's a very European city. When I have my work meetings at a café table in the sunshine, on those wide boulevards, under those gorgeous shady trees, listening to the ding-ding-ding of the trams gliding by, it feels like Milan, or Barcelona."

"But the shopping's not as good as London," said Fiona. "I miss Next, and Primark for the kids."

"You and your shopping. You can't beat Melbourne Central, the Emporium; the local Southland Mall stocks everything you need."

Fiona looked pensive.

"Back to my previous question," she said. "Suppose I'm a potential emigrant to Melbourne. What would you tell me?"

"Do your research," I said. "Become familiar with the way another country works. Expect differences. Don't try and export your old country to Australia. Just because both countries speak English doesn't mean Britain and Australia are anything like each other."

Fiona tipped the end of the shiraz into my glass while I warmed to my subject.

"Study the websites and social media groups," I continued. "Build relationships with people who've already emigrated. Burn your bridges. Sell your house. Don't make it easy to 'go home'. If you do, you won't solve the bigger problems you encounter; you'll run from them. And don't call your old country 'home'."

I paused for dark red refreshment.

"You'd never return, would you, Simon?"

"No. I liked our lives in England; I like our lives here more. What did that Scottish bloke I met say? 'Same shit; shinier bucket'."

"But do you feel Australian?" asked Fiona.

"I'm an English-born Australian. I'm 100% Australian, with English heritage. What's Australian, anyway? Half of Melbourne's population comes from overseas. What about you?"

"I think I'll always be a New Zealander. I love living here, but I'm not sure I'll ever be able to refer to myself as an Australian."

"In my opinion," I concluded, "the most important thing for someone preparing to emigrate is to look forwards. Start thinking

Australian while you're still in your previous home. Embrace all things Aussie. Read the news, watch the sport, drink the wine."

"Wine. Simon, can you believe we drank an entire bottle while we talked?"

"We'd better have another one."

"I agree, let's find the waiter. Excuse me? Hello? Could you bring another bottle of the shiraz?"

The Coconut Wireless
by Simon Michael Prior

A true story of love, travel, and South Pacific Island adventure.

When Simon and Fiona embark on a quest to track down the Queen of Tonga, they have no idea they'll end up marooned on a desert island.

No idea they'll encounter an undiscovered tribe, rescue a drowning actress, learn jungle survival from a commando, and attend cultural ceremonies few westerners have seen.

As they find out who hooks up, who breaks up, who cracks up, and who throws up, will they fulfil Simon's ambition to see the queen, or will they be distracted by insomniac chickens, grunting wild piglets, and the easy-going Tongan lifestyle?

"Laugh out loud funny, full of adventure, and wonderfully descriptive." – Jean Roberts, author of *A Kiss Behind the Castanets*.

Available from Amazon at
www.smarturl.it/thecoconutwireless
Or type B08Y85D19R in the search box on Amazon.

20

Living the Algarve Dream
ALYSON SHELDRAKE

It's 7 a.m. and time for a walk. Kat, our rescued Spanish Water Dog, peeps out from her bed under my desk in our home office where I have been writing since 5 a.m. Her soft milk chocolate brown eyes look up at me expectantly. The moment I glance over at her, she is up, and her little stump of a tail starts wagging. Our morning walk along the river path is my favourite time of day. We are up and out long before most people, including my husband Dave, have even stirred.

I grab her lead and a bottle of water, just as the first soft brushstrokes of peach light stretch across the sky. As I get ready to leave the house, I can hear an excited squeaking noise outside. That will be Valente, one of our neighbour's dogs. He always comes with us in the mornings. I've been training him to behave and walk nicely on a lead. He's a bit of a rogue, but I've grown quite fond of him.

I open the door, and sure enough, there's Valente at the gate, whirling around and whining with excitement. He's a real scruff of a dog, a little like an Irish setter, with a black coat, smiley face, and a waggy tail. I call him Wolfie, as he often sits in the road at night and howls at the moon. The name Valente, 'the valiant one', doesn't really suit him as he disappears if it is raining, and he is petrified of loud bangs. Which means he scarpers back home every Thursday and Sunday morning when the hunters start shooting at 8 a.m.

Kat looks at him quite disparagingly as we set off. She has cute curly black fur, a solid body and determined legs, and looks like a little black woolly sheep. She's about eleven now. We don't know her exact age, but I have photos of her from when she was rescued in Spain, and they are heart-breaking. We adopted her almost seven years ago and I adore her. She is my shadow and follows me everywhere and has the most placid, gentle nature. The locals call her *macaquinha* (little monkey) which seems to suit her slightly mischievous side.

Our house is nestled in a small hamlet called Igreja Nova, which means New Church. All our neighbours are Portuguese, and we have been made to feel so welcome since we moved here to live almost three years ago.

I head off down the road and stop to savour the view. The fields stretch out in front of me, parcelled off into imperceptible sections, all freshly tilled and planted. Most of our neighbours here own a small plot and they grow a host of fruit and vegetables on the land. This is Aljezur, the home of the sweet potato, and the soil is fertile and rich. From my viewpoint, I can look across and see the old part of town nestled into the sweep of hills. All the houses are painted white, many with the red sandstone-coloured roof tiles typical of this region.

I walk along the road for a little while, down to the footbridge that crosses the river. I love to breathe in the fresh cool air and enjoy the vast expanse of sky stretching far above me. The first strokes of sun are reaching upwards through the low mist and all is calm and quiet.

On our first day of living here, we walked down to a local café and ordered lunch. The owner, on finding out we had just become 'locals' said something we felt was the perfect phrase for us. He pointed to the cloud-free blue sky above us and said (in English),

"This place here is our little piece of sky."

The word for both heaven and sky in Portuguese is the same word, *céu*. Although he interpreted it incorrectly into English, we were thrilled with that translation, and thought it perfectly fitting for our new home. The skies do indeed seem larger and brighter here. You can stand amid nature and see the dome of the earth stretching far above you.

At the bridge, I turn right and head along the path beside the river, as I watch the two daft dogs snuffling and sniffing their way in front of me.

Aljezur is a land that has remote origins, as denoted by the various archaeological remains scattered around the region. Humans have inhabited this area since pre-history, as far back as 7000 B.C. It was invaded and conquered in the 10th century by the Moors, who quickly expanded the town, until 1250, when they were defeated by the Christians.

The Moors built the imposing Aljezur castle on the hilltop to defend the area. In its commanding position, it must have been a majestic sight when it was first constructed. The main walls are still there today, perched proudly above the town, with the Portuguese flag flying from the highest point.

The Aljezur river divides everything in half, with the original town on the seaward side, and the new Igreja Nova development stretching across to the fields on the other side. Today it is just a small babbling stream, home to a host of wildlife and surrounded by beautiful poplar trees, a bank of wild flowers, and an annoying plethora of bamboo plants.

The name Aljezur derives from the Arabic word Aljuzur (الجزر), which translates as islands. Historically, Aljezur would have been a key town in the Algarve region, as it had a port capable of hosting large boats. The river surrounded the village and turned it into an island, hence the Arabic name. Agriculture was the main economy here, and the cargo was shipped out through the port, which was near a creek close to the edge of the old town.

It's hard to imagine it now as I wander along beside the little stream, listening to the early morning birdsong, and enjoying the peaceful solitude. I hardly ever see anyone else out here at this time of day. I walk past my favourite tree, a magnificent edible pine tree that stands majestically in the centre of the ploughed field and stop to marvel at its size.

It's springtime, and the red poppies are scattered along the side of the path, dancing at the slightest touch of a breeze. They are surrounded by white daisies and a host of healthy plants and grasses. The poplar trees are covered in the drooping catkins that arrive even before their tender green leaves appear. In late spring, the floor around the trees is scattered with cotton wool, as they disperse their seeds. Tufts of fluffy cotton are everywhere, and from a distance it looks like snow has fallen.

I notice the chewed remains of some root plants as I walk along the path. That's where the *javali*, or wild boar, were feasting last night, and one reason why Kat and I wait until first light before we walk along the river path. I don't fancy meeting a full-grown angry *javali* any time soon. They weigh up to eighty kilogrammes and can be very aggressive, with sharp teeth. Not a pretty sight.

The end of the path widens out into a small car park and leads out across the main road beside the metal bridge that joins the old and new towns. I always pop over to the other side of the bridge to see the ducks. Yesterday I spotted a family of babies all hustling to be fed and exploring their new home. If I am really lucky, I'll spy an otter swirling in the water and coming up for air.

They share the river with the Mediterranean or Spanish pond turtles, alongside the resident greylag geese husband and wife team. The female goose is so tame that Paulo, the owner of the local café, can hand-feed her pieces of bread.

I spot Paulo ahead and also my friend Petra. She runs a stall in the daily market, and we meet every morning at Paulo's and have a *bica* coffee and a natter. Apparently, our laughter some mornings can be heard across the river in the old town, according to a local person who knows us well.

The market is where we buy our fruit and veg, all organic and fresh. Most of it comes from Petra's garden. You can't get much more local than something harvested the day before from a plot of land not five kilometres away. Catia is already in there too, setting up her stall, with the finest specimens of seafood and shiny fish on sale.

And then we head along the main road that leads back to Igreja Nova and then meanders on to the foothills of Monchique. That's a delightful winding road full of tiny hamlets and villages to explore too. Virtually every car that passes will have someone waving and beeping their horn at me as they drive by. This place really feels like 'home' and everyone knows me and Kat.

It's so different here to the main Algarve region and the village of Ferragudo where we lived previously. This is more rural and unspoilt. All our neighbours are so friendly, in the slightly reserved and polite way we have come to know and respect. They also provide us with loads of fruit and vegetables—whatever is in season that they have just harvested. We will often find a bag of lemons, sweet potatoes or a giant pumpkin sat on our front wall.

As we turn off the main road, I spot one of our dear friends, Maria Victoria, coming down the hill from her house, pushing a wheelbarrow. She's off down to the river to collect food for her chickens and rabbits. Kat adores her and her menagerie of animals and loves to visit her garden plot, which has a convenient set of concrete steps beside it. They are the perfect height for Kat to sit on and peer into the makeshift *escondidinho* (hideaway) which is usually home to a fat rabbit or three.

We walk past A Bica, the local pizzeria restaurant—they do the best pizzas in the whole of the Algarve! I always stop to look in their pond and listen to the cacophony of frogs croaking and filling the air with their raucous mating calls.

Once we're home, I sort out Kat's food and fix my breakfast. I have an enormous bowl of gluten-free porridge oats every morning, topped with a ridiculously sizeable amount of fresh fruit. Two sliced bananas, blueberries, raspberries, and chopped up strawberries balance precariously on top of the mound of porridge, and I settle down to scoff it all. I was diagnosed with Rheumatoid Arthritis just over two years ago, and, so far, I am managing it through a rigorous 'diet' and supplements. Most days I can function really well, although I have the odd bad day when I retreat back to bed and sleep.

Dave will be up by now. He'll be sitting in the office, probably editing some photos for a client. I walk through the kitchen and out into my studio and have a look round before I clear up from breakfast. That's where I do all my painting. The easel has my latest piece drying on there, ready for me to start work again this morning. I've completed well over two hundred paintings since we moved to Portugal ten years ago.

I wander out into our little courtyard garden and see the first fingers of sun creeping over our neighbours' wall and settling onto our plants. We had a builder create a lovely covered area outside where we sit and eat lunch every day. He persuaded us to go for a really large structure and I am so glad he did, as there was room to add a fabulous corner sofa. That's where you'll find me most afternoons sitting and reading a book. With Kat beside me, of course, curled up asleep.

And that's it. Our simple, rural, gentle Algarve life and home. Our dream come true. And more. I had no idea just how happy and content I could be in this little place, living an unhurried, stress-free existence, writing and painting, and savouring every moment of our time here.

But why the Algarve? And what is it really like when you move overseas and try to live a simpler life? For the answers to those questions, I'll have to take you back a bit and explain how we ended up living here in our own little corner of Portuguese paradise.

ჿഓჿെჿ

When I met Dave, we were both serving in the Devon and Cornwall police. I had relocated to Exeter and bumped into a rather cheeky and charming custody sergeant. We quickly fell in love, moved in together, and started our new life, juggling opposite shift patterns, long working hours, and stressful but exhilarating jobs.

We had a wish-list of places in the world that we had both always wanted to visit, and enjoyed some remarkable holidays to Venice, Hong Kong, and the Caribbean, amongst others. Our honeymoon in Cape Town was fabulous; it was such a spectacular and colourful region. We savoured fine food and delicious wines and explored the stunning unspoilt beaches and open countryside. We both said we would have considered moving there to live if it had been safer.

Our motto was always 'never go back to the same place twice'. Which was fine until one day we met friends that had just returned from a holiday in the Algarve. They knew someone who owned a little fisherman's cottage, and before we knew it, we had arranged to rent the cottage for a week. The plane touched down at Faro airport. We walked down the steps and breathed in the unmistakable scent of being 'abroad'. It's hard to describe; there's a warmth to the air that hits you immediately at Faro, alongside the hint of pine, the aroma of a distant shoreline, and something imperceptibly sweet and enticing.

We picked up the hire car and headed off. The directions were a scruffy set of handwritten scribbles, but the route was straightforward. Head along the N125 until you go through Lagoa, then look out for the turning for Ferragudo.

It was a moment that changed everything.

Heading into the village of Ferragudo, there is a bend in the road and then suddenly—there—in front of you—is the entire village sitting sleepily across the river, nestling into the hillside. The water glistens in the sunlight, the boats are bobbing and clanking against the tide, and the houses are all painted white, with the church sitting majestically above them. It all seems to say 'welcome, come and rest here for a while, leave your cares behind you'.

We both—inarticulately but excitedly—said "wow!" at the same moment as we rounded the corner and experienced that view for the first time.

We found the cottage at the end of the village on a little one-way loop. We parked up outside, unloaded our bags, and inserted the key into the front door. Inside was dark, cool, and a bit musty. We quickly flung open all the shutters and the windows, and a gentle breeze swirled into the rooms. Two bedrooms, both with traditional carved dark wood furniture. Then through into a small lounge/diner with a little kitchen at the back. Where was the bathroom? Ah, through the back door and into the extension, tucked away. And then out into the cutest small back garden, complete with a giant lemon tree, and the sound of chickens scuffling and squawking next door.

Home for the week was looking good. Time to dump our bags and explore. A five-minute walk and we were in the main square, with its cafés and restaurants and side streets leading off in every direction. Cobbled pavements, little local shops, and pretty, traditionally painted houses that all led eventually to the church at the top of the village.

The view from the church was spectacular, reaching across to the principal towns of Portimão and Praia da Rocha on the other side of the river. Nearby, we spotted the renovated old castle sitting majestically above the little locals' beach, with the promise of Praia Grande's large expanse of golden sand hidden round the corner. All that, and the bluest of skies, bright sunshine, and clean, fresh air. This was late September, one of the best months to enjoy the fine Algarve summer without the fierce heat of July and August. And we were smitten.

We wandered back down to the square, sat at Marina's café, and ordered two coffees. João, the owner, spoke a little English, and returned with two *galãos*, which is a milky coffee in a tall glass, reminiscent of a latté, but sweeter. He also brought out two small pastries, sitting enticingly on a plate, and so began our love affair with the famous *pastel de nata*. They were still warm from the oven, a pastry-based custard cream delight sprinkled with a little cinnamon on top. They were heavenly. We sat back in our chairs, turned our faces to the sun, and felt the strains of modern life melting away.

Ferragudo had everything we could have wished for in a holiday destination. It was small enough to feel cosy, not too busy with tourists, and it still retained a sense of real life with most of the occupants being locals and fishermen rather than holidaymakers. There were sufficient restaurants serving local food for us to eat out in a different place every night, although we soon discovered our favourites. And it was ideally located to explore the region, being situated slightly left of centre on the map.

The Algarve has around 150 kilometres of coastline, with everything ranging from bustling and busy tourist areas that are heaving with holidaymakers in the summer, through to almost deserted coves and beaches, with quaint villages where the locals still live in a time long lost to other countries.

We travelled to the town of Silves and marvelled at this medieval wonder, with its Roman bridge, historic castle, and 13th century Gothic cathedral. We scoffed piri-piri chicken and chips sitting in a café overlooking the river, washed down with a local beer, then traversed the narrow streets and explored the shops.

Next up was a day trip to the west coast, and we fell in love with this area's dramatic cliffs and coastline, which are reminiscent of the west of Ireland or Cornwall. The beaches were impressive—wide, deserted stretches of soft golden sand, backed by red and sandstone cliffs carved into the landscape, with hints of black volcanic rocks and views across the Atlantic.

We spent a morning travelling north to Monchique, and the highest point in the Algarve, Fóia, at 902 metres. The view from the top was spectacular. We wound our way back down the hill, stopping at the small spa retreat of Caldas de Monchique. Lunch was a posh affair at the restaurant nestled under the trees. We enjoyed a leisurely meal that stretched far into the afternoon.

Our week passed by all too quickly. How could we possibly lock up and leave 'our little house' and return to the UK and our work policing the streets? It was as if we had moved to a different planet. The two worlds were so far apart. We vowed before the plane had even left the runway that we would visit Ferragudo again as soon as we could.

And so it began. We saved up all our leave, rang up the owners of the cottage, and returned so many times over the ensuing few years that we ended up leaving clothes and small items behind 'for next time'. Maybe it was because we stayed in a traditional house, surrounded by locals, rather than a tourist resort, that it made us feel we were coming 'home' each time we arrived. We shopped, ate, and explored the area, avoiding the more 'touristy' destinations and discovering the hidden beaches, tucked-away villages, and local restaurants that are the real Algarve. And each trip made us more determined to return again.

So much for 'never going back to the same place twice'.

✧෪✧ଔ✧

It was perhaps inevitable that our love for the area, and Ferragudo in particular, would mean that we began to take more than a passing interest in estate agents' windows. Because of family circumstances, and a complete change of career for me, we were renting in Dorset, having sold our home in Devon. Our money was sitting in the bank, and due to an excellent pound to euro exchange rate in our favour at the time, it would stretch much further abroad than in the UK.

We suffered an aborted attempt to buy an apartment in Ferragudo, thanks to a less than scrupulous builder, and a dodgy 'money in an envelope' approach to financing that we eschewed. Eventually we found a newer house on the edge of the village. It was bigger than we had planned, with four bedrooms, and an enormous basement which would have been large enough to fit an entire separate apartment inside. A big garden, lovely Portuguese neighbours, and a stupendous view which reached across the Arade river and all the way up to the Monchique. The view alone made the property irresistible.

We did our sums, put in a crazy offer which was accepted, and on Dave's fiftieth birthday, it was ours. We owned a house in Ferragudo. Then we just had the small matter of biding our time until Dave retired from the police. After that, I could give up my lucrative, but utterly exhausting work as a Director of Education, and we could start a new life in the sun.

In reality, it took almost five years before that could happen. Five very long, tiring, and frustrating years. There is one piece of advice we always give to people. It is sensible to get to know an area before you buy. Take time to make sure you are in the right place, that it fits your particular needs and lifestyle, and that you feel comfortable with your choice. Don't rush things. We did all of that and were certain we had done the right thing. We loved the village, the local people, the location, everything.

But then, having bought our house, we kept having to lock it up and leave it behind and return to the UK to work. Every single trip we fell in love with it even more. And that made each journey back to the reality of life in the UK more difficult.

The basement of the house was the secret. I had always been interested in art and painting, but with work and other commitments, had never had time to do more than dabble with my paints and attend the occasional workshop or course. Dave had held a camera in his hands since he was a young boy, revelling in the mysterious and exciting world of the darkroom and developing films. And now the era of the digital camera had arrived.

We both had creative worlds we wanted to explore. And that large basement would be where we could bring our plans to life. There was room for a proper art studio, rather than the cramped corner of my bedroom where my easel and paints were stacked up, currently redundant. We could create a big, shared office area, and the back corner of the basement, which had no windows, was the perfect location for a home photographic studio. It was all there, waiting to be developed, if you can excuse the pun.

And then one day I snapped. Dave had retired by this time, but other circumstances were keeping us in the UK. My job had become almost impossible to sustain. It was stressful and fraught with major issues I had to manage on a daily basis. The 'top of the tree' can be a lonely and unrewarding place. I worked at least seventy hours every week, usually waking up at 4 a.m. with all the unresolved issues whirling around in my head.

I had a photo of that 'wow!' view of the harbour at Ferragudo pinned above my desk at work. It was the only thing that kept me sane and focused. I could close my eyes for a second, imagine ourselves back at our house, opening up the front door, checking everything was in order, then walking down to the square for a coffee. What on earth was I doing still slogging my guts out for an ungrateful and toxic employer when I could be there instead?

I went home, sat down, and looked at our finances. If we moved to Portugal, could we live on Dave's police pension alone? I took into account the fact we wouldn't need to pay rent in the UK anymore, run two posh cars, or constantly eat out because I got home so late from work every night it was too late to cook anything. Or keep paying for flights and holidays to the Algarve.

The sums astounded me. We would be £1.37 worse off a month. That included covering the small-ish mortgage we had taken out on the house in Ferragudo, and all our estimated bills and living costs over there.

That was the crunch point. We knew we could survive—just—if we lived simply and cheaply, based on the then unheard-of situation of a one-to-one euro to pound exchange rate. (Little did we know that within a year of moving out here, that is exactly what happened. One December morning the pound was worth less than a euro as the markets collapsed.)

The decision was swift and painless. I handed in my notice, giving them a generous five-month leaving period which stretched to the May half-term. That would allow them time to find my replacement and give us time to sort everything out. We booked the ferry crossing for the 25th of May. We were moving to Portugal. Permanently.

That was ten years ago now.

    I smile as I think back to that day when we finally arrived here. Skipping around our home, planning where all the furniture we had brought with us would fit around the items we already had in place. Opening the balcony door, now as full-time proper residents, breathing in the fresh air and savouring the view. And wondering, with excitement, what the future would hold.

The Algarve Dream Series
by Alyson Sheldrake

Could you leave everything behind and start a new life in the sun?

Have you ever been on holiday abroad and wondered what it would be like to live there?

Alyson and Dave Sheldrake did. They fell in love with a little fishing village in the Algarve, Portugal, and were determined to realise their dream of living abroad. They bought a house there, ended their jobs, packed up everything they owned and moved to the Algarve to start a new life.

Travel alongside them as they battle with Portuguese bureaucracy, set up their own businesses, adopt a rescue dog and learn to adapt to a slower pace of life. In the third book in the series, *A New Life in the Algarve, Portugal,* you will meet a whole range of other people who have also made the Algarve their home.

Part guidebooks, mostly memoir; the *Algarve Dream Series* of books are a refreshingly honest and often hilarious account of life abroad.

For more information, visit Alyson's website:
www.alysonsheldrake.com

About the Authors

Alyson Sheldrake

Alyson Sheldrake is the author of the award-winning *Algarve Blog*, and she is also a feature writer for the *Tomorrow Magazine* in the Algarve.
She is an accomplished and sought-after artist working alongside her husband Dave, a professional photographer. She has published three books about their Algarve Adventures: *Living the Dream – in the Algarve, Portugal*, *Living the Quieter Algarve Dream*, and an anthology of expat stories entitled *A New Life in the Algarve, Portugal*.
When she is not painting or writing, you can find her walking their rescued Spanish Water Dog called Kat along the riverbank in Aljezur.
www.alysonsheldrake.com

Ann Patras

Born in England, Ann has lived in Canada, Zambia, South Africa and now lives in Spain. She still has the same husband she was in most of those places with, as well as three 'kids'.

In her own chatting-over-a-glass-of-wine style, she has already written three books about their unusual, sometimes scary, often hilarious antics in Zambia: *Into Africa with 3 kids, 13 crates and a husband*; *More Into Africa with 3 kids, some dogs and a husband*; and *Much More Into Africa with kids, dogs, horses and a husband*.

She assures her eager fans there are more to come.

www.annpatrasauthor.com

Beth Haslam

Beth grew up on a farm estate in Wales and was mostly seen messing around with her beloved animals.

When she and her husband, Jack, bought a second home in France, their lives changed forever. Computers and mobile phones swapped places with understanding French customs and wrestling with the local dialect.

These days, Beth is occupied as never before raising and saving animals, writing, and embracing everything their corner of rural France has to offer. And she loves it!

Beth has written five bestselling books in her *Fat Dogs and French Estates Series*. Further episodes are planned for the future.

www.bethhaslam.com

Clare Pedrick

Clare Pedrick is a British journalist who studied Italian at Cambridge University before becoming a reporter on several UK newspapers. After moving to Italy to buy a tumbledown house on a whim, she became the Rome correspondent for the Washington Post and European Editor of an international features agency.
She still lives in Italy with her husband Mario, whom she met in the medieval hilltop village where she bought her house.
Now restored, the old ruin that first took her to Umbria is a much-loved weekend and summer retreat for Clare, Mario, and their three children.
Her book, *Chickens Eat Pasta*, is available in paperback or e-book and is also on Audible as an audiobook.
www.books2read.com/u/4EPYM0
Or type B012GZXOPY in the search box on Amazon.

Jean Roberts

Jean Roberts is a retired social worker, researcher, charity worker, and author of the bestselling memoir *A Kiss behind the Castanets* and the sequel *Life Beyond the Castanets*. She is also a contributor to several other books and articles.
In 2005 she bought a run-down house in Andalucia and fell in love with the country and the people. She continues to share her time between her house in Spain and her home in the Essex countryside. When she is not writing you will find her in the kitchen or walking in the woodland that surrounds her home.
www.jeanroberts.me.uk

Linda Decker

Linda is an award-winning travel writer. Her memoir, *Bombs and Bougainvillea, an expat in Jerusalem,* was given first place for a non-fiction book in 2018 by the Scottish Association of Writers.
Her second book, *Impressions of Andalucía,* featuring 70 new watercolour paintings by watercolourist Peter Lawrence, will be published in 2021 with contributions by bestselling authors Chris Stewart and Victoria Hislop.
Linda spent nearly thirty years living and travelling overseas. When she is not writing she loves walking, yoga and reading.
Her latest memoir *Andalucía Forever, a new life in southern Spain* is coming soon.
www.linda-decker.com

Lisa Rose Wright

In 2007, Lisa left a promising career as an ecologist catching protected reptiles and amphibians, and kissing frogs, to move to beautiful green Galicia with her blue-eyed prince (now blue-eyed husband).
She has written two books of their adventures: *Plum, Courgette & Green Bean Tart* and *Tomato, Fig & Pumpkin Jelly.* The third book in the series *Chestnut, Cherry & Kiwi Sponge* is due out in 2021.
Lisa divides her time between growing her own food, helping to renovate a semi-derelict house and getting out and about to discover more of the stunningly beautiful area she calls home.
www.lisarosewright.wixsite.com/author

Lucinda E Clarke

Lucinda was born in Dublin, dragged up in the Cotswolds in England and finished off in dockland Liverpool. She was then hauled from one country to another by her first husband, and many hair-raising adventures later, she collected husband number two and retired to Spain.
Within six months, she was bored witless—after running her own video company and working in the exciting world of radio and television—she continued to write. She now scribbles 24/7 in a bid to earn that mega yacht she believes she deserves, but frankly, time is running out.
She recently published her sixteenth book, the last in the *A Year in the Life… Series* of psychological thrillers. She has been invited to host her own show on Ex Pat Radio chatting to authors about their books and writing in general.
www.lucindaeclarke.com

Nick Albert

Nick Albert was born and raised in England. In 2004, in search of a simpler life, he and his wife Lesley, bought a run-down farmhouse in the rural west of Ireland, a country they had never before visited. With little money or experience and armed only with a DIY manual, they set about refurbishing their new home, where they now live happily alongside several unruly, but delightful dogs.
In 2017, Nick was signed by Ant Press to write a series of humorous memoirs about his quirky life in rustic County Clare. The *Fresh Eggs and Dog Beds* four-book series are available on Amazon and in audiobook format.
www.nickalbertauthor.com

Nikki McArthur

In 2004 Nikki and family traded in their lives in the UK, to live in rural south-west France. She now has five children, runs several businesses and has also found the time to pursue her love of writing. Nikki is currently writing a series of books about the family's experiences. The first volume *What have we got Toulouse? A family moving to France* was released in April 2020.

A dedicated mother and natural organiser, Nikki enjoys sharing the knowledge and experience she's gained over the years. Her practical and down to earth approach to life shines through in her work.
www.amotherinfrance.com

Rachel Caldecott

Rachel studied Expressive Arts in Brighton. She has worked for a film production company, a Japanese travel agency, and some well-known NGOs.

She currently lives in southern France with her husband, two children, and six rescue cats. When not writing, she helps in her husband's glassblowing business and makes her own handmade jewellery.

Her interests include human and animal rights, the environment, and politics. Since 2015, she has been involved in helping refugees and collecting medical donations to send to Syria.

Rachel Caldecott usually writes YA fiction. Her first memoir about life in France, *Blown Out of Proportion - Misadventures of a Glassblower in France*, is now available.
www.rachelcaldecott.com

Rob Johnson

Rob Johnson is an English author and reluctant olive farmer who lives halfway up a mountain on the west coast of Greece with his wife Penny and various rescue dogs and cats.

According to his father, Rob has only had one 'proper job' in his life because working as an administrator and publicist for touring theatre companies apparently didn't count. Nor did writing four plays which were professionally produced and toured throughout the UK.

Since then, he has published five novels and *A Kilo of String*, a memoir about his and Penny's often bizarre experiences of living in Greece.

www.rob-johnson.org.uk

Ronald Mackay

Ronald Mackay lives happily with his wife Viviana on the shores of Rice Lake, Ontario, Canada.

As a child he mastered Scots first and then English. He has also worked in French and Romanian. Spanish is now the language of the home. Ronald has farmed in Scotland, Mexico, Canada, and Argentina, fished commercially in the North Sea and the Atlantic, taught at universities in Europe, Asia and the Americas, and has engaged in community development projects around the world.

He has published two memoirs in English, one in Spanish and many short stories. He also writes plays for community theatre. He recounts many shorter international experiences in the travel anthologies edited by Robert Fear.

www.fd81.net

Roy Clark

Roy grew up in Liverpool where he spent much of his youth seeking solace and adventure in the small pockets of nature within the city's confines while dodging the truant officer.
Becoming the owner of a bicycle meant trips into the North Wales countryside became possible. Eventually, he moved north in search of new adventures among the wild mountains and lochs of the Scottish Highlands. In 2002, an idea of a holiday morphed into relocating to Slovenia where he spent sixteen years living in the mountainous north-west region of the country.
Roy currently lives with his wife Justi in the west of Ireland.
The Sunny Side of the Alps: From Scotland to Slovenia on a Shoestring.
www.smarturl.it/sunnyside1
Or type B0848R8479 in the search box on Amazon.

Simon Michael Prior

Simon Michael Prior inflicts all aspects of life on himself so that readers can enjoy learning about his latest exploits.
During his forty-year adolescence, he's lived on two boats, sunk one of them; sold houses, street signs, Indian food and paper bags; visited fifty countries, lived in three; qualified as a scuba diving instructor; learnt to wakeboard; trained as a Marine Rescue skipper, and built his own house without the benefit of an instruction manual.
His new book *The Coconut Wireless*, a fun travel memoir about a quest to find the Queen of Tonga, is now available on Amazon.
www.smarturl.it/thecoconutwireless
Or type B08Y85D19R in the search box on Amazon.

Todd Wassel

Todd Wassel is an international development professional, author and traveller. Currently Todd is the Country Representative for the Asia Foundation in Lao PDR. Originally from the United States, he has been out in the world for more than two decades, living and working in over forty-five countries.

Todd won the People's Choice Award in the Southeast Asia Travel Writing Competition and has been featured in Lonely Planet, The Diplomat, as well as on ABC Australia.

He currently lives with his wife and their two kids in Laos, along the banks of the Mekong.

www.toddwassel.com

Tonia Parronchi

Tonia Parronchi met her Italian husband in 1990. He invited her to Rome for a week, and she has never left.

When their son was born, Guido took VERY early retirement and bought their first sailing boat, Whisper. A total land-lubber, Tonia had mixed feelings about setting sail with a small baby. Varied experiences such as high seas, stuck anchors, marauding mosquitoes and severe sunburn led to her humorous memoir, *A Whisper on the Mediterranean*.

She has written two novels, *The Song of the Cypress* and *The Melting of Miss Angelina Snow*. There is no doubt about it … Italian men are her downfall. The food's not bad either!

www.amazon.com/Tonia-Parronchi/e/B00GNTVLG4
Or type B00GNTVLG4 in the search box on Amazon.

Val Poore

Val is an English language teacher by day and a writer during her free time. Born in the UK, she spent twenty years in South Africa and has since spent another twenty living on a historic barge in the Netherlands, a lifestyle she adores despite the hard work it involves. These diverse worlds have given her some wonderful experiences, and she enjoys sharing her stories in her books and on her blog, which she started in 2006.

To date, Val has written nine memoirs and two novels, but she also writes barge-related articles for the women's sailing magazine, *Sistership*.

www.rivergirlrotterdam.blogspot.com

Vernon Lacey

Vernon Lacey is the author of *South to Barcelona* (Ant Press), a memoir about moving to Catalonia. He has published a range of journalism articles on sports and current affairs in Spain.

In 2020 his account of travelling in Cornwall was a winning entry in the annual Bradt Guides Travel Writing Competition, published in the anthology of new writers *Kidding Around*.

He is a teacher of English and Philosophy and lives in Munich with his German wife and three children. He has performed and recorded works by Johannes Kreusch and Tulio Peramo for classical guitar.

www.vernonlacey.com

Victoria Twead

(aka Beaky, crazy chicken lady, etc)

Victoria Twead is a New York Times, Wall Street Journal and Amazon bestselling author and usually works in her pyjamas. Eleven years in a tiny remote mountain village in Spain, rescuing a vulture and owning probably the most dangerous cockerel in Europe inspired Victoria to write *Chickens, Mules and Two Old Fools* and the subsequent books in the *Old Fools Series*.

Her husband has been unable to wrestle the laptop from Victoria's vice-like grip and she continues to write and publish books in Australia where another joyous life-chapter has begun.

www.victoriatwead.com

Itchy Feet - Tales of travel and adventure

"**W**here's my passport?"
"I need to go travelling again…"

From the Indonesian jungle, to an epic journey out of Africa, and rafting the Zambezi, twenty intrepid and inspiring authors share their adventures with you in this anthology of travel stories.

Find out what Egypt is like in a heatwave, and hunt down Dracula in Transylvania.

Catch a rare glimpse into the lives of the last Pech indigenous people of La Moskita, Honduras.

Experience history first-hand through four continents, three wars and a desperate message in a bottle with a story of heartbreak, poverty and travel in the 19th century.

Be entertained by a teenager's first glance of foreign soil, and an Australian view of England. Ride a Harley through France and Spain or motorbike around India and find out what makes someone a perpetual nomad.

Travel around the world from the comfort of your own armchair. No passport required.

Itchy Feet – Tales of travel and adventure is the second book in the *Travel Stories Series*, curated by Alyson Sheldrake. **To be published in the autumn 2021.**

For more information visit:
www.alysonsheldrake.com/books

We Love Memoirs

The Facebook group *We Love Memoirs* was founded by Victoria Twead and Alan Parks, two memoir writers who created the opportunity to start a community on social media for both readers and authors to get together. The group now has almost 6,000 members and continues to grow.

The group covers a whole range of different memoir themes from comedy, and travelogues, to other people who have also upped sticks and started a new life abroad. There are inspirational and moving accounts of people overcoming abuse, illness, and adversity, and tales of animals, adventures, and resilience. There is an enormous selection of books to choose from, and the group's page is full of recommendations, new releases, special offers, quizzes, and prizes.

Many people describe this as their 'happy place' on Facebook:

www.facebook.com/groups/welovememoirs

Acknowledgements and Dedication

My special thanks go to all the authors who contributed to this book. Thank you for your willingness to share your stories about life abroad with me.

A warm and hugely appreciative thank you to Val Poore for her tremendous work proof-reading this for me. Her attention to detail and enthusiasm for the project was infectious.

To the beta readers who helped to shape this book, namely Beth Haslam, Lisa Rose Wright, Julie Haigh, Jules Brown, Simon Michael Prior, Kevin JD Kelly, and Kathleen Van Lierop—my sincere and heartfelt thanks.

A big shout out must also go to Dorothe Wouters for her creative talents in designing the fabulous suitcase images that adorn the covers of the *Travel Stories Series* of books. She perfectly understood what I wanted to create and delivered exactly what I imagined in my head.

Thank you to the wonderful members of the Facebook Group We Love Memoirs. This really is the best bunch of friendly authors and memoir readers. I have made new friends and read so many wonderful books through this group.

My special thanks must also go to Victoria Twead, of Ant Press publishing company, for her continued support, advice, and encouragement. She is an inspiration to us all as authors.

As always, thank you to Dave, my talented and supportive husband. I love you.

Free Photo Album

To view a series of free photographs which accompany this book, please visit my website:

www.alysonsheldrake.com/books/

Keeping in Touch

If you would like to be notified when I publish the next book in the *Travel Stories Series*, please contact me via email and I will add you to my mailing list.

author@alysonsheldrake.com

I also write a monthly newsletter, which is full of art, photographs, book reviews, and articles. You can sign up to this free via the link here:

www.alysonsheldrake.com/news/

About the Curator

Alyson Sheldrake was born in Birmingham in 1968. She has an honours degree in sport and has a PGCE (Secondary) qualification in physical education, English, and drama. She has always loved art and painting, although she found little time for such pleasures, working full time after graduation. She joined the Devon and Cornwall Police in 1992 and served for thirteen years, before leaving and working her way up the education ladder, rapidly reaching the dizzy heights of Director of Education for the Church of England in Devon in 2008.

Managing over 130 schools in the Devon area was a challenging and demanding role. However, after three years her husband Dave retired from the Police, and their long-held dream of living in the sun became a reality.

Alyson handed in her notice, and with her dusty easel and set of acrylic paints packed and ready to move, they started their new adventure living in the beautiful Algarve in Portugal in 2011.

Alyson is the author of the award-winning and popular Algarve Blog, and has also been a keynote speaker for several years at the annual Live and Invest in Portugal international conference. She is also a feature writer for the *Tomorrow Magazine* in the Algarve.

She is an accomplished and sought-after artist working alongside her husband Dave, a professional photographer. Being able to bring their much-loved hobbies and creative interests to life has been a wonderful bonus to their life in the Algarve. She was also delighted to add the title 'author' to her CV, with the publication of her first book, *Living the Dream – in the Algarve, Portugal*, in April 2020. The subsequent sequel, *Living the Quieter Algarve Dream*, was published in November 2020, and the *Algarve Dream* series of books was completed with the publication of *A New Life in the Algarve, Portugal – An anthology of life stories* in April 2021.

Chasing the Dream – A new life abroad, is the first anthology in her new *Travel Stories Series*.

Your Review

I do hope you have enjoyed reading this book. If you have a moment, I would love it if you could leave a review online. I read and learn something from every review that is posted, and I do a happy little dance for every lovely comment shared.

All of the authors represented in this book are always keen to hear what you think about their work, and all strive to write the very best books they can for your enjoyment.

Thank you.

Printed in Great Britain
by Amazon